UNPLUG

365 FUN, FAMILY-FRIENDLY ACTIVITIES FOR KIDS

ÜNPLUG
365 FUN, FAMILY-FRIENDLY ACTIVITIES FOR KIDS

CONTENTS

FUNNY

1 Conjure Up a Fortune Teller
2 Play Wink Murder
3 Play Balloon Ping-Pong
4 Make Pipe-Cleaner Puppets
5 Guess What's in the Bag
6 Remember the Tray
7 Play Forty, Forty
8 Levitate Cards
9 Bowl with Aliens
10 Slalom a Ping-Pong Ball
11 Play Stick Charades
12 Spot the Difference
13 Go on a Treasure Hunt
14 Enjoy a Day at the Spa
15 Play P-I-G
16 Spy Cloud Shapes
17 Play Rock Dominoes
18 Make and Play Ladybug Tic-Tac-Toe
19 Build a House of Cards
20 Make a Coin Jump
21 Invent a Secret Handshake

22 Get Tricky
23 Play with Shadows
24 Try a Balloon Trick
25 Make and Fly a Quick Kite
26 Fly Paper Planes
27 Twist a Swan
28 Be a Ventriloquist
29 Play with Pen and Paper
30 Blow Giant Bubbles
31 Never Be Bored Again
32 Play No-Numbers Dominoes
33 Play Battleships
34 Nail That Number
35 Play ABC Knockout
36 Play Kittycat Draw
37 Play Would You Rather?
38 Do Magic Tricks
39 Make a Square
40 Balance a Spoon on Your Nose
41 Send a Message in a Bottle
42 Build an Extreme Indoor Fort

43 Play Pooh Sticks
44 Bob for Apples
45 Create Your Own Obstacle Course
46 Play Frogs and Flies
47 Play Dress-Up Relay
48 Splat the Rat

ARTSY

49 Knit without Needles
50 Decorate Eggs
51 Make Mini Pom-Poms
52 Print Your Own Wrapping Paper
53 Paint a Portrait
54 Create a Coral Reef
55 Make a Mega-Mouth Pop-Up Card
56 Transform a T-Shirt
57 Draw Your Hand in 3-D
58 Make Marbled Paper
59 Make Salt Dough
60 Weave Fabric
61 Make a Room Sign

62 Top Your Pencil

63 Decorate a Pencil Case

64 Make a Seashell Pet

65 Throw a Monster Mural

66 Make Potato Prints

67 Put on a Clothes-Line Art Show

68 Make Bark and Leaf Rubbings

69 Make Sun Prints

70 Create Twinkling Lanterns

71 Sketch a Tree

72 Make Stationery

73 Ping a Masterpiece

74 Draw a Comic Strip

75 Use a Mini-Loom

76 Give a Sock Puppet Attitude

77 Fashion a Journal

78 Shoot a Short Film

79 Paint Like a Famous Artist

80 Tie-Dye a T-Shirt

81 Fold a Chewing Gum
Wrapper Bracelet

82 Print a Block Picture

83 Design a Coat of Arms

84 Make Bag Tags

85 Scrapbook it

86 Draw a Racing Car

87 Draw a Plane

88 Design a Jigsaw Puzzle

89 Make a Mardi Gras Mask

90 Create Coffee-Filter Butterflies

91 Invent a Board Game

92 Be a Fashion Designer

93 Photograph the Alphabet

94 Collect Your Garbage

95 Walk Your Pencil

3

YUMMY

96 Create Crunchy Snacks

97 Make Traffic Light Jellies

98 Cook Up a Muffin in a Mug

99 Make Tortilla Pinwheels

100 Challenge Your Taste Buds

101 Use Chopsticks

102 Make Cake Pops

103 Make Edible Slime

104 Concoct Coconut Ice Balls

105 Twist Pizza

106 Toast Marshmallows

107 Harness the Power of the Sun

108 Make the Ultimate Pizza

109 Grow Rock Candy

110 Throw a Super Sleepover

111 Shake Some Ice Cream

112 Make Hot Chocolate

113 Make Lemonade

114 Roll Your Own Breadsticks

115 Make Chocolate Slime

116 Create Art on a Plate

117 Invite Friends to a Picnic

118 Play the Menu Game

119 Bake Farmyard
Cupcakes

HANDY

120 Construct a Piñata
121 Fashion a Paper Bouquet
122 Make a Samurai Warrior's Helmet
123 Build a Periscope
124 Make a Photo Box
125 Form Pasta Monsters
126 Fashion an Indoor Teepee
127 Build a Solar System Mobile
128 Get Organized
129 Sew Cards
130 Upcycle Your Toys
131 Catapult a Marshmallow
132 Make an Origami Bookmark
133 Pin Your Photos

134 Build a Helicopter
135 Catch the Sun
136 Race in a Regatta
137 Make a Piggy Bank
138 Make a Flick Book
139 Run Your Marbles
140 Make Music
141 Make Glove Monsters
142 Hold Your Earphones
143 Make an Ice Mobile
144 Frame Your Day
145 Store in a Robot
146 Make an Outdoor Photo Booth
147 Launch a Parachute
148 Make a String Telephone
149 Light Up a Lava Lamp
150 Make a Hammock
151 Press Flowers
152 Make a Wind Chime
153 Hang a Wreath
154 Make Two Natural Instruments
155 Build a Box City
156 Make a Snow Globe
157 Be a Real "Sew" Off

158 Make Paper-Cup Speakers
159 Tell Time Without a Clock
160 Make a No-Sew Bag
161 Hold Your Pencils
162 Make a Finger Bunny
163 Make an Outdoor Silhouette Theater

BRAINY

164 Challenge Your Memory
165 Write a Mini-Mystery
166 Make a Spectrometer
167 Make a Dinorama
168 Outline Your Family Tree
169 Revamp Your Room
170 Write a Sequel
171 Design a Board Game
172 Grow Crazy Cress Heads
173 Defy Gravity
174 Try the Pencil Trick
175 Make a Code Wheel

176 Make Quicksand
177 Build a Mini-Museum
178 Construct a Barometer
179 Calculate Storm Distance
180 Talk by Flashlight
181 Send a Semaphore
182 Forecast the Weather
183 Make a Balloon Rocket
184 Create a Geyser
185 Find the Age of a Tree
186 Launch a Vinegar Rocket
187 Make a Time Capsule
188 Make Your Own Compass
189 Write a Spooky Story
190 Count to Ten in Five Languages
191 Go Star Gazing
192 Invent a Superhero
193 Learn to Read Music
194 Boost Your Memory
195 Create Three Cool Codes
196 Deal with an Emergency
197 Prepare for Disaster
198 Learn About Your Star Sign
199 Make a Thaumatrope

200 Be a Mad Scientist
201 Learn about the Seven Wonders of the Ancient World
202 Understand Clouds
203 Learn Moon Phases
204 Say Thank-You Ten Ways
205 Trick Your Brain
206 Write with Invisible Ink
207 Read Your Own Palm
208 Make a Kitchen Volcano
209 Make Your Own Newspaper
210 Make Glow-in-the-Dark Goo
211 Measure Rainfall
212 Find Your Chinese Zodiac Animal
213 Test Your Pizza Brain
214 Take the Wheels Quiz
215 Make a Tangram
216 Have a Spelling Bee
217 Be a Human Lie Detector
218 Create a Spy Code
219 Be a Know-It-All
220 Dream Big
221 Create a Super Pseudonym
222 Be a Myth Buster

6

MESSY

223 Grow Pizza Sauce
224 Build a Willow Tunnel
225 Melt Your Crayons
226 Attract Butterflies
227 Dig a Dino Park
228 Grow Potatoes in a Bag
229 Make a Stick Family
230 Throw a Seedball
231 Build a Bucket Pond
232 Feed the Birds
233 Make Drip Castles
234 Lay a Stick Trail
235 Carve a Pumpkin
236 Make Mud Faces
237 Build a Bottle Tower Garden
238 Grow a Bag of Strawberries
239 Create a Sand Palace
240 Thread a Flower Garland
241 Take Lavender Cuttings
242 Use Natural Dyes
243 Build a Woodland Den

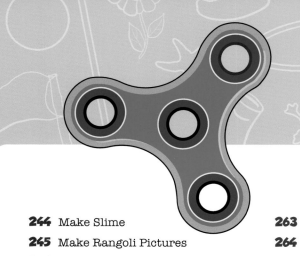

244 Make Slime

245 Make Rangoli Pictures

246 Create a Walk of Fame

247 Make a Papier-Mâché Bowl

248 Grow Mint Tea

249 Go Pond Dipping

250 Create a Boot Garden

251 Make Bouncing Slime

252 Make Spooky Black Flowers

253 Grow a Worm Farm

254 Make a Daisy Chain

255 Make a Recycled Birdhouse

256 Spin a Picture

257 Build a Bug Hotel

258 Make a Birdbath

7

SPORTY

259 Do Perfect Push-Ups and Sit-Ups

260 Bunnyhop on a BMX

261 Relax with Yoga

262 Master a Ribbon Maze

263 Try Chinese Jump Rope

264 Play Glow-in-the-dark Ring Toss

265 Get the Goal

266 Shoot a Bow and Arrow

267 Have a Water Cup Race

268 Throw Paper-Plate Frisbees

269 Play Beanbag Ladder Toss

270 Sail a Leaf Boat

271 Transfer a Spinner from Finger to Thumb

272 Play Sand Darts

273 Go Rock Pooling

274 Play Hopscotch

275 Build a Snow Penguin

276 Do the Pinch-Grip Toss

277 Try Stone Skipping

278 Win an Egg and Spoon Race

279 Build a Spudzooka

280 Walk Your Camera

281 Race Mini Junk Rafts

282 Catch the Dragon Tail

283 Learn to Juggle

284 Play Red Light, Green Light

285 Spot Five Animal Footprints

286 Get Tied Up in Knots

287 Toss Hand-to-Hand

288 Play Elbow Tag

289 Walk Through Paper

290 Get Wet in a Water Relay

291 Go on a Ghost Hunt

292 Spin a Basketball

293 Do Transfer Tricks

294 Play Water Balloon Volley

295 Make Your Own Boomerang

296 Play Up-Duck!

297 Thumb Wrestle

298 Play Pencil Spin

299 Do a Skateboard Trick

300 Ready Your Camping Gear

301 Play Rock, Paper, Scissors

302 Play Bottle Spin

303 Make Snow Angels

304 Play H-O-R-S-E

305 Play Drop Catch

306 Play Cup Catch

307 Skip Yourself Fit

308 Go Sledding

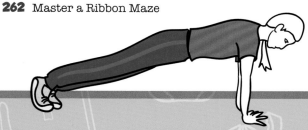

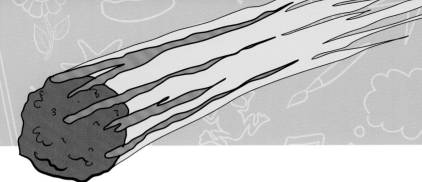

309 Play Water-Balloon Dodge

310 Go Hill Rolling

311 Do the Table Spin

312 Stick the Spider's Web

313 Go on a Nature Hunt

314 Ride the Waves

8

BUSY

315 Make a Checklist

316 Set Some Goals

317 Map It

318 Play Eye Spy

319 Try Travelspeak

320 Fill Your Farm

321 Play Travel Bingo

322 Play Alien, Alien, Rock Star

323 Play Why? Because!

324 Play Who Am I?

325 Name That Place

326 Guess the Weather in Skyway

327 Find the Food Counter

328 Spot the Crazy House

329 Plan a Planet

330 Make Up a Fast Story

331 Know Your Trucks

332 Be a World Traveler

333 Create Napkin Origami

334 Assign a Letter

335 Play Describotron

336 Take a Travel Quiz

337 Be a Design Genius

338 List It

339 Collect Tickets

340 Look for Symbols and Flags

341 Create a Memory Corner

342 Make Travel Art

343 Frame Holiday Photos

344 Play Quick-Fire Cars

345 Try 60-Second Speak

346 Plan a Movie

347 Get Map Smart

348 Bust Your Boredom

349 Spot the Souvenir

350 Go on a Scavenger Hunt

351 Word Chains

352 Design Your Own Sticker

353 Draw a Self-Portrait

354 Play a Trick on Yourself

355 One Day I'll...!

356 Doodle Dudes

357 I Saw Elephants

358 Fold and Fly a Perfect Paper Plane

359 Learn a New Language

360 New Names

361 Today I Am

362 Master the Art of Origami

363 Eye in the Sky

364 Retro Post

365 Language Lab

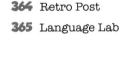

INTRODUCTION

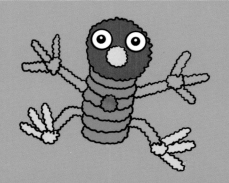

THERE'S ALWAYS SOMETHING TO DO!

Turn off your screen, and try something new! This book is packed with a whole year's worth of things to play, create, eat, build, grow, and do.

Games don't need to be electronic—learn how to play rock dominoes or ladybug tic-tac-toe. Embrace your inner engineer by building an indoor fort or flying a paper airplane. If you're feeling artsy play doodle dudes or draw a self-portrait.

And, it's never a bad time to show off your smarts. Embrace your brainy side by writing a mini-mystery, developing a new language, or making a code wheel to send secret messages. On a long journey, it's often all too easy to plug into a screen—why not challenge your companions with I-spy games instead?

Whether you're alone or in a group, at home or on the road, indoors or outside, remember to play safe and be super hygienic. (Remember to wash your hands often, sneeze into your elbows, and avoid touching your face). And, of course, be aware of the social distancing guidelines in your local area.

1

FUNNY

Have you ever bowled with aliens?
Played ping-pong with balloons?
Can you master shadow puppetry?
Perfect your magic tricks? Build a
house of cards? These fun
games and activities are
sure to bust
your boredom!

1 CONJURE UP A FORTUNE TELLER

A fortune teller is great for entertaining your friends and family. Try to think up some funny fortunes that will amuse your audience.

you will need
• Piece of paper
• Scissors
• Colored pencils or markers

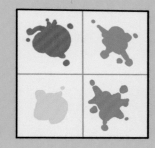

1 Fold the paper diagonally as shown and cut off the rectangle at the top to create a perfect square. Fold it again to make a smaller triangle. This will give you the center point.

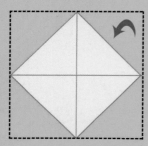

2 Open out the paper and fold the four corners into the center.

3 Turn the square over and fold the four corners into the center again. Write the numbers 1 to 8 on each of the small triangles.

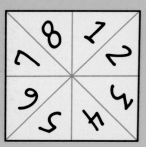

4 Open up the flaps and write a fortune underneath each number.

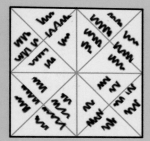

5 Turn the square over and fold it in half across the middle widthways, then unfold it and fold it in half the other way. Write the name of a color on each of the four flaps (or color the flaps instead).

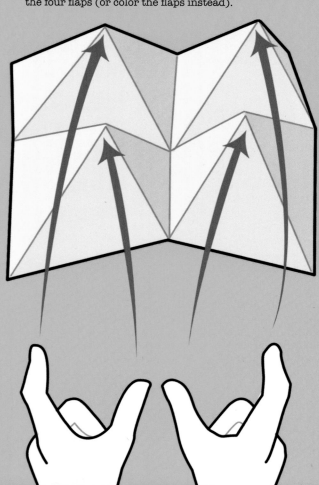

How to use your fortune teller

Ask a person to choose a color and spell out the letters, e.g. R-E-D, moving the fortune teller in and out with each letter. Stop on the last letter and ask the person to choose one of the four visible numbers. Move the fortune teller in and out that number of times, then ask them to choose a second number. Open up the flap they choose and reveal their fortune. Here are some suggestions in case you run out of ideas:

You will be eaten by a shark.

You will win a game show.

You will go to jail.

You have a secret admirer.

You will be kidnapped by aliens.

You will be top of the class.

You will swallow a spider in your sleep.

You will walk on the moon.

6 Now carefully put your fingers and thumbs inside the flaps and open and close them to reveal the numbers.

DONE!

2 PLAY WINK MURDER

You'll need a large group of people for this game. It works best with at least eight players.

you will need
- Playing card (including one joker) for each player except one.

1 Choose someone to be the detective and send him or her out of the room, then deal the cards face down to each player. Players should look at their cards without showing the others. Whoever has the joker is the murderer.

2 The detective comes back in and the players wander around the room chatting to one another. Meanwhile, the murderer "kills" people by winking at them. When a player is killed, they should wait for 10 seconds, then die dramatically and leave the room.

3 The detective has three chances to find the murderer. If they fail, they remain the detective for the next round. Otherwise, the murderer becomes the detective.

DONE!

3 PLAY BALLOON PING-PONG

You can play this with any number of people. Make sure you move anything that could be knocked over before you start playing.

you will need
- Paper plate for each player
- 2 craft sticks for each player
- Packing tape or duct tape
- At least one balloon

Why Not? Use more than one balloon if you have lots of players.

1 Decorate the plate if you want to personalize your paddle, then tape two craft sticks to the back to make the handle.

2 You can either play across a table (like traditional ping-pong) if there are two or four players, or bat the balloon to one another across the room. Try to stop it touching the ground.

DONE!

4 MAKE PIPE-CLEANER PUPPETS

Pipe cleaners are quick and easy to work with. If you make a mistake, just unwind them and start again.

Safety First!

Pipe cleaners can be difficult to cut and might damage your scissors, so ask an adult to cut them with wire cutters.

you will need

- Pipe cleaners
- Mini pom-poms of various sizes
- Glue
- White card
- Coloring pens or pencils
- Googly eyes
- Scissors
- Wire cutters (optional)

1 Wind a pipe cleaner around your finger to make each puppet's body. Leave the top sticking up, like a neck, so you can attach the head.

2 Twist more pipe cleaners to make arms, legs, hands, and feet, as shown above, and attach them to the puppet's body. Dab some glue on the end of the neck and push the pom-pom head down onto it, then glue on a tiny pom-pom button.

3 Complete your puppet by attaching a tiny pom-pom nose and googly eyes.

4 Here are some other ideas for your puppet-show cast. You could draw features and accessories on card stock, then color them and ask an adult to help you cut them out.

5 Make a pipe cleaner top hat for this penguin puppet and give him gray wings and a yellow pipe cleaner beak and feet.

6 Put the puppets on your fingers and let the show begin!

DONE!

5 GUESS WHAT'S IN THE BAG

This is a good game for a group of friends and family members of different ages.

you will need
- Cloth bag
- Collection of everyday objects

Top Tip
If you're playing with younger children, give them some clues.

1 One player puts something into the bag without showing the others.

2 The others have to guess what's in the bag just by feeling it.

3 The first player to guess correctly gets a point. Then the next player chooses something to go in the bag. The first player to get five points wins the game.

DONE!

6 REMEMBER THE TRAY

How good is your memory? Test yourself by playing this classic game, then try the memory method below to see if it improves your score.

you will need
- Tray or large plate
- 10-20 small everyday objects (such as a comb, pencil sharpener, coin, spoon, etc.)
- Cloth to cover the tray
- Pencils and paper

Place It!
Here's a trick to help you remember everything on the tray. Imagine you're getting up to go to school and place each of the items along the way.

For example, you get up and "Ouch!" you step on the pencil sharpener. Then you go into the bathroom and comb your hair.

You eat your breakfast with the spoon, then get on the bus and pay with a coin and so on, until each of the objects has a place in your daily routine.

1 Take turns putting objects on the tray (or ask an adult to do this), then cover them with the cloth. Remove the cloth and give everyone one minute to remember as many items as possible.

2 After a minute, cover up the tray and ask the players to write down all the items that they can remember. How well did they do? Now change the objects and keep practicing.

DONE!

7 PLAY FORTY, FORTY

This game is based on hide-and-seek but with a twist.

98... 99... 100

1 Choose a base and a seeker. The seeker stands facing the wall at the base with his/her eyes closed and counts to 100 while the players hide, then shouts, "Ready or not, here I come!"

2 While the seeker is searching for the players, they must try to get back to the base without being caught. If they make it, they shout, "Forty, forty, I'm free!"

3 If the seeker spots someone hiding, he/she shouts, "Forty, forty, I see you under the bed" (or wherever). Then the hider must try to run back to the base without being caught.

4 The last person to be caught becomes the seeker for the next game.

DONE!

8 LEVITATE CARDS

Practice this trick in front of a mirror before you perform it in front of an audience.

1 Cut the plastic strip so it is slightly longer than the width of the card. Stick it to the center of the card, as shown.

2 Carefully place the card in your palm, then show it to your audience and tell them that you are going to make the card rise out of your hand.

3 Wave a magic wand, or your other hand, over the card. Flex your palm slightly at the same time and the card will lift as the plastic strip arches.

DONE!

9 BOWL WITH ALIENS

Defeat these alien invaders by bowling them over.

you will need

- 6 or 10 small plastic bottles, all the same size, with lids
- Liquid paints
- White card
- Scissors
- Black marker pen
- Glue
- Lightweight ball
- Newspaper to protect your work surface

1 Spread out some newspaper, then pour a little paint into each plastic bottle. Put the lids on tightly and swirl the paint around until the bottles are fully colored.

2 Draw some alien shapes the size of the bottles onto white card and paint the shapes to match the bottles.

3 Ask an adult to help you cut out the aliens, along with some eyes, from the white card.

4 Stick the eyes onto the aliens and use the black marker to draw the pupils. Don't forget to give your aliens mouths!

5 Stick the alien shapes onto the matching bottles and leave the glue to dry.

Top Tip
You could stick numbers on the back of each alien pin and award points for each one knocked down.

6 Arrange the alien pins in a triangle formation at one end of the room, where the ball can't damage anything. Now roll the ball along the floor and try to knock over as many aliens as you can.

DONE!

10 SLALOM A PING-PONG BALL

Play this game on your own and try to beat your previous time, or race with friends. If you knock down a flag, add on ten seconds.

1 Make the flags by folding strips of paper in half and cutting triangle shapes. Place a toothpick in the fold and glue the two halves of the triangle together.

you will need
- Colored paper
- Toothpicks
- Glue
- Modeling clay or sticky tack
- Ping-pong ball
- Bendy straws
- Timer

2 Stand the flags in bases made of modelling clay or sticky tack and arrange them on a tabletop in pairs to form "gates."

3 Time yourself as you use the straw to blow the ball from one side of the table to the other, passing through all the gates on the way. How quickly can you complete the course?

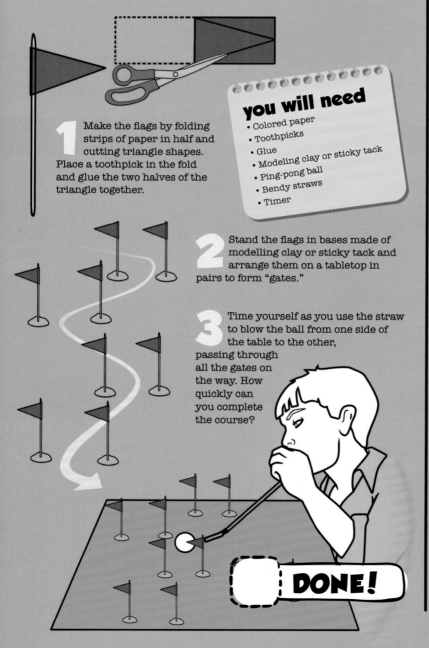

DONE!

11 PLAY STICK CHARADES

You can play this game in teams or as individuals, with each person acting out their charade for everyone else to guess.

you will need
- Popsicle or craft sticks
- Colored markers or paints
- Black marker pen
- Container large enough to hold all the sticks

1 Write the names of books, plays, films, or TV shows in the center of the craft sticks.

2 Color the backs and ends of the sticks to show the category, such red for books, yellow for plays, green for films, and blue for TV shows. If your title is a book and a film, draw red and green candy stripes.

Top Tip
If you point to your ear, it means that the word you are acting out sounds like the word in the title.

3 Each player picks a stick from the jar and shows the back to the audience, so they know the category. The player then acts out the title, without speaking, for the others to guess.

DONE!

12 SPOT THE DIFFERENCE

Would you make a good detective? This game will test your powers of observation. You'll need at least three players and a room with a lot of things in it.

1 All the players take a look around the room, then one stays behind while the others leave. The remaining player moves three objects around.

Safety First!
Check with an adult before you start moving things (or ask an adult to move them for you, then everyone can play the game).

2 The players come back in and have to list the things that have been moved.

DONE!

13 GO ON A TREASURE HUNT

Organize this treasure hunt for your friends and family, or ask an adult to do it so you can play, too. If you don't have any sticks, use a piece of paper and cut it up.

you will need
- 8–10 popsicle or craft sticks
- Tape
- Marker pens
- Treasure, such as sweets or a small toy

1 Stick the craft sticks together with tape, then write down where to find the treasure by writing one letter on each stick.

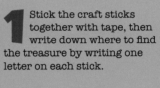

2 Turn the sticks over and draw a picture on the front, then take the tape off to separate the sticks and hide them all in one room.

3 The treasure seekers will need to find all the sticks and arrange them in the right order, using the picture on the front as a guide, so they can discover where the treasure is hidden.

DONE!

14 ENJOY A DAY AT THE SPA

When your feet are fresh and your face is glowing, have some fun with a game of musical manicures.

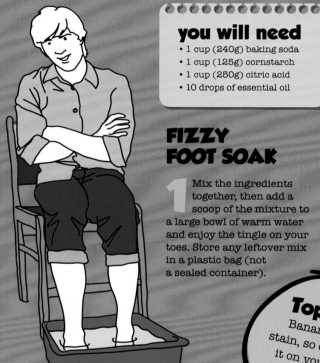

you will need
- 1 cup (240g) baking soda
- 1 cup (125g) cornstarch
- 1 cup (250g) citric acid
- 10 drops of essential oil

FIZZY FOOT SOAK

1 Mix the ingredients together, then add a scoop of the mixture to a large bowl of warm water and enjoy the tingle on your toes. Store any leftover mix in a plastic bag (not a sealed container).

Top Tip
Banana can stain, so don't get it on your best clothes or towels.

BANANA FACE MASK

1 Mash the banana with a fork until you have a smooth paste, then mix in the honey and lemon juice. Spread the mask over your face, avoiding your eyes. Leave it for 10 minutes, then wash it off.

you will need
- A ripe banana
- 1 teaspoon lemon juice
- 1 teaspoon honey
- An old towel and an old T-shirt

MUSICAL MANICURES

1 Players sit in a circle and pass around a bottle of nail polish while the music plays, as if playing musical chairs.

you will need
- Nail polish (various colors if possible)
- Nail polish remover
- Music

2 When the music stops, the person holding the polish has to paint one nail, then the game continues. Change the color of the polish between rounds if possible.

3 The first person to have a full set of painted nails is the winner.

 DONE!

15 PLAY P-I-G

You'll need a set of four matching cards (e.g. four aces, four jacks, etc.) for each player, so you can play this game with up to 13 people.

1 Shuffle the cards well, then deal four cards to each player. Players take one of their four cards and pass it to the person on their left. At the same time, they receive a card from the player on their right, and so on.

2 When a player has a full set of matching cards, they quietly touch the end of their nose with their index finger (this player is now out of the game). All the other players should then do the same, even if they don't have a full set.

3 The last player to touch their nose is given a letter: first P, then I, then G. The first player to complete the word PIG is the loser.

Charlie P I
Emily P
Liam P I
Jo P I G

DONE!

16 SPY CLOUD SHAPES

It's been said that clouds are the sky's imagination. Why not catch a little of its creative magic and try some cloud shaping?

Top Tip
Cloud pictures don't just appear in blue summer skies. Try cloud shaping at sunrise and sunset and during a storm, too.

1 Lie down on your back and stare into the sky. Watch the clouds drift by.

2 Let your mind wander. What do you see? Are there castles, horses, monsters? Keep looking until you see something. Relax and let your imagination flow.

3 Now look at the blue spaces between the clouds. Pictures lie hidden there, too.

DONE!

17 PLAY ROCK DOMINOES

It's so tempting to collect those lovely smooth, flat stones on the beach or in the garden. But what do you do with them? With a little bit of paint and a steady hand, you can turn them into dominoes. This game has been popular since ancient times — a set was found in Tutankhamen's tomb!

you will need
- 28 smooth, flat stones
- White paint pen (or acrylic paint, a small brush, and a steady hand)

Domino Piece Guide

1 Collect 28 smooth, flat stones. Wash them to remove any sand or soil and paint a white line across the center of each.

2 Then, on either side of the lines, mark with two sets of dots in every combination from zero to six. Use this guide to make sure that you don't miss any.

3 When the paint is dry, play with your dominoes on the lawn or at an outdoor table. You need at least one other player. First, place the dominoes facedown (with no dots showing and shuffle them around. This is the boneyard. This is because dominoes were originally made out of bone. Yuck!

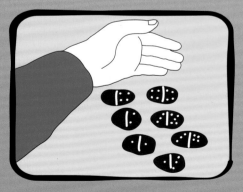

4 Each player takes 7 dominoes. The players should see their own dominoes, but not the other players'. No peeking! Decide who starts by each picking up a domino from the boneyard. The player with the highest number of dots goes first.

5 Lay the first domino. The next player places one of his or her dominoes at one end of the first domino by matching the number of dots. If he or she can't go, then he or she should pick up a new pebble from the boneyard.

6 The game continues with each player matching one end of the domino chain in turn. If a double is laid, set the pebble vertically rather than horizontally. Every time you can't go, pick up from the boneyard. If you run out of space, start turning corners with the pieces. The first player to use up all his or her pebbles wins!

DONE!

18 MAKE AND PLAY LADYBUG TIC-TAC-TOE

You might know this game as X's and O's. The ancient Romans called it *terni lapilli*. Whatever you call it, it's super cool when you have pet ladybug rocks to play with!

you will need
- 10 smooth flat stones
- Acrylic paints in red, black, white, blue, and yellow
- Chalk
- Paintbrushes
- Sticks and twigs
- Garden twine

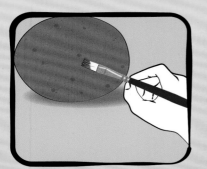

1 Find 10 ladybug-shaped stones in your garden or park. Paint 5 of them red and the other 5 yellow. Give them a couple of coats of paint to make sure they're well covered. Let them dry thoroughly between coats.

2 Use chalk to mark the head and wing line on each. Use a thinner brush to paint over the wing line with black paint, then paint in the head. You can rub off the chalk when it's dry.

3 Now add the dots. You can either paint on the dots with a brush or dip a finger into the paint and finger paint them on.

4 When the black paint is dry, add other details — eyes, mouth, nose, and antennae. The end of the paintbrush is great for making dots for the antennae.

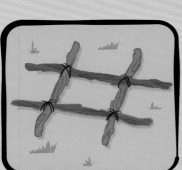

5 When you've painted all 10 stones, you have all the pieces for the game. Make the grid by crisscrossing sticks and branches on the ground. You can make them sturdy by tying them with garden twine.

6 Play tic-tac-toe! One player uses the red ladybugs, the other uses the yellow ladybugs. Take turns placing a ladybug in a square. The first to get three in a row wins!

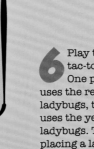

DONE!

19 BUILD A HOUSE OF CARDS

Start with a three-story house, then add more triangles at the base to build higher. A six-story house will need a six-triangle base.

1 Balance two cards against each other to make a triangle shape and carry on until you have a line of three.

2 Carefully lay two cards on top of your line of triangles.

you will need
- Playing cards
- A flat surface and a steady hand

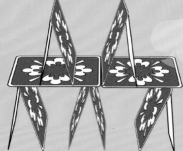

3 Build the next story using four cards to make two triangles and lay one card on top. Then make a triangle with two cards on top of that to make the third story.

Why Not? Challenge a friend to see who can build the tallest house.

DONE!

20 MAKE A COIN JUMP

Take time to practice this trick in front of a mirror before you show it off to your audience.

1 Place the coin in the palm of your right hand, just in front of your index finger.

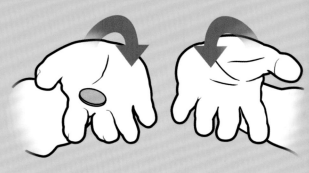

2 Show the audience both your palms, then quickly flip your hands over and clench your fists. The coin should have flown into your other hand.

Top Tip The coin must be in the right place for the trick to work. If it didn't work, try swapping hands.

3 Now open your hands and show the audience that the coin is in your left hand.

DONE!

21 INVENT A SECRET HANDSHAKE

Psssst! What's the coolest way for best friends to say hi? A super-secret handshake, complete with tugs, snaps, and other slick moves.

1.

2.

3.

whoop-whoop!

1 Decide on 5 or 6 moves for the handshake. Check out the list below, and see what works for you and your pals.

2 Any secret handshake should involve all your senses. Add hoots, whistles, tongue-clicks, and a shriek or two.

3 Make an order for your handshake steps. Remember to add in something unique to your handshake — a move you think of together.

Why not try...
- Fist bump
- Clasp
- Pinky swear
- Touch fingertips
- Shoulder bump
- Fingers in the air
- Itsy Bitsy Spider fingertips
- High fives (up high and down low)
- High tens (that's with both hands)
- Hug it out
- Hip check
- Palm swipe
- Finger pulls

Top Tip
Practice, practice, PRACTICE. You may have five or more steps in the shake, but you want to make it look effortless.

DONE!

---

22 GET TRICKY

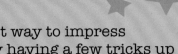

Hey, presto! The easiest way to impress friends and family is by having a few tricks up your sleeve. Try this one at your next party.

THE FLOATING KETCHUP

1 Before you start, empty a plastic bottle and fill it with water almost all the way to the top. Explain to your audience that you can make a tomato ketchup packet move at your command, then open the bottle and insert the packet. Close the lid.

2 With one hand, hold the bottle by the side so you can clearly see the ketchup packet. With the other hand, point at the packet, giving it commands as you go: "Ketchup up!" "Ketchup down!"

3 The trick: As you tell the packet to move, you gently squeeze on the bottle. The water pressure will make the ketchup packet rise and fall and even stop on command!

DONE!

23 PLAY WITH SHADOWS

You can make an entire zoo come to life on your wall, using only your hands, fingers, and some clever lighting.

SHOWTIME!

Shine a flashlight onto an empty wall. The fun of making animal shadow puppets is the practice! Try different shapes and animals to see what looks best.

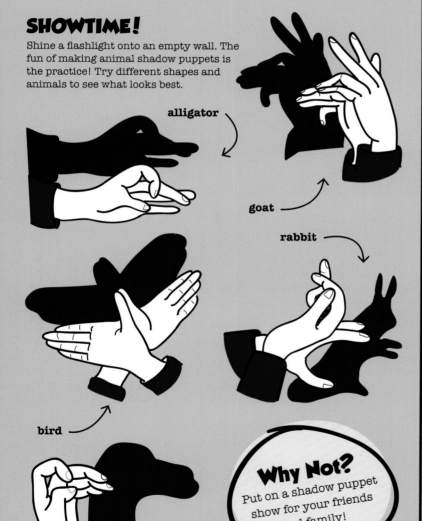

alligator

goat

rabbit

bird

camel

Why Not?
Put on a shadow puppet show for your friends and family!

DONE!

24 TRY A BALLOON TRICK

Push a pin into a balloon and it goes pop, right? Wow your friends with this simple trick!

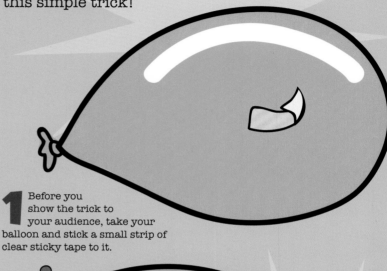

1 Before you show the trick to your audience, take your balloon and stick a small strip of clear sticky tape to it.

BANG!

2 Now for the trick! Hold the balloon so that the tape is facing away from your audience. Say the magic words while you take a pin and carefully, (watch your fingers!) push the pin into the balloon through the tape. The balloon shouldn't pop!

3 Lastly, to prove that the balloon wasn't a fake, use the pin to pop the balloon and end your trick with a bang!

DONE!

25 MAKE AND FLY A QUICK KITE

There are many different types of kite. Here's a quick kite you can create from a simple brown bag!

1 Get the bag ready. Decorate it with markers and doodle whatever you want!

Why Not?
Experiment with kite materials. If you use a larger bag, will it fly faster? If you use a plastic bag, will it fly higher?

sticky tape

2 Open the paper bag and punch one hole at each of the four corners at the top of the bag. The hole should be about 1 inch (3cm) away from the rim.

hole punch

4 Tape a few pieces of crêpe paper to the closed end for your kite's tail.

5 Time for takeoff! Run fast and drag the kite behind you until it catches a gust of wind and flies into the air.

you will need
- Brown paper bag
- Markers, crayons, or whatever else to design and decorate your kite
- Hole punch
- Four pieces of string 20 inches (50cm) long
- Piece of string at least 8 feet (2.5m) long
- Pencil or stick
- Sticky tape
- Several torn pieces of crêpe paper 8 inches (20cm) long

3 Push one 20-inch (50cm) piece of string through each of the holes and tie a knot so it stays in place. Once you have attached all four strings, tie their ends together and connect them to your 8-foot (2.5-m) long piece. Wrap the long string around a pencil or stick to make a handle.

DONE!

26 FLY PAPER PLANES

This game tests your plane-making skills as well as your aim. Play with friends and keep a list of the scores, or practice on your own.

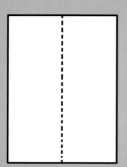

1 To make the planes, fold the paper in half lengthways, then fold the two top corners into the middle.

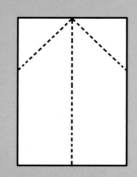

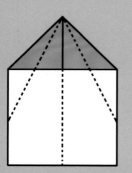

2 Fold the two angled sides inwards to meet at the center fold.

3 Now fold along the center line, so the folds are on the inside, then fold down the flaps on either side to form the wings.

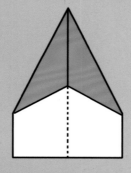

you will need
• Sheets of paper
• Large piece of cardboard
• Scissors
• Paints (optional)
• Masking tape (optional)

Top Tip
The secret to making a good paper plane is to keep the folds crisp. Press them down with your nail at each stage.

4 While you make the planes, ask an adult to cut some holes in the cardboard. Some should be just large enough for the planes to fly through and some should be bigger.

5 Paint a sky background on the cardboard (if you like) and give each hole a score depending on its size — smaller holes are worth more points than large ones.

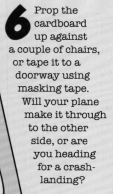

6 Prop the cardboard up against a couple of chairs, or tape it to a doorway using masking tape. Will your plane make it through to the other side, or are you heading for a crash-landing?

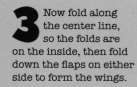

DONE!

27 TWIST A SWAN

Turn a balloon into a beautiful swan and impress your party guests!

Twist here

1 Use a long, thin balloon for this trick. Inflate your balloon most of the way, leaving 2–4 inches (5–10cm) at the end. Bend the whole balloon into a large circle so that the knot is halfway inside the circle. Grab the balloon at the center and twist all the way around, holding the knot.

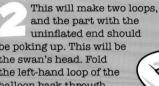

2 This will make two loops, and the part with the uninflated end should be poking up. This will be the swan's head. Fold the left-hand loop of the balloon back through the right hand loop to make a "balloon body."

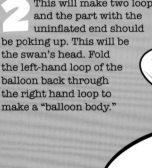

Squeeze here

3 While holding the top end, squeeze the air from the inflated part around the bend in the balloon. This makes the balloon stay in a bent position that's just right for the swan's head!

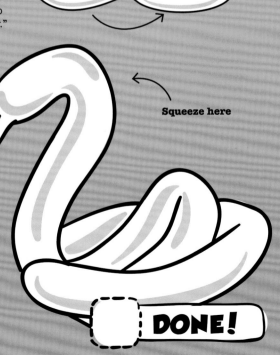

DONE!

28 BE A VENTRILOQUIST

Got a sock puppet? Time to teach it how to talk!

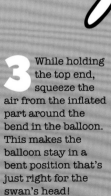

BLAH BLAH BLAH BLAH

1 Capture your audience's attention by saying something as simple as, "Did you hear that?" The question will make them listen more closely.

2 "Swallow" your actual voice and speak, moving your mouth as little as possible. You want to control your breathing and talk from "inside" your mouth.

3 Saying the letters B, F, M, P, Q, V, and W is very challenging. Try using the substitutions in this chart:

SOUND	TIP
For B	replace it with a "geh" sound at the back of the throat
For F	use a "th" sound so "fabulous" becomes "thabulous"
For M	use "nah" or "neh" instead so "master" becomes "nah-ster"
For P	use "kl" in the back of your throat, so "paint" becomes "klaint"
For Q	stretch out the sound so it's "koo"
For V	just like F, use the "th" sound
For W	use "oooh" at the start of a word so "welcome" would sound like "oooh-elcome"

DONE!

PLAY WITH PEN AND PAPER

Get set for gaming fun! All you need is a pen, some paper, and a friend or two!

HANGMAN

Think of a word and give your friend the subject (such as a place, person, sport, film, or TV show). For example, we've used Italy below. Next, draw a line for each letter in your word. Your friend then chooses letters they think could be in the word, one at a time. If a letter is correct, write it on your lines in its position. However, if it's wrong, add a line to your hangman! Your friend has six tries to guess the word before the hangman drawing is complete. These are the steps to complete your drawing:

b ⫽ E ⫽ E TA Y

CHARADES

You'll need at least three people to play this one. First, cut or rip paper into little slips. Write names of books, TV shows, and films on separate slips of paper. Now fold them and mix them up in a pile. Take turns to pick out a slip of paper, then "act" out silent clues to get your friends to guess what it is. There's only one rule — you can't make a sound! Here are ways to show what you're acting out:

Book

Film

TV Show

You Got It!

DONE!

30 BLOW GIANT BUBBLES

Make your own oversized wand to blow gigantic bubbles!

you will need

For the bubble solution:
- 3 cups (700ml) water
- ½ cup (120ml) dish soap
- ½ cup (60g) cornstarch
- 1 tablespoon baking powder
- 1 tablespoon golden syrup

For your super-bubble wand:
- 2 plastic straws
- 6.5 feet (2m) string
- Tape measure
- Scissors
- Dishwashing bowl

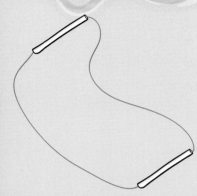

1 Measure out 6.5 feet (2m) of string and thread through both straws. Tie the ends of your string together, then space out your straws to make the handles of your bubble wand.

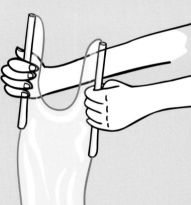

2 Put all of the ingredients for your bubble mixture into a dishwashing bowl, and mix them together.

3 Dip your bubble wand into the mixture. Raise it up into the air, and slowly walk backwards. Don't be put off if it doesn't work the first time — you'll soon be making mind-blowing bubbles!

 **DONE!**

31 NEVER BE BORED AGAIN

If you're alone, there's no reason to be bored! Even when you're all by yourself, there is always something fun to try.

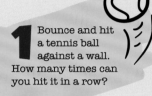

1 Bounce and hit a tennis ball against a wall. How many times can you hit it in a row?

5 Create a small shadow puppet theater using a box, a flashlight, and some small toy figures.

2 Twirl a hula hoop indoors or out. How long can you keep it spinning without dropping it?

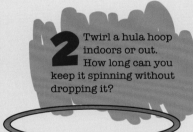

6 Find a book you've never read before and start it.

3 Make up a dance routine to your favorite song.

7 Write a letter to yourself in the future.

4 Find three things in your bedroom that could be used to make instruments.

8 Invent and draw your own comic book character.

 **DONE!**

32 PLAY NO-NUMBERS DOMINOES

You don't need tiles to play dominoes. All you need are some craft sticks, colored pens, and a flat surface to play on!

you will need

- Pack of wooden popsicle or craft sticks— check how many there are in the pack. You will need 28.
- Felt-tip pens. You need 7 colors: blue, green, purple, yellow, and red. Leaving a popsicle stick blank counts as one color, too.
- Envelope big enough to store your craft sticks.

you will need to use seven different colors

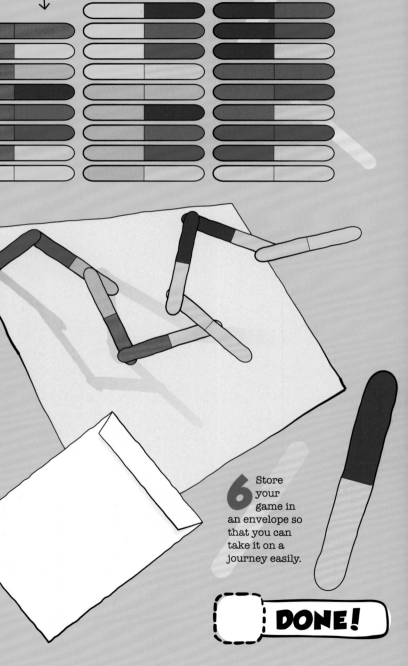

3 To play, deal all the craft sticks out between players.

4 Each player takes turns laying down a craft stick. You must match the color of a craft stick tip already on the table (you can match either end). If you can't make a match, you must miss a turn.

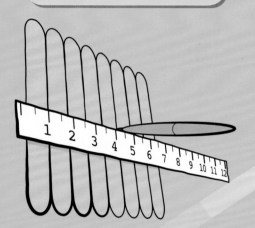

1 Lay some craft sticks in a row and use a ruler to draw a line across the middle. Do this to all the craft sticks.

2 Color the craft stick halves, following the colors indicated in the chart above.

5 The winner is the player to get rid of all their craft sticks first.

6 Store your game in an envelope so that you can take it on a journey easily.

DONE!

33 PLAY BATTLESHIPS

This is a great game to play when you and a friend have time on your hands. Before you start, make some battleship grids.

you will need
- Paper and pens
- Ruler
- Envelope to store your grids

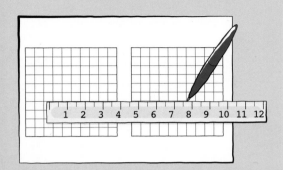

1 Draw some grids using your ruler and pen. Draw two grids on one letter-size sheet of paper to make a set. Each grid should be 10 squares across and 10 squares down. You don't have to be too accurate about the square size.

2 Number the grids — from 1 to 10 across the top and from A to J down the sides.

3 To play, each player gets a set of two grids. They mark their fleet of battleships on the first grid, using the instructions in the blue box below. You can place your ships anywhere on the grid, going up or across (not diagonally).

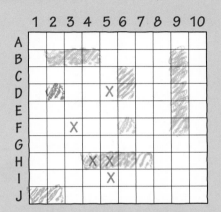

Where will you hide your aircraft carrier?

5 If you eventually hit all the squares and sink a ship, your opponent must tell you.

6 The winner is the player who knocks out all the opponent's ships first.

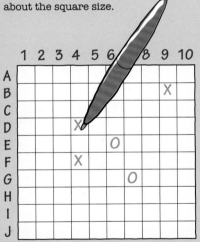

4 Take turns to call out a square coordinate — 4D or 9B, for example. Your opponent must tell you if you hit one of the ships on their grid or if you missed. If you make a hit, mark the corresponding square on your second grid with an X. If you miss, mark the square with a O.

SHIPS PER PLAYER:
1 aircraft carrier: 5 squares
1 battleship: 4 squares

1 cruiser: 3 squares
2 destroyers: 2 squares each
2 submarines: 1 square each

DONE!

34 NAIL THAT NUMBER

Play this spot-the-number challenge next time you are in the car! Play in teams so that everyone can join in.

Why Not?
If you are on a longer trip, you can keep an eye out for numbers all the way through your adventure.

2 ✓   10 ✓
3 ✓   11 ✓
4 ✓   12 ✓
5 ✓   13 ✓
6 ✓   14 ✓
7 ✓   15 ✓
8 ✓   16 ✓
9 ✓   17 ✓
       18 ✓

1 Spot three single digit numbers in a row. These could be on a license plate or on a building, for example.

3 Vary the game by adding up two numbers only, and keeping a note of the sum answers. See if you can get every answer from 2 (1 + 1) to 18 (9 + 9) during your trip.

2 Add up the numbers. The idea is to see how high an answer you can get during your trip. The top answer would be 27 (9 + 9 + 9).

DONE!

35 PLAY ABC KNOCKOUT

This is a fun game to play with others when you are on a longer car trip. Show off your mad detective skills!

Why Not?
You can play this game without spotting things. Come up with a category such as animals, girls' names, or boys' names, and then write your alphabet list.

1 Write the alphabet down the left-hand side of your paper.

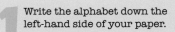

you will need
- Pencils and paper for each player
- A watch to time your game

3 If two players have the same answer, these cancel each other out and don't score. Score one point for every answer you have that nobody else does.

2 Spot one object for each letter and write it down. Play for 10 minutes, then read out your answers.

DONE!

36 PLAY KITTYCAT DRAW

You probably know how to play an old game called "hangman." It's a little gruesome so we've given it a furry feline makeover!

1 The first player must think of a word. Draw dashes where the letters go. For example the word "book" would have four dashes.

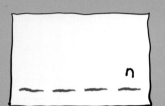
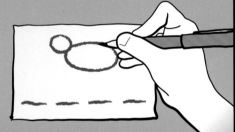

2 The second player guesses a letter. If it's in the word, write it on the dash.

3 If the letter isn't in the word, start drawing a cat. It has ten sections to draw.

4 Each time a player makes a wrong guess, draw a section of the cat. Will you finish it before the player guesses the word?

There are 10 separate sections of the cat's body, and the face (eyes, nose, and mouth) is one final section.

DONE!

37 PLAY WOULD YOU RATHER?

Here's a question game, just for fun.

Why Not? Come up with your own cool "would you rather" questions.

WOULD YOU RATHER

Be a shark or a whale?

Be a grizzly bear or a polar bear?

Be a tiger or a lion?

Be a dog or a cat?
Be a bird or a bee?
Be a horse or a deer?

Be a worm or a spider?

1 Ask your friend one of the "would you rather" questions.

2 They must pick one of the answers, and explain why!

DONE!

38 DO MAGIC TRICKS

Wow your friends and family with some magic tricks! With a little practice you'll be able to impress without any special equipment, though it helps to wear the right clothes.

MAGIC GROWING ARM

you will need
• Wear a short-sleeved T-shirt under a long-sleeved jacket or coat

1 Hold your right arm across your body, clamped firmly against your chest.

2 Grip your right wrist and try to pull, making it look like hard work. Say "Grow, arm!" in a loud voice.

3 Start to pull your right arm across to your left, making sure your long sleeve stays where it is, clamped to your chest. Your arm will appear to magically grow!

MOVE A PEN WITH YOUR MIND

you will need
• Pen, pencil, or straw — any will do as long as it's round
• Wearing a baseball cap helps
• Flat surface

1 Tell your audience that you're going to try to move the pen with the power of your mind. Lay the pen on the table as shown.

2 Do a bit of performing to distract your audience. Show them you're getting ready to use the power of your mind!

3 Bend over and very gently blow. Don't make a noise, but it will help mask any blowing if you're doing this in a noisy location such as a café. Your baseball cap will shield your face, too.

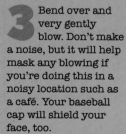

DONE!

39 MAKE A SQUARE

Here's a pen-and-paper game for two players to play on a rainy day or on the go.

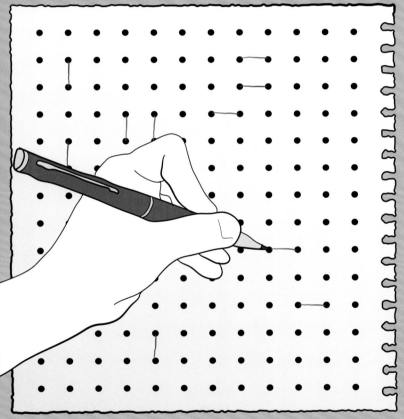

1 Draw a grid of dots as shown. You could draw eight dots down and eight dots across, but make the grid bigger if you want a longer game.

2 The first player draws a line between two dots (no diagonal lines, please). The second player draws another line between two dots. Take turns drawing lines.

3 If you can draw the last side of a square, you win that square. Put your initials in it. You then get another turn to draw a line.

4 The winner is the player with the most squares at the end of the game.

DONE!

40 BALANCE A SPOON ON YOUR NOSE

At your next party, try this trick!

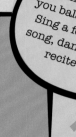

Why Not?
Do something else while you balance the spoon. Sing a few verses of a song, dance around, or recite a poem.

1 Grab a small spoon to perform your trick with. A teaspoon is perfect.

2 Rub the concave side of the spoon on your nose to get friction. Gently tilt your head back and keep rubbing. Once the spoon starts sticking to your nose, let go of the handle!

3 Having trouble becoming "attached" to your spoon? Breathe on it or rub it a few times with your index finger before trying again. That should help!

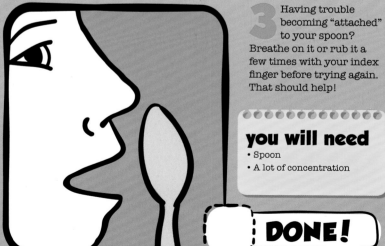

you will need
- Spoon
- A lot of concentration

DONE!

41 SEND A MESSAGE IN A BOTTLE

What if you wrote a note, stuck it into a bottle, and tossed it into the ocean? How far would it go? Who would find it? If you don't live near the ocean, why not imagine what would happen if you sent a message, and write story about it?

1 Find a medium-sized glass bottle with a strong lid to keep the water out.

3 Write your message. Include an adult's email address so that whoever finds the bottle can contact you!

2 Find some thin card, if you can, and a permanent marker to write your note.

4 Make sure the tide is on its way out when you throw your bottle into the sea, otherwise it will just end up back on land. Off it goes!

DONE!

42 BUILD AN EXTREME INDOOR FORT

What's better on a wintery day than a super-sized, homemade fort? Gather together blankets, cushions, and chairs to see what you can make!

Put all breakable objects away. Try not to use weak or small pieces of furniture that might fall down on the people inside the fort.

Drape blankets, sheets, and towels over large pieces of furniture like a dining table, or the back of an armchair or sofa.

Use chairs to prop up your sheets, too. Turn them around so they can be used as tables inside the fort.

The inside of your fort must be comfy and cozy. Fill the floor with cushions so you've always got somewhere squishy to sit.

Fill your fort with fun things to do. Books, games, and snacks are perfect!

Sheets make the best roofs because they are light. Keep them in place with large clips or cushions.

 DONE!

43 PLAY POOH STICKS

You can thank Winnie the Pooh for the invention of this super simple game. Pooh played it on a warm, sunny day with his friends. Play it with yours the next time you cross a bridge over a stream.

1 Each find a stick. Look at each other's sticks, and agree whose is whose. You could even tie a piece of different-colored string to each stick to remind you which is yours.

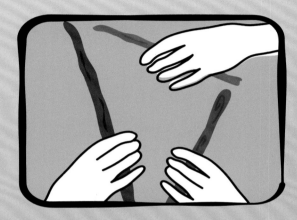

2 Gather on the side of the bridge where the stream runs in (upstream). Stand side by side, holding your sticks at arms length over the stream.

4 Run to the other side of the bridge (downstream). Who-ever's stick appears first wins!

3 Ready, steady, GO! Drop your sticks at the same time.

 **DONE!**

44 BOB FOR APPLES

Traditionally a Halloween game, this is great fun on any occasion — you just need a bowl of water and some apples. Be warned, though, you WILL get wet!

1 Put a bowl on a sturdy surface at roughly waist height, like a strong outdoor table. Fill it three-quarters full with water and float the apples on the top. Add as many apples as will fit, but not so many that they can't move around in the water.

3 When a player has caught an apple, the counting stops and that is their score. Everyone takes a turn, and the person with the lowest score wins!

2 Players must put their hands behind their backs while trying to catch an apple between their teeth. Decide how long each player has — for example, 20 seconds. All other players should count them down by saying one-Mississippi, two-Mississippi, and so on.

DONE!

45 CREATE YOUR OWN OBSTACLE COURSE

Next time you are stuck indoors, make a homemade obstacle course! Use objects from around your home to make yours.

START

1 Toy toss: Put a laundry basket at one end of the room, grab an armful of cuddly toys and cushions, and try to throw them in. Get three out of five in the basket before moving on to the next stage!

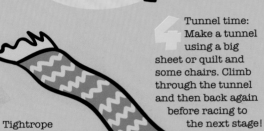

2 Funny jumps: At this stop on the course, each player does a sequence of jumps in the air. Do a star jump, a frog jump, and a bunny hop.

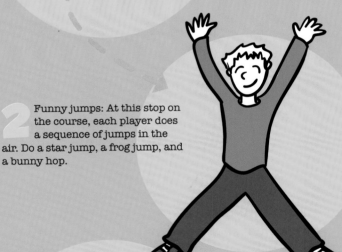

3 Hula-paloola: Place a hula hoop on the floor and jump in and out of it ten times with your feet together.

4 Tunnel time: Make a tunnel using a big sheet or quilt and some chairs. Climb through the tunnel and then back again before racing to the next stage!

5 Tightrope walk: Place a scarf in a straight line along the floor and pretend you are a circus performer! Walk across the scarf without stepping over the edges, and hold your arms out to the side to help you balance.

6 Hat's the way to do it! Get a pile of hats, scarves, and gloves. Each player must put them all on, strike a pose, then take them all off again!

FINISH

DONE!

46 PLAY FROGS AND FLIES

Are any of your friends super sleuths? Maybe one or two are heading for a career on the stage? If so, they'll enjoy this game.

Why Not?
If there's quite a large group of you, you could also select a fly saver. This is a person who can bring the flies back to life with a special signal (for example, pointing). But if the detective works out who the fly saver is, then he or she also becomes a dead fly.

1 Sit in a circle and choose a detective. This person must now go away from the group, out of earshot, until he or she is called back. Now decide who is going to be the frog. Everyone else is a fly.

2 Call the detective back. The frog is going to "kill" the flies secretly while the detective isn't looking by sticking his or her tongue out at them.

3 The flies should "die" as dramatically as possible, with lots of spinning and buzzing. They eventually fall into a heap on the floor.

4 The detective needs to work out who the frog is before the flies are killed off. If the frog kills off all the flies but one, he or she wins. If the detective guesses who the frog is before that, he or she wins. But the detective only has 3 guesses.

5 For a new game, start all over again with a new detective.

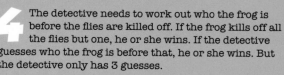

DONE!

47 PLAY DRESS-UP RELAY

This is a game for at least four players. If you have an odd number, choose one person to be the referee or allow one player to have two turns.

1 Put two boxes containing the same items of clothes at one end of the room and two empty boxes at the other end. Divide the players into two teams and get half of each team to line up next to the empty boxes and half next to the boxes of clothes.

you will need
- 4 large cardboard boxes
- 2 matching sets of dressing-up clothes, big enough to fit all players (shirts, shorts, jackets, hats, scarves or ties, gloves, and so on)

2 At the word "go," two of the players standing next to the empty boxes race to their team's box of clothes, put them all on, then race back to the empty box, take off the clothes, and put them in the empty box.

3 The players standing at the opposite end (by the empty boxes) then take a turn and so on. The first team to finish, once everyone has had a turn, wins.

DONE!

48 SPLAT THE RAT

This is a game for two or more players. If you don't have a large tube, join two paper towel tubes together and use a smaller sock to make a mouse instead of a rat.

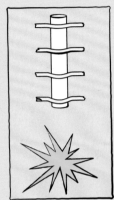

1 Fill the sock with dried peas, beans, or rice, then tie the open end with string, leaving a piece to make a tail. Decorate the sock to look like a rat if you want to.

you will need
- Old sock
- Dried peas, beans, or rice
- String
- Long cardboard or plastic tube
- Large piece of strong cardboard or wood
- Tape
- Roll of newspaper

2 Tape the tube firmly to the cardboard or wood, leaving about 30 inches (75cm) free at the bottom.

3 Make a "splatter" by rolling up a newspaper and fastening it with sticky tape. Prop the cardboard or wood up against a wall and drop the rat into the top of the tube. The other player should try to splat it before it hits the floor.

DONE!

2

ARTSY

Who knew you were a creative genius?
Make your own pop-up cards,
transform your T-shirts, star in your
own movie, or craft fun pom-poms and
twinkly lanterns to style up your
room. Put your heart into your art and
create mini-masterpieces.
No beret necessary.

49 KNIT WITHOUT NEEDLES

Finger knitting is really easy. It produces a long rope that you can use to make necklaces, belts, lanyards, and much more.

Top Tip
To save your knitting for later, slip a pencil, chopstick, or paintbrush through the loops and lift them off your fingers.

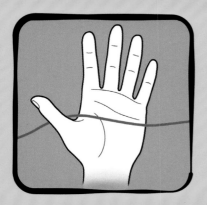

1 Let the end of the ball of yarn hang between the thumb and palm of your left hand if you're right-handed, or your right if you're left-handed.

2 Take the yarn across your palm, loop it around your little finger and weave it backward and forward through your fingers.

3 When you reach your index finger, wrap the yarn around it and weave it back the other way toward your little finger.

4 Now loop the yarn around all four fingers at once.

you will need

- Yarn (thicker yarn is best because your knitting will grow more quickly)
- Scissors
- A pen, paintbrush, or chopstick if you want to save your knitting for later
- A needle if you want to sew strips of knitting together

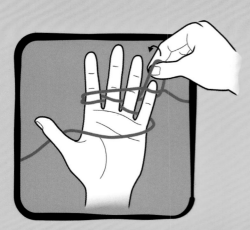

5 Slip the bottom loops over the top loop of yarn, working from your little finger to your index finger. Repeat steps 4 and 5 until the knitting is as long as you want it to be.

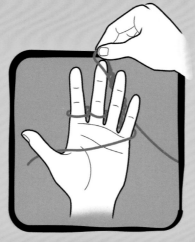

6 To cast off, hook the loop from your little finger over your ring finger, hook the bottom loop from that finger over the top one and so on, until you just have one loop left on your index finger. Cut a tail of yarn about 6 inches (15cm) long, pull that through the last loop, and tie it off.

7 You could braid ropes of finger knitting together to make bracelets for your friends.

DONE!

You could use hard-boiled eggs for this activity, but you can only keep them for a week. If you want your eggs to last longer, blow out the insides so you have a clean, empty shell. Here's how to do it.

Top Tip

Don't waste the eggs! Use them to make omelettes, scrambled eggs, or cakes.

you will need

- Eggs at room temperature
- Sharp object, such as a needle or the point of a compass
- Drinking straw
- Bowl
- Food coloring
- Vinegar
- Optional: rubber bands, felt pens, stickers, googly eyes, stick-on jewels, ribbon, tape, etc.

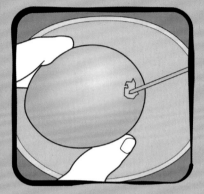

1 Ask an adult to make a hole in the wider end of the egg with a sharp object and gently enlarge it so the contents of the egg can pass through. Poke around in the hole to mix the egg up, then make a smaller hole in the other end of the egg.

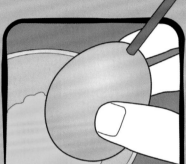

2 Hold the larger hole over a bowl and place a drinking straw on top of the smaller hole. Blow through the smaller hole until the egg is empty.

5 Now it's time to get creative! Here are a few eggcellent ideas for decorating your eggs.

3 Clean the inside of the eggshell by holding it under the faucet (take care, it will be quite fragile), then leave it to dry.

4 Color the eggs by dipping them in a glass half-filled with hot water, a teaspoon of food coloring, and a teaspoon of vinegar. You can create stripes, spots, or other patterns on your eggs by placing rubber bands or stickers on the eggs before you dip them.

DONE!

51 MAKE MINI POM-POMS

Pom-poms are useful for all kinds of craft activities. Here's how to make them quickly and easily, using a fork.

you will need
- A fork with four prongs
- Thick yarn (light worsted is best)
- Scissors

1 Wrap the yarn around the fork. You'll need to do this at least 40 times.

2 Cut a separate 8-inch (20-cm) length of yarn, then thread one end between the second and third prongs at the bottom and pull the other end through the second and third prongs at the top. Tie the ends together as tightly as you can.

3 Carefully slip the bundle of yarn off the end of the fork and ask an adult to help you snip through all the loops. Roll the pom-pom between your hands to fluff it up and give it a trim to get rid of any uneven ends.

Why Not?
Glue or sew two mini pom-poms together to make baby birds. Just add eyes and a beak.

DONE!

52 PRINT YOUR OWN WRAPPING PAPER

If you have a present to wrap, why not make your own hand-printed paper? Use your stamp to make gift tags, cards, and stationery, too.

you will need
- Plain paper big enough for your package
- Evenly shaped potato
- Knife
- Cookie cutter(s)
- Paper towel
- Paint and a paintbrush

Safety First!
Ask an adult to help you cut the potato.

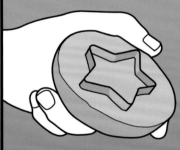

1 Cut the potato in half, widthways or lengthways, depending on your design, and press the cookie cutter firmly into the cut side of one half.

3 Apply paint to your potato stamp with a paintbrush and press the stamp evenly onto the paper. Leave until completely dry before using.

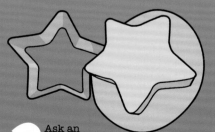

2 Ask an adult to help you cut away the potato around the cookie cutter shape, and dry the potato with paper towel.

Why Not?
Make two-tone designs using the other half of the potato to print a background in a different color.

DONE!

53 PAINT A PORTRAIT

If you can't find someone willing to sit still for you, try drawing a self-portrait or copy a face from a magazine. Every face is different, of course, but these tips will help you to get the proportions right.

you will need
- Paper
- Soft pencil
- Black marker pen
- Paints and brushes
- Mirror, if you're doing a self-portrait

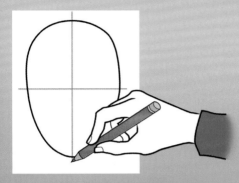

1 Draw an egg shape in the middle of the paper, then draw a faint cross through the center. This will help you to place the features.

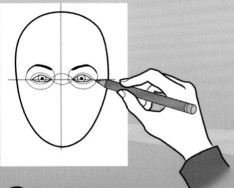

2 Draw two circles across the central horizontal line and sketch in the eyebrows along the top of the circles, then draw the eyes in the center of the circles. They should be almond-shaped and about an eye's width apart.

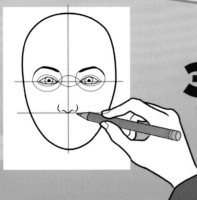

3 Now divide the lower half of the face by drawing a faint line halfway between the central line and the chin. Sketch the bottom of the nose resting on this line.

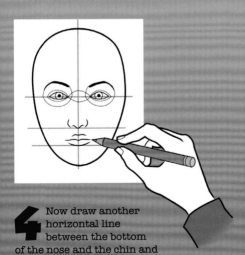

4 Now draw another horizontal line between the bottom of the nose and the chin and draw the mouth. The bottom lip should rest on this line.

5 Add the ears. The bottom of the ear should be in line with the bottom of the nose and the top in line with the top of the eye.

6 Complete your drawing by adding the neck and hair. Go over the lines (except the guidelines) using a marker pen, then erase your guidelines. Now your portrait is ready to paint.

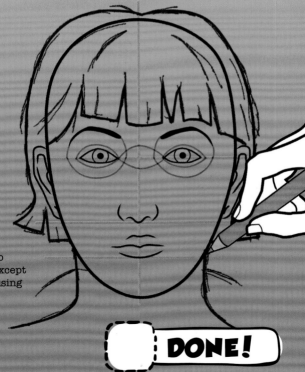

DONE!

54 CREATE A CORAL REEF

Create a coral reef on your wall with these colorful tropical fish — then give your ocean art more bite by adding a hungry shark looking for lunch!

you will need
- 6 small white paper plates
- 2 large white paper plates
- Paints
- Paintbrush
- 6 googly eyes
- Glue
- Scissors

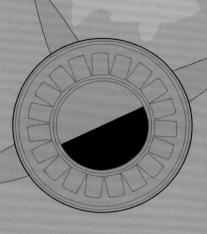

1 To make the tropical fish, paint the backs of four of the small paper plates in bright colors. While they are drying, cut fins and tails from the other two small plates and paint them, too.

4 Cut three fins from the other large plate and paint them gray, then cut triangular teeth from the leftover white card.

5 When the gray paint is dry, draw a semicircular mouth at the bottom of the plate and paint it black. Then glue the fins to the other side of the plate, two either side of the shark's face, and the third at the top of its head.

3 To make the shark, paint the back of one of the large plates gray.

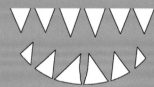

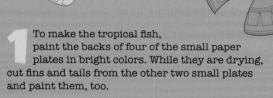

2 Glue the fins and tails to the other sides of the small painted plates, and decorate the fish with stripes, dots, and other patterns. Then glue on the googly eyes and arrange the fish on your wall.

Why Not?
Paint a coral reef background to complete your underwater scene.

6 Stick on the googly eyes and give your shark some fearsome teeth. Place it on your wall, sneaking up on the fish.

DONE!

55 MAKE A MEGA-MOUTH POP-UP CARD

You can make this greeting card super-cute or super-scary, depending on the occasion.

you will need

- 1 letter-size sheet of thin light-colored card stock
- 1 letter-size sheet of thin red card stock
- Ruler
- Pencil
- Scissors
- Paints or marker pens

1 Fold the sheet of light-colored card stock in half. Measure halfway along the crease, make a mark, then draw a 1-inch (3-cm) line across the card stock and cut along it.

2 Fold the flaps back to make two triangles.

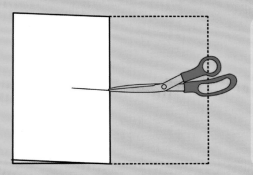

3 Fold the triangles back to the center and open out the card stock. Push the triangles upward and pinch them together to make a pop-up mouth.

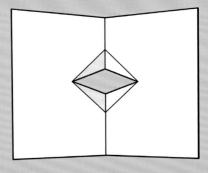

4 Now fold the sheet of red card stock in half and glue the two sheets of card stock together. (Don't put glue around the mouth.)

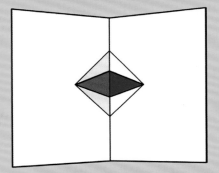

5 Draw a fierce or friendly face around your mega-mouth. Here are some ideas.

DONE!

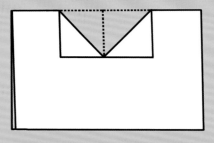

56 TRANSFORM A T-SHIRT

If you have a boring old T-shirt in need of upcycling, try this quick and easy makeover.

1 Choose a design for your T-shirt from a book or magazine and trace it onto thin card or sticky back plastic (or print a design onto thin card stock), then cut it out.

Safety First!
Ask an adult to help you cut out the shape. Some fabric paints need to be ironed. Ask an adult to do this.

2 Lay the T-shirt on a flat surface and put the cardboard inside to stop the paint going through to the back. Lay your shape in position. Use double-sided tape to keep it in place, or peel the backing off the plastic.

3 Carefully dab paint around the shape using the sponge or paintbrush. Leave it to dry, then lift up the shape and follow the instructions on the paints for setting them.

DONE!

57 DRAW YOUR HAND IN 3-D

This is simple to do and the result is really impressive.

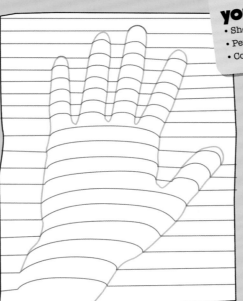

1 Place your hand in the center of the paper and trace around your hand and wrist with a pencil.

2 Draw a straight pencil line from the edge of the paper to the hand outline, draw a curved line across the hand, then draw a straight line to the other edge. Repeat these lines about 0.8 inch (2cm) apart across the hand and fingers.

3 Use colored markers to follow the pencil lines and fill in the gaps between them.

Voilà! Now take a look around the house. What else could you draw in 3-D using this technique?

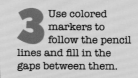

DONE!

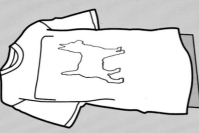

58 MAKE MARBLED PAPER

Marbled paper is great for wrapping gifts or covering books. You can use it to make cool greetings cards and stationery, too. Just be sure to ask the owner of the shaving cream before you use it!

Top Tip
If your paper curls up as it dries, try putting a weighted baking tray on top to flatten it out.

you will need
- Shaving cream
- Large tray or baking pan
- Ruler or spatula
- Food coloring or paint
- Wooden stick (a skewer or chopstick, for example)
- Heavy white paper
- Paper towels
- Plenty of newspaper to keep the table clean

1 Squirt a small amount of shaving cream into the tray or pan and spread it out using the ruler or spatula. You need a thin layer just a bit bigger than your sheet of paper.

2 Drip evenly spaced drops of food coloring or paint onto the shaving cream.

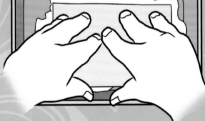

3 Use the stick to swirl the colors together, so they make streaks in the shaving cream. Don't mix it up too much — you want the colors to stay separate.

4 Carefully lay the paper on the shaving cream and press it down gently and evenly.

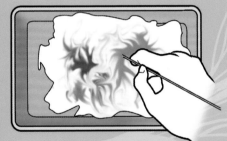

5 Lift up the paper and lay it painted side up on some paper towels.

6 Use the ruler or spatula to scrape off the shaving cream, leaving the paint behind. Leave the marbled paper to dry.

DONE!

59 MAKE SALT DOUGH

Salt dough is easy to make and it can be molded or cut into all kinds of shapes, but don't eat it!

1 Mix the flour and salt together in a bowl, then gradually add the water. Add more flour if it's too sticky. Knead the dough with your hands until it's completely smooth.

2 Salt dough is perfect for making decorations for all kinds of celebrations. Roll out the dough and use cookie cutters to cut out the shapes. Make a hole with a straw or chopstick before baking so you can hang them up.

3 Place the shapes on baking parchment on a baking pan. Cook at 212°F (100°C) until the dough is completely dry. This should take between one and three hours depending on thickness. Paint the dough when it's cool.

you will need
- 2 cups (256g) of flour
- 1 cup (273g) of salt
- 1 cup (235ml) of lukewarm water
- Cookie cutters
- Drinking straw or chopstick
- Parchment paper
- Paints

How to use your salt dough

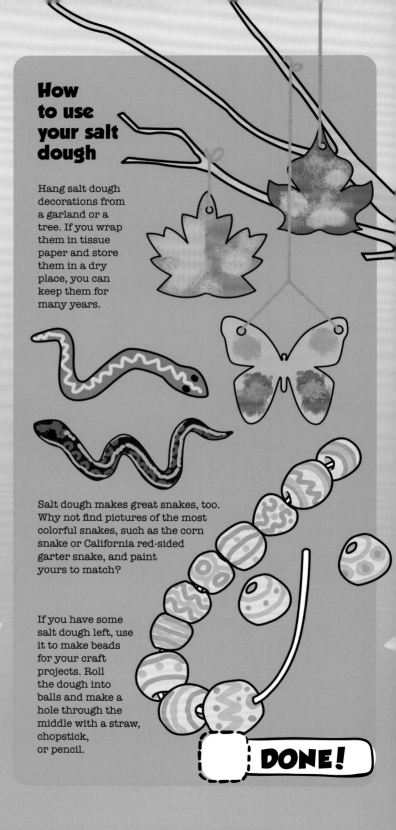

Hang salt dough decorations from a garland or a tree. If you wrap them in tissue paper and store them in a dry place, you can keep them for many years.

Salt dough makes great snakes, too. Why not find pictures of the most colorful snakes, such as the corn snake or California red-sided garter snake, and paint yours to match?

If you have some salt dough left, use it to make beads for your craft projects. Roll the dough into balls and make a hole through the middle with a straw, chopstick, or pencil.

DONE!

60 WEAVE FABRIC

Weaving with fabric strips is much faster than using yarn. Hang your finished piece on the wall, or use it as a mat or coaster.

you will need
- Strong piece of cardboard
- Ruler
- Pencil
- Scissors
- Thick yarn
- Strips of fabric (or ribbon) about 0.8 inch (2cm) wide
- Glue

Safety First!
Thick cardboard can be hard to cut, so ask an adult to help you.

1 Measure the top of the cardboard and make a mark in the center, then make marks 0.6 inch (1.5cm) apart along the top either side of the center point. Do the same at the bottom and use scissors to cut slits about 0.4 inch (1cm) long where you made the marks.

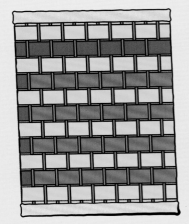

2 Slide the yarn through the top left slit, leaving a tail of about 4 inches (10cm). Then wind the yarn through the bottom slit, around the back and up through the top, and so on until you reach the end. Tie the yarn to the tail you left and cut it off.

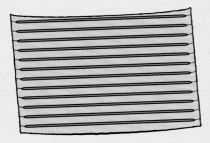

3 Weave the fabric through the yarn on the front, leaving a little overhanging on each side. Glue the ends to the back of the cardboard. Glue a piece of fabric or ribbon to the top and bottom of the loom to cover the cardboard.

DONE!

61 MAKE A ROOM SIGN

Mark your territory with this personalized room sign.

1 If the cardboard isn't the right size and shape, ask an adult to cut it for you. Make two holes in the top to hang it, then paint it along with the smaller piece of cardboard.

you will need
- Piece of thick cardboard the size of your sign, plus a smaller piece for your name
- Paints and a paintbrush
- Pictures from the Internet, phone, catalogs, or magazines
- Glue
- Ribbon
- Letters cut from a magazine to spell your name

2 Print pictures from the Internet or your phone or cut images from catalogs and magazines that show things that are important to you, such as your favorite sports, bands, hobbies etc., and make a collage on the sign.

3 Glue the letters on the smaller piece of card to spell out your name and attach it to the sign, then thread ribbon through the holes and hang it on your door.

DONE!

62 TOP YOUR PENCIL

Give your pencils attitude with these cool toppers. Quilling is great for making greetings cards, gift tags, and tree ornaments, too.

you will need
- Quilling tool, cotton swab, or plastic straw
- Strips of colored paper, 0.4 inch (1cm) wide
- Glue

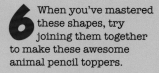

1 To make your own quilling tool, ask an adult to cut one end off a cotton swab and cut a slit in the end about 0.4 inch (1cm) long, or cut a slit in the end of a straw.

2 Slide the end of a strip of paper into the slit and twirl the tool until you reach the end. Dab some glue on the end of the paper and stick it to the coil, then slide it off the quilling tool. This is a tight coil.

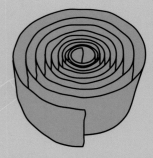

3 To make a loose coil, slide the paper off the tool and let it unravel a little before sticking the end down.

4 Make a teardrop shape by pinching one end of a loose coil.

6 When you've mastered these shapes, try joining them together to make these awesome animal pencil toppers.

Top Tip
You can buy strips of paper for quilling, or ask an adult to cut them for you with a craft knife.

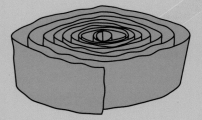

5 To make an eye shape, pinch both ends of a loose coil.

DONE!

63 DECORATE A PENCIL CASE

You'll always have your pencils close at hand if you make this quick-and-easy pencil case.

you will need
- Ring binder
- Large ziplock plastic bag
- Washi tape (or plain duct tape, decorated)
- Scissors
- Hole punch

1 Line the bag up with the rings of the binder and fold over the bottom of the bag, so it fits well within the covers. Stick the folded end down with tape.

2 Cover one side of the bag with tape, leaving a little tape overhanging on both sides. When one side is covered, turn it over and fold the overhanging tape over to the other side, then cover the other side with tape.

Top Tip
If the edges look untidy, run some tape along them to neaten them up.

3 Punch holes in the case so it clips into your binder. (You might need an adult to help push the punch through the tape.)

DONE!

64 MAKE A SEASHELL PET

Next time you're on the beach, collect shells to take home. Try to find different shapes and sizes, and make sure there aren't any creatures left inside!

you will need
- Collection of shells
- Craft glue
- Paintbrush
- Modeling clay
- Small beads

1 Take a look at these shell creatures. Are any of them cute enough to be your pet? Use them as inspiration as you sift through your shell collection to find shapes and sizes that you could use.

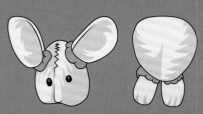

2 Experiment with different shell combinations before gluing them together. Modeling clay is a great way to fix them in position while you get your glue ready. Build the heads and bodies separately, and glue on smaller parts, like eyes, ears, and noses, before joining them to the other bits. If you don't have any tiny shells for eyes and noses, you can use beads.

3 When you're happy with your arrangement, glue it together. Use the brush to paint glue onto the more delicate pieces. The clay is also useful to support your pet while it dries.

DONE!

65 THROW A MONSTER MURAL

You can just "throw" this one together. It's super-easy to create a super-size mural with just paint and play balls.

1 Find a place to hang your paper or sheet. A shed wall or fence is ideal (check with the owner that it's okay first, though). Sheets can also hang from a clothesline. Spread out the dust cover in front.

2 Squeeze different colored paints into different containers. Roll a ball into one of the paints until it is covered. Stand about 5 feet (1.5m) from the paper and throw the ball.

3 Throw more and more balls until the paper is suitably splattered. You can "sign" it by dipping your hand into the paint and pressing it onto the corner of the paper.

you will need
- Large roll of paper or an old sheet
- Thumbtacks
- Dust cover or old sheet
- Tempera paint
- Paint trays or disposable containers
- Textured play balls, such as spike balls
- Permanent markers
- Googly eyes (optional)

4 Now get creative with the marker pens and googly eyes to make silly, serious, and seriously silly monster faces.

DONE!

66 MAKE POTATO PRINTS

Potatoes are great to print with, but you can use other homegrown or bought veggies, too. Try halving peppers and cauliflowers, and experiment with celery leaves and carrot tops.

1 Cut a large potato in half and press a cookie cutter into the center of the potato.

2 Ask an adult to slice around the cookie cutter. Remove the excess potato and the cookie cutter.

3 Squeeze the paint into the saucer, then dip the potato into the paint. Press your potato shape onto the paper you want to decorate. Try doing this with your other vegetables too, and see what amazing artwork you can come up with!

DONE!

67 PUT ON A CLOTHES-LINE ART SHOW

You don't need a huge space to set up an outdoor art studio — a balcony, patio, porch, or small lawn will do.

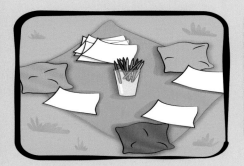

you will need
- Clothesline or rope
- Clothespins
- Paper
- Art materials
- Blanket and cushions (optional)

1 Set up your studio. It can be as simple as a pile of paper and a pot of colored pencils on a rug. A few cushions might be nice, too.

2 Be sure to ask an adult to help you to put up the clothesline or tie a rope between two posts or trees. It should be at a height that you can reach. Put a bag or box of clothespins near the line.

3 Ask a few friends to come and make some art. Pin your masterpieces to the line as you do them. Now invite more friends or your family to your art show.

DONE!

68 MAKE BARK AND LEAF RUBBINGS

Using paper and crayons, take rubbings of bark textures and leaf patterns, and start your own collection. Mount them in a scrapbook and use the Internet or a guide to identify them.

1 Place a piece of paper on the bark of a tree, and hold it in place with one hand. Rub a crayon smoothly across it, keeping all the strokes in one direction using the side of the crayon. The pattern of the bark and its ridges will be transferred to your paper.

2 Choose a leaf. It should be dry. Leaves that have lots of veins and ribs on them work best.

3 Place your leaf on a firm surface and put a thick piece of paper over it. Use your crayon in the same way that you did for the bark rubbing — keeping all the strokes in the same direction. One side of your leaf will be smoother than the other. Try rubbing both sides.

DONE!

69 MAKE SUN PRINTS

Get creative with sun print papers. Special chemicals in the papers react to sunlight and help you to create awesome shadow prints. They're so cool, you'll want to hang them in your room!

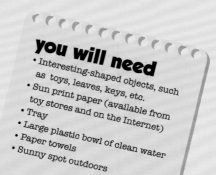

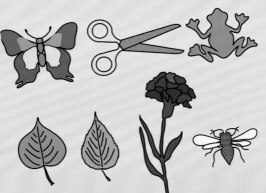

1 Find some fun-shaped objects. Small toys, plastic insects, leaves, keys, scissors, and flowers all work well.

2 Choose a shady spot, or do this part indoors, away from the window. Place a couple of sheets of sun-print paper onto the tray. Make sure they don't overlap. Arrange your objects onto the papers.

3 Carry the tray to a sunny spot, taking care not to move the objects out of place. Leave the tray in the sunshine for 2 to 5 minutes. (If it's a little cloudy, leave it for up to 20 minutes.)

4 Take a bowl of clean water out to the tray. When the sun paper has faded to white, take the objects off. Put the paper into the bowl. Leave it in the water for a few minutes. This is where the magic happens — the shapes of your objects will become white, and the faded blue background will become a dark blue color.

5 Take your sun prints out of the water and rest them on some paper towels to dry. Impressed? Why not hang them in your room?

DONE!

70 CREATE TWINKLING LANTERNS

The flickering light of a lantern is all you need to enjoy your outdoor space after sundown. If you decorate it with magical creatures and tell imaginative stories, who knows what'll happen!

1 Decorate your jam jar with acrylic paint pens. You could draw patterns and shapes or fairies, dragons, and other magical creatures. Leave to dry.

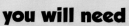

2 Now make the handle. Bend a loop at one end of the garden wire. Thread your beads from the other side until half the wire is covered.

you will need

- Old jam jar (or several)
- Acrylic paint pens
- 20 inches (50cm) thin garden wire
- Beads
- Play sand
- Container with lid
- Food coloring
- Tea light (if possible, use Citronella to ward off mosquitoes and other biting insects)

3 Wrap the leftover wire around the neck of the jam jar, twisting the end to secure it.

4 Bend the beaded wire over the jam jar. Undo the loop you made in Step 2, and thread this wire through the neck wire. Twist to secure, and tuck in any ends.

5 Take the lid off your container and put in a couple of spoonfuls of sand. Add a few drops of food coloring. Replace the lid and secure tightly. Shake for a minute.

6 Pour the sand into the bottom of your jam jar and add in a tea light. Hang your lantern up outside, ask an adult to help you light it up at twilight, or use battery-operated tea lights. What sort of magic can you make happen?

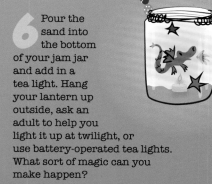

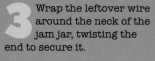

DONE!

71 SKETCH A TREE

Do you have a favorite tree in your garden or on your way to school? Why not capture it on paper? It's easy if you focus on one part at a time.

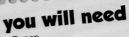
you will need
- Paper
- Pencil
- Pencil sharpener
- Eraser
- Cushion to sit on (optional)

1 Sit down in front of your favorite tree, and get comfy. Look carefully at its overall shape, trunk, branches, and leaves. Start drawing it from the bottom and work your way up. Draw the sides of the tree trunk and any roots at the base of the tree.

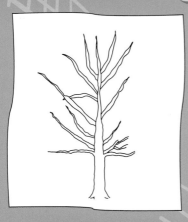

2 Now draw the main branches. Notice how they get thinner as they spread out. Allow some branches to be behind others. Include the unusual shapes that branches often make.

3 Draw the bark patterns on the trunk and branches. Add as much detail as possible. Shadows and lines will make it more realistic.

4 Draw the smaller branches and twigs. Notice how the smaller twigs branch off the larger ones, and even smaller twigs branch off of those.

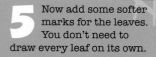

5 Now add some softer marks for the leaves. You don't need to draw every leaf on its own.

6 Take a look at where the shadow falls on your tree. Start with the trunk, and add shade and tone. Now shade the branches that fall into shadow. Shade the leaves last. When you've finished, don't forget to sign your masterpiece!

DONE!

72 MAKE STATIONERY

Personalize your stationery with spray paint and found objects. You can create all sorts of patterns and textures for that special thank-you note, birthday card, or wrapping paper.

you will need
- Empty spray bottles
- Paint
- Water
- Thick paper or blank writing paper
- Newspaper
- Found objects (leaves, pebbles, shells, feathers, recycled materials)

1 Wash the spray bottles out thoroughly. Squeeze the colored paints into different bottles and add water. They shouldn't be too runny. Spray some onto some old newspaper to check the consistency.

2 Lay the newspaper on the lawn or patio and put your blank paper on top. Arrange collected objects such as pebbles, leaves, feathers, or other interestingly shaped recycled materials, onto the paper.

3 Spray the paint mixture over the paper and objects. Leave to dry, and then remove the objects carefully to reveal your spray-paint patterns.

DONE!

73 PING A MASTERPIECE

This is fun, messy art — perfect for sensory play. You'll ping a masterpiece together in no time!

you will need
- White paper that is twice as wide as the cardboard
- Rubber bands (different thicknesses if possible)
- Different colored paints
- Sponge
- Paintbrush
- Cardboard, such as the side of a cereal box
- Containers for paint mixing

3 Use the paintbrush to drip some paint onto a couple of the bands and ping them. The colors will splash over the paper randomly.

1 Fold the white paper around the cardboard to cover both sides. Stretch and wrap the rubber bands over it to make a pattern of lines.

2 Squeeze colored paints into different containers. Dip sponges into the paints and dab them onto the paper with the rubber bands. For clean colors, use a different sponge for each paint.

4 Let your art dry on one side, and then paint the other. When the second side is dry, remove the rubber bands and unfold the paper to see the patterns you've created.

Why Not?
Use your rubber band art as wrapping paper or stationery!

DONE!

74 DRAW A COMIC STRIP

Comic strips can be funny, thoughtful, or packed with adventure! Here are some important pointers to help you draw your own.

1 Figure out what your style will be when you write and draw your comic. If you don't care so much about the details, that's okay! Draw stick figures and come up with clever punchlines or a silly joke.

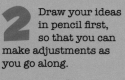

2 Draw your ideas in pencil first, so that you can make adjustments as you go along.

3 Invent cool characters. Name them and give them simple and distinct features like funky glasses, big hair, or scary teeth. What are their best and worst qualities? Funny comic strips need to end with a punchline, while adventure strips might end on a cliffhanger!

4 Tell as much of the joke or story through your pictures and keep words in speech bubbles brief.

FACE FACTS

Show some emotion!
Here are a few secrets to drawing basic facial expressions.

Anger
A frown, slanted eyes, and possibly a red face.

Happiness
A smile and wide eyes.

Sadness
A frown and small eyes.

Shock
A gaping mouth, wide eyes, and possibly several lines near the forehead.

Mischief
A grin and slanted eyes with one eyebrow raised.

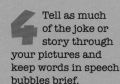

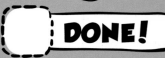

NO WAY!

YES!

HMMMMM

What?

NO!

DONE!

75 USE A MINI-LOOM

Weaving has been around since the beginning of civilization. Make your own mini-loom — and learn to weave your own teeny tapestry.

you will need

- Large piece of sturdy cardboard
- Scissors
- Tape
- Ruler to measure and pencil to mark measurements
- Strong string/yarn (in different colors)
- Needle with a wide hole

1 Measure an even number of lines across the cardboard at about 0.4 inch (1cm) apart. At the top and bottom of the cardboard, cut little notches for the string to sit in as you wrap it around the loom.

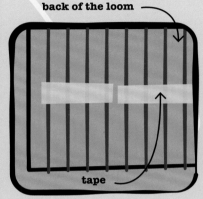

back of the loom

tape

2 Choose a specific color for the threads stretched on the loom. Carefully wrap the thread around so it catches in the notches on either end. Then tape the threads down on the back side of your board, so they stay put while you weave.

3 Choose another color string and, using a needle, carefully begin to weave it under and over each string in turn. When you reach the end of a row, start a second row above the first, starting above the last string you ended on.

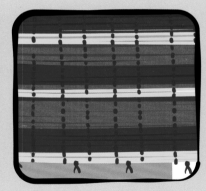

4 Keep weaving until the entire loom has been filled. You can change to different colors of string along the way. Carefully push each row together keeping the rows straight. Remember not to pull the sides in too tight.

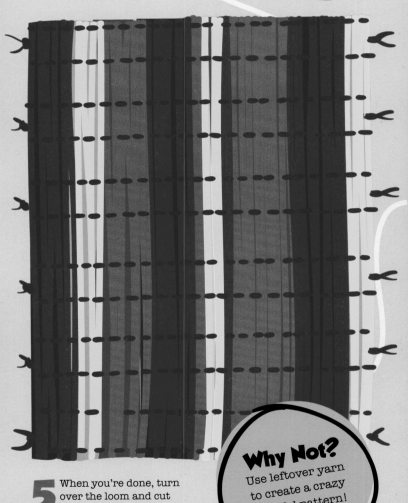

5 When you're done, turn over the loom and cut across the stuck-down threads. Now take one end off of the loom and tie the threads together in pairs to close the weaving. Your masterpiece is finished!

Why Not?
Use leftover yarn to create a crazy colorful pattern!

DONE!

76 GIVE A SOCK PUPPET ATTITUDE

You can make an effortlessly cool puppet from the simplest of items: a sock!

Why Not?

Once you've made your sock puppet, give it a personality. Then teach it to talk for itself (see #28)!

you will need
- Piece of thick cardboard
- Scissors
- Large sock
- Yarn (optional)
- Two buttons, googly eyes, pipe cleaners, and other craft bits you can find
- Fabric glue

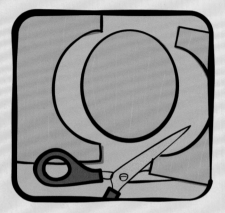

1 Cut a large oval from the cardboard and fold it in half. This will be your puppet's mouth.

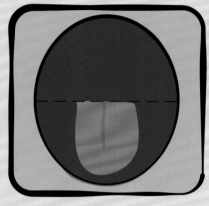

2 Decorate the oval so it looks like a mouth. You could add a tongue, teeth, or even words!

3 Stick your hand inside the sock and find the "mouth." Put your thumb in the heel of the sock and your other fingers in the toes.

4 Dot some fabric glue inside the crease and insert the cardboard mouth. Leave to dry.

yarn hair

button eyes

cardboard tongue

5 Finally, decorate your puppet with whatever other materials you want to make it more like an original character: a fake wig (with yarn), funny ears (with pipe cleaners), or perhaps a swatch of fabric for a cape!

DONE!

77 FASHION A JOURNAL

Writing a journal is really fun, and could even help you become a great writer! Follow these simple tips to make your very own journal.

1 Take a piece of tabloid card and fold in half (like a birthday card). This will be the cover for your journal, so decorate it however you like!

you will need
- Tabloid card
- Lined letter paper
- Crayons, stickers and markers for decoration
- Stapler
- Ribbon

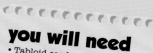

MY JOURNAL

2 Now use a hole punch to punch two holes halfway down your cover, close to the fold. You may need to ask an adult to help you.

3 If your lined letter paper does not have holes, use your hole-punch to make holes halfway down the paper on the left hand side. These will make up the inside pages of your journal.

6 Your journal is ready to use! You could also make one with plain paper to use as a sketch book.

5 Thread a length of ribbon through the holes in your cover and inside pages, then tie in a bow.

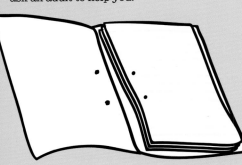

4 Place your letter sheets inside your cover, and make sure that all the holes match up.

Why Not?
Create a code that only you can understand to keep snooping eyes away from your journal!

DONE!

78 SHOOT A SHORT FILM

Making a film with friends can be a lot of fun! Follow the tips below and create your own masterpiece. Start with the four S's.

STORYBOARD

1 Make up a storyboard (a rough, comic-strip style version of your story) to use as a guide along the way. Draw a quick sketch of how you want each shot to look.

SCRIPT

2 Once you've got an idea of your story and characters, you can write a script for each of your actors to learn.

SET AND SCENERY

3 You don't need to go to any special locations to get great shots. Your own house is an excellent place to start. See if you can get your family and friends to be in your cast!

SPECIAL EFFECTS

4 Makeup, wigs, and other costume elements can turn a friend into a superstar actor!

The Wide Shot
Use this shot to show where the action is taking place and to set the scene.

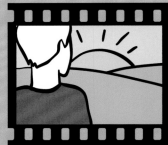

Over the Shoulder
This shot shows the action from your character's point of view.

Extreme Close-Up
This shot is great for focusing attention on small details. Using an extreme close-up of a character's face is a great way of creating a sense of tension.

Close-Up
Use this shot to clearly show your character's emotions and reactions.

DONE!

79 PAINT LIKE A FAMOUS ARTIST

You can create art in the style of some of the world's greatest artists! Here are two famous artist's techniques to inspire you.

you will need
- Newspaper
- Paper and card
- Paints
- Paintbrushes
- Sticky tape
- Pencil
- PVA glue

IMPASTO PAINTING

Impasto is a way of painting where the paint is layered on very thickly so the brush marks can still be seen. The Dutch artist Vincent van Gogh often used this technique.

1 Sketch out the outline of what you want to paint onto the card using a pencil.

2 Start to paint with thick brush strokes. Don't add water to your paint, you want it to be as thick and gooey as possible. Acrylic paint works best.

SPLATTER PAINTING

The American artist Jackson Pollock used this technique to create some of his most famous works. Why not have a go yourself?

1 First, tape your newspaper onto the floor. This will keep the floor from getting too messy. Put your blank canvas or paper on top of the newspapers.

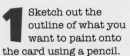

2 Stand over the canvas and dip your paintbrush in the paint, then shake and splatter color from left to right. Do this several times with different colors.

3 Allow the first layer of paint to dry before adding another. You can use the hard side of your brush handle to trace swirly patterns on the picture, too.

Why Not?
If you don't have acrylic paint, try adding a blob of PVA glue to poster paint.

DONE!

80 TIE-DYE A T-SHIRT

Be creative and turn a plain white T-shirt into a cool new top!

you will need
- Disposable tablecloth or garbage bags
- White T-shirt
- Rubber bands
- Salt
- Fabric dyes in your favorite colors
- Small bowl
- Large bowl
- Rubber gloves
- Plastic squeeze bottles
- Plastic bag

1 Cover your work surface with the tablecloth or garbage bags. Roll the T-shirt up from the collar to the bottom and tie rubber bands around it.

2 Wearing rubber gloves, carefully mix up the fabric dye with water in a jug (following the instructions on the packet), and pour the mixture into your squeezy bottle. You can do this with as many colors as you like!

3 Put warm salt water into a bowl and dip the shirt into the water. Take it out after a minute or two.

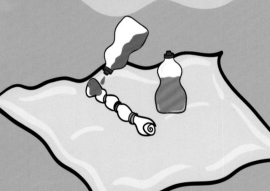

4 On your protected work surface, squeeze your fabric dye on to each section of the rubber-band tied T-shirt.

Why Not?
Try different colors and ways of tying your T-shirt to get different effects.

5 When you have applied the color, put the dyed T-shirt into a plastic bag and leave it overnight. The next day, run your T-shirt under cold water while wearing your rubber gloves to protect your hands. Rinse the shirt until the water runs clear. Then remove the rubber bands!

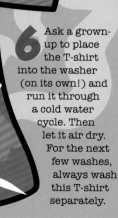

6 Ask a grown-up to place the T-shirt into the washer (on its own!) and run it through a cold water cycle. Then let it air dry. For the next few washes, always wash this T-shirt separately.

DONE!

81 FOLD A CHEWING GUM WRAPPER BRACELET

This bracelet is not only fun to make — you'll be recycling when you make it! You can make this bracelet from any candy wrapper or scrap paper, but chewing gum wrappers are perfect.

1 Fold one long side in toward the middle of the wrapper, then do the same with the other side. Next, fold the whole thing in half lengthwise, to form a thin strip.

2 Bend your wrapper in the middle, then fold in each long end in to meet the middle.

3 Repeat steps 1-2 with your next bit of wrapper. Using different colors will create a pattern.

4 Insert the flat ends of one folded wrapper into the side openings of the next, so that they slot into each other and make a V shape.

5 Repeat the first four steps with your folded wrappers to form a zigzag chain.

6 When your bracelet is long enough to fit around your wrist, make one more link, but don't fold the last two folds.

7 Insert these sides into the openings of your first wrapper, and close the bracelet by folding the long strips in. After a bit of practice, your bracelet should look like this!

Why Not? Try different color combinations and make bracelets for all of your friends!

DONE!

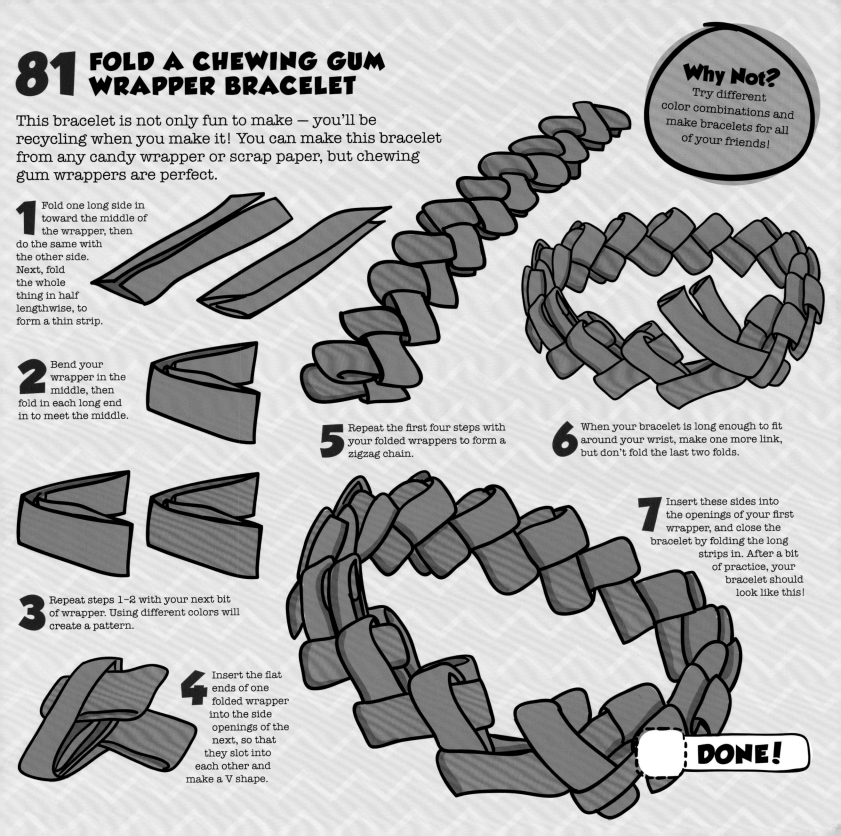

82 PRINT A BLOCK PICTURE

The next time your meal comes in a to-go box, make sure to keep hold of it. You can use it to make a cool piece of art!

you will need
- Leftover food container
- Pencil
- Poster paint
- Paper plate
- Paint roller
- Paper

1 Lightly sketch out your design on one of the flat sides of your food box. When you are happy with it, press harder with your pencil to leave an imprint.

2 Put your paint on your paper plate and dip your roller into it. Make sure all of the roller wheel is lightly and evenly covered in paint.

Why Not?
Use different colors on your stencil and layer them on to the page.

3 Roll the paint onto the lunch box, making sure you have covered the whole surface. Try not to put the paint on too thickly, or your design won't show.

4 Press a sheet of paper onto the painted box. Rub over it gently with your palm so that the paint spreads evenly.

5 Peel the paper off to reveal your art! You can repeat this many times to make things like posters, wrapping paper, or even to decorate greeting cards!

DONE!

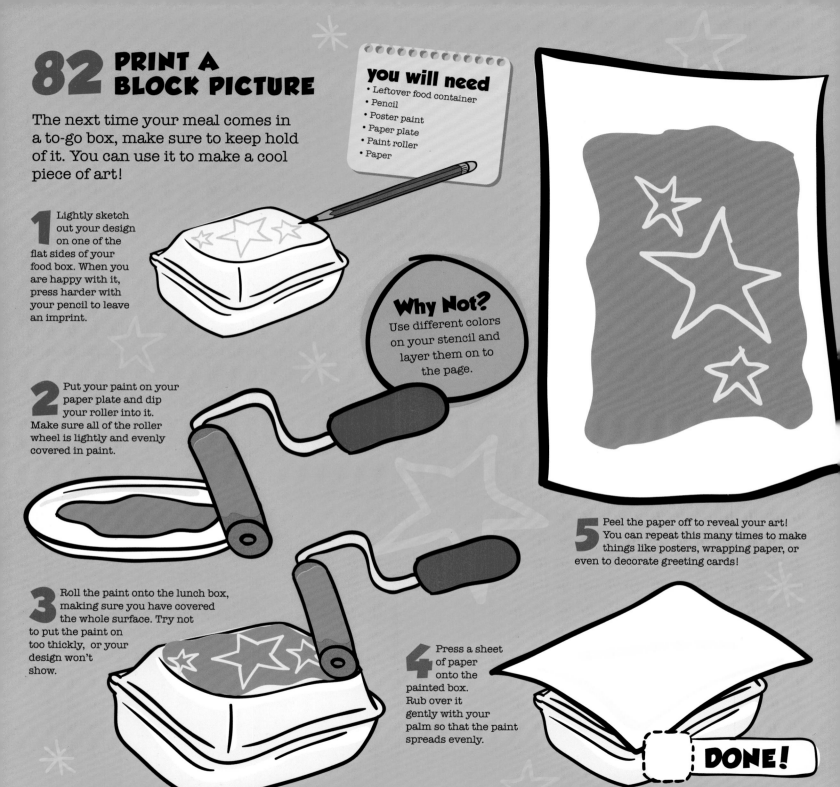

83 DESIGN A COAT OF ARMS

A traditional coat of arms is a decorated shield that features all kinds of things related to your family. Have a go at making your very own!

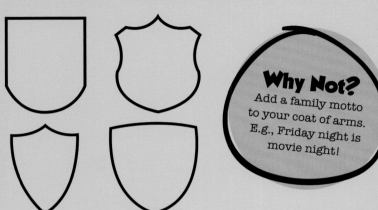

Why Not?
Add a family motto to your coat of arms. E.g., Friday night is movie night!

1 First, draw a basic shape for your coat of arms. The most common shapes are shown above, or you can design your own!

2 Write a list of words that spring to mind when you think about your family. These will make up symbols of your shield! Write down the name of each family member and something cool about them.

3 Split your coat of arms into sections, one for each member of your family. Now take one thing about them from your list and draw it into that section.

DONE!

84 MAKE BAG TAGS

Tie tags or ribbons to your travel bags so you'll recognize them. Making tags is easy using recycled card.

you will need
- Some plain card stock
- Scissors
- Felt tip pen
- Sturdy string

1 Ask an adult to help you cut a tag shape from card stock. Decorate it with your name. It could be any shape or size you want.

2 Punch or push a hole through the tag with a pencil. Loop some string through to tie it to your bag.

3 If your bags go on a baggage carousel at an airport, it can be hard to pick them out from all the other bags. It's a good idea to tie a colored ribbon on to the handles. That way you'll be able to spot your bags as they appear.

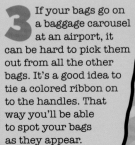
DONE!

85 SCRAPBOOK IT

Scrapbooking means making your own unique book of memories. Here are some tips for making a trip scrapbook look good.

Why Not?
There are lots of scrapbooking ideas on the Internet. Take a look to get some inspiration.

1 Decide what will go on which spread (open double-page). Each spread could have a theme, such as "days out" or "food," for instance.

2 Before you glue anything down, decide what the "layout" will be. Where will you glue photos and where will you add writing?

3 When you're ready, glue down your images. Then begin decorating around them by drawing frames around the pictures, using felt-tips and a ruler.

you will need
- Scrapbook (you can buy one from a stationery store)
- Any tickets, postcards, or photos you may have collected on your vacations
- Glue stick
- Felt-tip pens
- Ruler
- Stickers, wrapping paper, etc., to decorate your album. You can also buy all sorts of special scrapbooking decorating material on the Internet if you like
- Pen to write down your memories
- Magazines, leaflets, or photo printouts, to cut or tear up for the collage

4 Now label your photos and memory images, and add any writing you want.

5 It's time to decorate your pages. Add stickers or even snippets of pretty wrapping paper. Fill in spaces with mini doodles. You could also cut out letters and words from magazines and glue them on to create a cool look.

6 When your scrapbook is complete, decide how you want to decorate the cover. You could cover it with wrapping paper or collage pieces, or draw a picture on a sheet of paper the size of the cover and glue it on.

DONE!

86 DRAW A RACING CAR

Here are some simple steps to help you draw a racing car. Once you get the basic shape you can decorate it however you want.

1 Start with two wheels on the ground. Add in details to the wheels as shown.

2 Add in the main body of the racing car.

3 Add the back of the racing car and the driver.

Why Not?
Add some speed lines to make your car look like it's going fast. Decorate the side with stripes and badges. Think up a name for your racing car team.

DONE!

87 DRAW A PLANE

Draw a plane in three easy steps. Then use it to create different pictures.

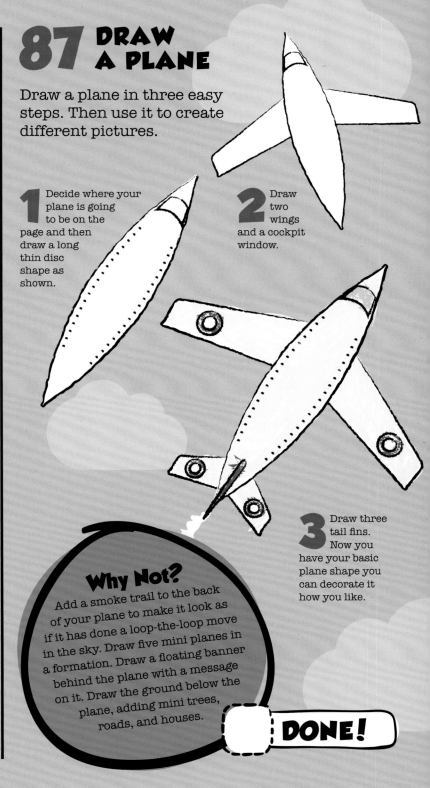

1 Decide where your plane is going to be on the page and then draw a long thin disc shape as shown.

2 Draw two wings and a cockpit window.

3 Draw three tail fins. Now you have your basic plane shape you can decorate it how you like.

Why Not?
Add a smoke trail to the back of your plane to make it look as if it has done a loop-the-loop move in the sky. Draw five mini planes in a formation. Draw a floating banner behind the plane with a message on it. Draw the ground below the plane, adding mini trees, roads, and houses.

DONE!

88 DESIGN A JIGSAW PUZZLE

Make your own jigsaw puzzle! You will need a flat surface to work on when you piece it together.

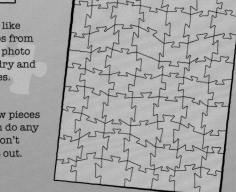

1 Print out a photo you like or choose some photos from magazines. Paste the photo to the board. Let the glue dry and then trim any uneven edges.

2 Draw a plan of jigsaw pieces on the back. You can do any shape you like but don't make them too hard to cut out.

3 Ask an adult to help you cut out the pieces. Store your jigsaw puzzle in an envelope until you are ready to use it.

DONE!

89 MAKE A MARDI GRAS MASK

Give yourself an air of mystery with a traditional Mardi Gras mask. If you base it on your hand prints, it should be just the right size.

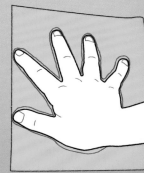

1 Place your hand on the card and spread your fingers. Trace around your hand and carefully cut out the handprint. Flip the cut-out hand over and use it as a template for the other half of the mask.

2 Overlap the palms and glue the two hands together. Try the mask for size and mark where the eye holes should be, then ask an adult to cut them out with a craft knife.

Safety First!
Ask an adult to help you to cut out the mask and eye holes.

3 Decorate the mask with feathers and add sequins, jewels, and glitter for extra sparkle. Fix the stick to one side with tape.

DONE!

90 CREATE COFFEE-FILTER BUTTERFLIES

These butterflies make a pretty window decoration, or you could hang them from a mobile.

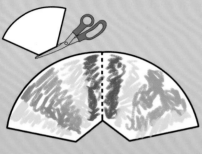

1 Cut along the bottom and one side of two standard coffee filters and flatten them out, or just flatten out a large round one, then scribble on them with colored markers.

you will need
- 2 standard coffee filters (or 1 large round one) for each butterfly
- Scissors
- Washable markers (must be washable or the colors won't blend)
- A spray bottle of water (or a paintbrush)
- A pipe cleaner for each butterfly
- Paper towel and newspapers

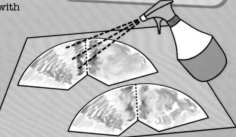

2 Lay the filters on some paper towel with plenty of newspaper underneath and spray the centers with water, then watch the colors blend.

Top Tip
If you don't have a spray bottle, use a paintbrush to dab water onto the filters.

3 When they are dry, twist a pipe cleaner around the center of the filters, and curl the ends to make two antennae.

DONE!

91 INVENT A BOARD GAME

The next time it's a rainy day, don't just play any old game — design your own!

1 First up, design your board. The simplest board shape is square with 10 smaller squares on each side. Choose some of the squares to be "active" squares and color them in.

Don't Forget!
You need game pieces to move around the board! You could use beads, coins, figures, or candy.

TELL A JOKE!

2 Choose what kind of game you'd like to make. Do you like answering questions or doing dares? Come up with fun things to do each time you or your friends land on one of your active squares. Write them on small cards or bits of paper and place them face down in the middle.

3 Before you start playing, come up with some fun rules to stick by. Roll a dice and take it in turns to move around the board.

DONE!

92 BE A FASHION DESIGNER

In this challenge, you can all turn into fashion designers and create the perfect vacation outfit.

1 Write the name of each person on a scrap of paper. Fold the scraps and ask everyone to choose one. Keep the name you get a secret. Choose again if you get your own name.

2 Now design a vacation outfit for the person you chose. Add labels and color in the outfit. It could be a costume for the beach, a day out in the countryside, or maybe a visit to town.

3 Fold up your drawing and label it with the person's name. Then present it to them at a "designer fashion ceremony"!

DONE!

93 PHOTOGRAPH THE ALPHABET

When you're out and about, either in the city or the countryside, find and collect your very own alphabet. If you look carefully, letters are everywhere, even in the most unexpected places.

1 Go for a walk in your neighborhood to begin the letter hunt. Always take an adult with you, or let one know where you're going. First of all look for the obvious letters on signs, stores, and cars. When you see a letter that you like the look of, take a photo of it. Try to capture just the letter without anything else around it.

2 Now look for less obvious letters. There are lots of shapes in buildings, plants, and all sorts of objects that look like different letters. The letter "E" might be half a window frame or a gate, a set of traffic lights, or the shadow of some telephone lines.

3 Then, make your own letters. You might trace them in the sand or the earth, or you might lay them out with leaves and pine cones or paper clips and pens. You could even ask a friend to make the shape of a letter with his or her body.

4 Try to collect the whole alphabet. Then, print them out to write messages to your friends. They're great for interesting greeting cards, and especially impressive on Valentine's!

DONE!

94 COLLECT YOUR GARBAGE

Cars can get messy! Make a "garbage guy" that you can stash in your car to keep it tidy!

you will need
- Scrap paper
- Recycled shoebox
- Glue
- Felt-tip pens

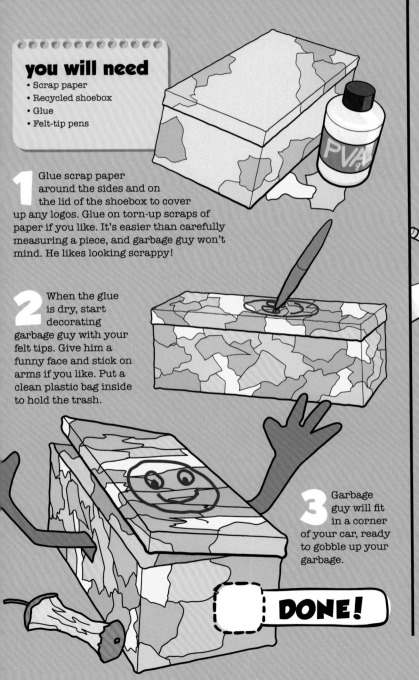

1 Glue scrap paper around the sides and on the lid of the shoebox to cover up any logos. Glue on torn-up scraps of paper if you like. It's easier than carefully measuring a piece, and garbage guy won't mind. He likes looking scrappy!

2 When the glue is dry, start decorating garbage guy with your felt tips. Give him a funny face and stick on arms if you like. Put a clean plastic bag inside to hold the trash.

3 Garbage guy will fit in a corner of your car, ready to gobble up your garbage.

DONE!

95 WALK YOUR PENCIL

The tiny tip of a pencil or pen can create amazingly intricate patterns on paper that are great to color in.

you will need
- Pencil or pen
- Blank sheet of paper
- Colored pens or pencils

1 Start in one corner. Move your pencil around the page, creating loops and waves.

2 Don't stop. Keep the line going — round, along, up, down — until you have filled the page with a random pattern.

3 If you have colored pens, you could color in the shapes you have made with your line.

DONE!

3

YUMMY

Want to make a stir in the kitchen? Try these fun projects that are simply delicious to eat. From rock candy to candy slime, pizzas to pinwheels, toasty marshmallows to mini-muffins, cook up some serious (and seriously yummy) fun.

96 CREATE CRUNCHY SNACKS

You can make these crunchy snacks in just 30 minutes. They don't need baking and you can measure everything using a mug and spoon.

you will need
- 1½ mugs chocolate chips
- 3 tablespoons softened butter
- 2 tablespoons golden syrup (optional)
- Microwave oven
- 1 mug mini marshmallows
- 1 mug plain broken cookies
- 1 mug raisins or other dried fruit
- Plastic wrap or baking paper

1 Put the chocolate chips, butter, and syrup (if using) into a large microwavable bowl. Heat in the microwave for 30 seconds, or until melted.

3 Put blobs of the mixture onto a baking tray lined with cling film or baking paper, then place it in the fridge until the chocolate is hard.

Safety First!
Ask an adult to help you use the microwave.

2 Take the bowl out and stir the mixture, then add the other ingredients. Mix until everything is coated with chocolate.

DONE!

97 MAKE TRAFFIC LIGHT JELLIES

You need to start this recipe a day in advance because each layer of flavored gelatin will take about three hours to set.

Safety First!
The gelatin needs to be dissolved in boiling water, so ask an adult to help with this.

you will need
- Large glass jug
- 1 packet lime gelatin
- 1 packet orange gelatin
- 1 packet strawberry gelatin
- 8 clear plastic cups (or glasses)

1 Make up the lime jelly in the jug according to the instructions on the packet and allow to cool for about an hour. Pour some jelly into each cup until it is one-third full. Leave in the fridge to set.

2 When the lime jelly has set, make the orange jelly and allow to cool for about an hour. Pour the orange jelly on top of the lime jelly until the cup is two-thirds full and leave in the fridge to set.

3 When the orange jelly has set, make the strawberry jelly and allow to cool for about an hour. Pour the strawberry jelly on top of the orange jelly and leave in the fridge to set.

DONE!

98 COOK UP A MUFFIN IN A MUG

Follow this super-quick recipe and you'll be munching on a chocolate muffin within minutes.

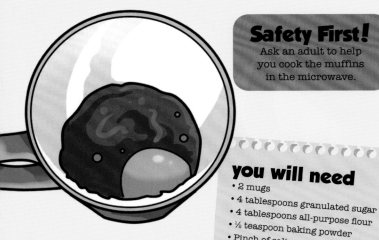

Safety First!
Ask an adult to help you cook the muffins in the microwave.

you will need
- 2 mugs
- 4 tablespoons granulated sugar
- 4 tablespoons all-purpose flour
- ¼ teaspoon baking powder
- Pinch of salt
- 4 tablespoons milk
- 4 tablespoons cooking oil
- 3 tablespoons cocoa powder
- 1 egg

1 Put all the ingredients in a mug and stir them together. Divide the mixture between two mugs.

2 Microwave on high for 60 to 90 seconds.

Enjoy!

Top Tip
Add chocolate chips to make your muffins extra yummy!

99 MAKE TORTILLA PINWHEELS

For lunch in a hurry, try these rapid wraps.

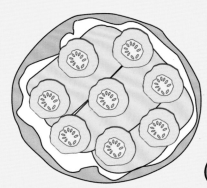

you will need
- Cream cheese
- 4 tortilla wraps
- 4 oz (120g) sliced meat, fish, or roasted vegetables
- Thinly sliced cucumber
- Toothpicks
- Butter knife

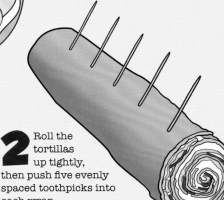

1 Spread the cream cheese over the tortillas and lay the other ingredients on top.

2 Roll the tortillas up tightly, then push five evenly spaced toothpicks into each wrap.

3 Cut between the sticks with a butter knife, so each wrap is divided into five, and serve.

Why Not?
Get creative with the fillings. Try using hummus or pesto and adding ready-prepared salad for crunch!

Safety First!
Ask an adult to slice the ingredients for you.

100 CHALLENGE YOUR TASTE BUDS

Test your taste buds with this blindfold taste test.

Safety First!

Make sure all the foods are safe to eat, and don't give anyone raw meat or fish. Check that none of the players has an allergy before you start. Ask an adult to cut up the fruit and vegetables, and wash them before eating.

1 Keep the foods hidden and blindfold one or more players.

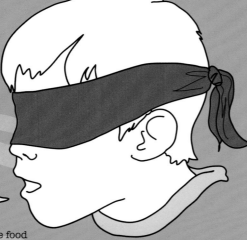

2 Put a little bit of one food on a spoon and ask the blindfolded player(s) to taste it and guess what it is.

3 Players get a point for each food they guess correctly.

you will need
- Blindfold
- Plastic spoons
- Selection of foods, such as peanut butter, mayonnaise, mashed banana, cheese, chocolate, cucumber, ketchup, apple, kiwi, strawberries, jam, or honey

Top Tip
If you have lots of players you could play in teams, with one team preparing foods for the other.

DONE!

---

101 USE CHOPSTICKS

Before eating, Japanese people say "itadakimasu," which means, "I receive this food." Then they grab their chopsticks and eat! Can you do it?

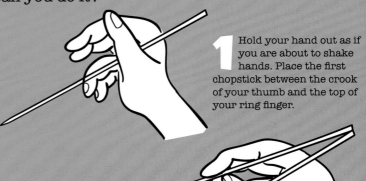

1 Hold your hand out as if you are about to shake hands. Place the first chopstick between the crook of your thumb and the top of your ring finger.

2 Hold the second chopstick like a pencil with your thumb, index and middle finger. Important: the bottom chopstick does not move.

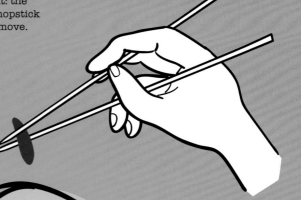

Guess What?
In Japan, it is considered rude to wave your chopsticks over your food. Go straight for the easiest piece!

3 Use your thumb to hold the chopsticks firmly while you pivot the top chopstick to meet the bottom one. Use this motion to grasp the food!

DONE!

102 MAKE CAKE POPS

These cute cakes on a stick come with an explosive surprise. If you don't have any popping candy, they'll taste just as good without it.

MAKE A CAKE-POP HOLDER

To keep your cake pops round, they need to stand upright in the fridge. You can make a cake-pop holder from an egg carton. Turn the box over and make a hole in the bottom of each cup with a skewer. Then insert the sticks.

1 Ask an adult to melt the milk chocolate in the microwave or over a pan of hot water. Crumble the cake into the melted chocolate and stir it in.

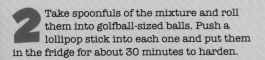

3 Ask an adult to melt the white chocolate in the microwave or over a pan of hot water, then stir in the popping candy.

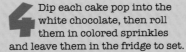

2 Take spoonfuls of the mixture and roll them into golfball-sized balls. Push a lollipop stick into each one and put them in the fridge for about 30 minutes to harden.

4 Dip each cake pop into the white chocolate, then roll them in colored sprinkles and leave them in the fridge to set.

Top Tip
If your cake pops slide down the sticks, try dipping the tops of the sticks in the chocolate coating, then pushing them back into the cakes.

DONE!

103 MAKE EDIBLE SLIME

This slime is satisfying and delicious. It's totally safe and super sweet, if you feel like sampling your work. Just make sure you wash your hands before you make it!

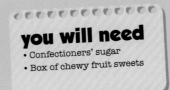
you will need
- Confectioners' sugar
- Box of chewy fruit sweets

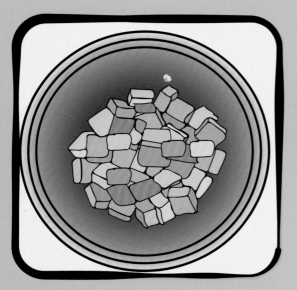

1 Unwrap the sweets and place them in a bowl. You could choose to separate the colors that work well together, such as orange and yellow, and red and pink.

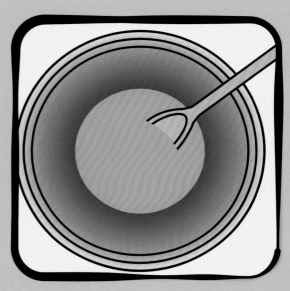

2 Ask an adult to boil a pot of shallow water on the stove. Using an oven mitt, place the bowl inside the pot. Stir with a spoon until the sweets melt completely. Using an oven mitt, take the bowl out of the water and turn off the stove.

3 While the sweets cool, dust confectioners' sugar over a clean cutting board or mat. When the mixture is cool enough to handle, scrape it out of the bowl onto the sugar.

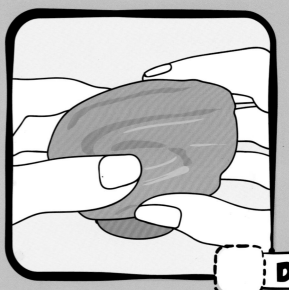

4 Knead in the confectioners' sugar and add more to thicken your slime.

DONE!

104 CONCOCT COCONUT ICE BALLS

You'll need to use your hands to mix and shape these coconut balls, so make sure they're really clean before you start.

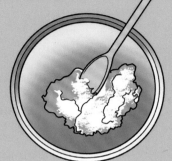

1 Mix the condensed milk and confectioners' sugar together in a large bowl using a wooden spoon. (It will get very stiff.) Mix in the coconut using your hands.

2 If you want to color half the mixture, put it in a separate bowl and mix in a few drops of pink coloring.

3 Sprinkle some confectioners' sugar and coconut onto a clean surface and roll the mixture into balls. Put them into candy cups, or onto a plate or tray, and leave overnight to set.

DONE!

you will need
- ¾ cup (250g) sweetened condensed milk
- 2 cups (250g) sifted confectioners' sugar, plus extra for rolling
- Wooden spoon
- 2 cups (200g) desiccated coconut, plus extra for rolling
- Pink food coloring (optional)
- Paper sweet cases (optional)

105 TWIST PIZZA

Puff pastry is hard to handle if it gets warm, so keep it in the fridge until the last minute and work as quickly as you can.

1 Ask an adult to preheat the oven to 375°F (190°C), and spread a little oil over the baking trays.

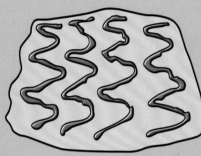

you will need
- 2 baking trays
- A little oil
- Pack of ready-rolled puff pastry
- Tube of tomato purée
- Butter knife
- Oregano or mixed herbs
- Grated Parmesan cheese (or other hard cheese)

2 Lay the puff pastry on a clean surface and squeeze zigzags of tomato purée across it. Spread the purée out with a butter knife.

3 Sprinkle a couple pinches of herbs over the tomato, then scatter the cheese on top. Cut the pastry into strips about ¾ inch wide and carefully lift them onto the baking trays.

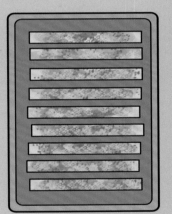

4 Prick the strips with a fork and give each one two or three twists. Ask an adult to put them in the oven for about 10 minutes, until golden and crispy.

DONE!

106 TOAST MARSHMALLOWS

Whether you're sitting around a fire on the beach at night, snuggling around a campfire in the woods, or just having a barbecue, it's the perfect time to toast some marshmallows — YUMMY!

Safety First!
Never light a fire without an adult. If your marshmallow catches fire, blow it out, don't shake it.

Why Not?
Add toppings! Dip your toasted marshmallows into chocolate or caramel sauce, and then cover in chopped nuts!

1 Poke a marshmallow onto a stick. Make sure that the end of the stick goes through the other end of the marshmallow so that it won't slip off into the fire.

2 Put the marshmallow over (not in) the fire or hot barbecue coals. Rotate the stick to cook it evenly. If you like your marshmallow gooey, take it away from the fire as soon as it's puffed up, or wait until it turns a golden brown colour on the outside.

3 Remove the marshmallow from the fire. Let it cool for a minute. Then bite off the marshmallow from its stick and let it melt in your mouth. Delicious! Time for another?

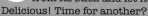

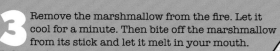

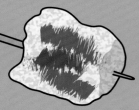

DONE!

107 HARNESS THE POWER OF THE SUN

Using a simple box on a hot day, you can focus the sun's energy and make an oven that will cook a gooey tasty treat!

Safety First!
Ask an adult to help you cut the shoe box lid.

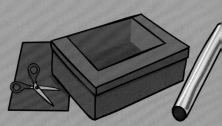

you will need
- Shoe box
- Tin foil
- Plastic wrap
- Glue stick
- Graham crackers
- Marshmallows
- Chocolate

1 Prepare your shoe box. Carefully, cut a large hole in the lid. Using the glue stick, line the inside of the box with tin foil. Put the shiny side facing up so that it reflects the sun's heat. Place the open lid on top.

2 Place your oven in the sun to preheat. After 30 minutes, put a graham cracker in the bottom, with a marshmallow on top. Now cover the top of box with plastic wrap.

3 Leave the oven in the sun until the marshmallow gets gooey and warm. Take it out and add a square of chocolate on top of the mushy marshmallow and top off with another graham cracker. Press down gently to melt the chocolate. Yum!

DONE!

108 MAKE THE ULTIMATE PIZZA

Eating a pizza is even better when it's got all your favorite toppings — so why not make one yourself!

Safety First!
Ask an adult to help you put your pizza in the oven and take it out again.

1 For the quickest pizza, head to your supermarket and look for premade pizza bases. Preheat the oven as instructed on the packet.

3 Spoon out some sauce (made from canned tomatoes and a sprinkling of basil). Add mozzarella or cheddar cheese on top.

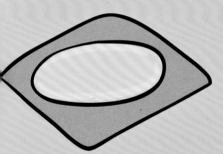

4 Sprinkle your favorite toppings on top, such as chopped peppers, spinach, ham, or mushrooms, then carefully put your pizza in the oven.

2 Place your base flat on a pizza stone or a baking sheet that's been drizzled with a bit of oil first.

5 Cook until the dough edges are brown and the cheese bubbles. This should take about 10 to 15 minutes. Now take the pizza out of the oven, take a bite, and enjoy!

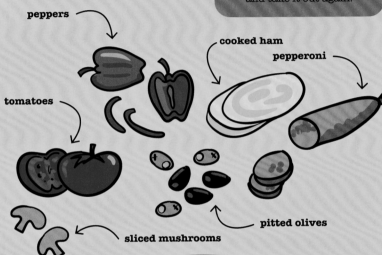

peppers

cooked ham

pepperoni

tomatoes

pitted olives

sliced mushrooms

Why Not?
Make your cool pizzas during October, also known as National Pizza Month!

Delizioso!
(which means "yummy" in Italian!)

DONE!

109 GROW ROCK CANDY

There's nothing better than a science experiment you can eat! You'll definitely be sweet on this treat.

you will need
- String
- Pencil
- Glass jar
- 1¾ cups (400ml) water
- 4 cups (800g) sugar
- Food coloring
- Lemon juice

5 Add a couple of drops of food coloring to your mixture and a squeeze of lemon for flavor, then pour into the jar, almost to the top. Place the pencil over the jar and let the string dangle into the liquid. Don't let it settle on the bottom or sides.

6 Find a safe place to leave your jar (not the fridge) and, after a day or so, you should start to see crystals forming around the string. Leave it for several days until more crystals form, then leave to dry before enjoying your sweet treat!

1 Tie a piece of string around the middle of your pencil.

2 The string should be long enough that it almost reaches the bottom when the pencil is placed over the top of the jar.

final rock candy crystal

3 Ask an adult to help you carefully bring the water to a boil and add ½ cup (115g) of the sugar.

4 When the mixture starts to bubble, begin adding the rest of the sugar, ½ cup (115g) at a time. Once done, take the pan off the heat.

Remember

Do not mess around with the jar or put your fingers in it. This disrupts the forming process of the crystalline structure!

Why Not?
Indian rock candy is mixed with fennel as a mouth freshener! What will you add to yours?

DONE!

110 THROW A SUPER SLEEPOVER

Hosting a sleepover is so much fun! Make sure you have lots of yummy treats for your guests.

THE INVITE

Make your invitations! These can be on paper or by email or text message. Choose a party theme such as sports, music, or a movie marathon.

FOOD

Stock up on your favorite snacks! Popcorn, chips, cookies, fruit, and vegetable sticks with dips are great.

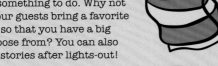

STUFF TO DO

Make a list of games and activities that you and your friends like, so you aren't ever stuck for something to do. Why not have each of your guests bring a favorite movie or game so that you have a big selection to choose from? You can also make up ghost stories after lights-out!

SLEEP (NOT!)

Find the best place for everyone to get into their sleeping bags. Gather up loads of squashy pillows and blankets and get comfortable!

Why Not?
Use some other activities in this book to keep you and your friends entertained!

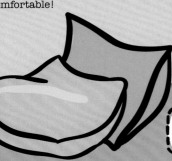

 **DONE!**

111 SHAKE SOME ICE CREAM

You can make real ice cream with nothing more than a plastic bag and a few other simple items!

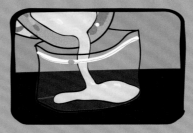

you will need
- 2 tablespoons sugar
- 1 cup (230ml) cream
- ½ teaspoon vanilla extract
- 1 small lock-top bag
- 3 tablespoons rock salt
- Lots of ice cubes (to fill a large plastic bag)
- 1 large lock-top bag
- Yummy items to flavor the ice cream, like chocolate chips, nuts, or fresh fruit

1 Combine sugar, cream, and vanilla in a bowl and pour into the small bag. Seal tightly.

2 Place the salt and ice in the large bag. Then put the sealed smaller bag inside the large bag.

3 Seal the larger bag. Shake until the mixture hardens. It should take about 5–10 minutes. Ta-da! You've got ice cream!

Why Not?
Add toppings to your ice cream once it's frozen. You could use fresh fruit or chocolate syrup!

chocolate syrup   cherry

DONE!

112 MAKE HOT CHOCOLATE

If you've only ever tried powdered hot chocolate, then you're in for a real treat!

you will need
- 1 cup (250ml) milk
- 1 (1½ oz) bar dark chocolate
- Mini marshmallows (optional)

1 Ask an adult to heat up some milk. Meanwhile, break up a small bar of dark chocolate into a heatproof jug.

2 Carefully, pour a third of the hot milk over the chocolate, and whisk. Let stand for a minute.

Why Not?
Sprinkle some mini marshmallows on top of your hot chocolate for an extra treat!

3 Add in the rest of the milk, whisking all the time, until the milk and chocolate are completely combined. Enjoy in your favorite mug!

 **DONE!**

113 MAKE LEMONADE

What could be better than a glass of cool, homemade lemonade on a hot summer day? This recipe makes enough for six glasses.

you will need
- 8 lemons
- 6 cups (1.5L) water
- 1 cup (250g) granulated sugar
- Lemon slices for garnish

1 Squeeze the juice out of the lemons into a jug — make sure you take out any seeds!

2 Ask an adult to heat a third of the water in a pan with the sugar. Make sure to keep stirring until the sugar has completely dissolved, then mix with the lemon juice.

3 Add the rest of the water to the jug, then leave in the fridge to chill. Serve with ice and a slice of lemon.

 **DONE!**

114 ROLL YOUR OWN BREADSTICKS

These delicious mini breadsticks are easy to make and are yummy snacks. You can store them in a plastic lunch box if you like.

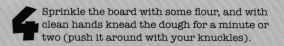

1 Heat an oven to 400°F (204°C). Line a baking sheet with foil and lightly spray with cooking spray; set aside.

Safety First!
Always ask an adult to help you before you use the oven, and ask them to help you when using knives.

2 Combine the flour, sugar, baking powder, and salt. Whisk until thoroughly incorporated.

3 Gradually add the milk and gently stir and mix until dough forms a ball; dough should be soft, but not sticky (add more milk or flour as necessary).

4 Sprinkle the board with some flour, and with clean hands knead the dough for a minute or two (push it around with your knuckles).

5 Roll the dough out and cut it into bars the size of a finger, then put them on the baking sheet. Ask an adult to put the tray in the oven. Bake the fingers for around 15–18 minutes until they are golden-brown, then ask an adult to take them out of the oven.

Enjoy!

DONE!

115 MAKE CHOCOLATE SLIME

For chocoholic slime-oholics! This is a slime you can take a bite out of — if you've made it with clean hands.

you will need
- 1⅓ cups (400g) sweetened condensed milk
- Confectioners' sugar
- Cornstarch
- ¾ cup (110g) plain chocolate, broken into squares

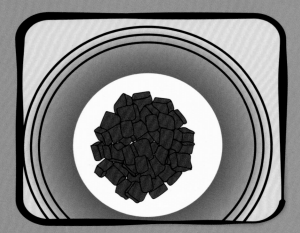

1 Place the sweetened condensed milk into a bowl. Add the chocolate pieces.

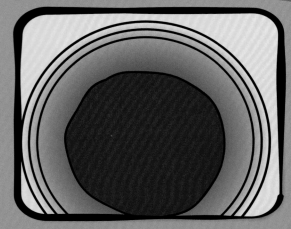

2 Ask an adult to boil a pot of shallow water on the stove. Using an oven mitt, place the bowl inside the pot. Stir with a spoon until the chocolate melts completely. Using an oven mitt, take the bowl out of the water and turn off the stove.

3 While the chocolate mixture cools, dust icing sugar and cornstarch over a clean cutting board or mat. When it is cool enough, pour the chocolate mixture onto the confectioners' sugar and cornstarch.

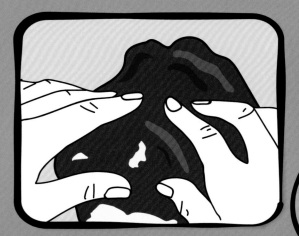

4 Using the spoon and your hands, fold the dry ingredients into the chocolate mixture until it is a slime consistency and mixed together well.

Science Alert!

The cornstarch acts as a thickener and your activator in this recipe, turning the mixture from liquid to moldable slime.

Top Tip

This slime will keep in a sealed container in the fridge for a few days only.

DONE!

116 CREATE ART ON A PLATE

Turn your meal into a work of art. Think about some of the other things you could make, too (and remember that you should never waste food).

SUNFLOWER SALAD

you will need
• Round slice of cheese
• Cherry tomatoes
• Stick of cucumber
• Small salad leaves
• Small pieces of fruit or vegetable to make the features

1 Lay the slice of cheese at the top of the plate and arrange the cherry tomatoes around it.

2 Put the stick of cucumber at the bottom to make a stalk and arrange salad leaves on either side, then use small pieces of vegetable to give your flower a smiley face.

BANANA OCTOPUS

you will need
• 1 banana
• Butter knife or scissors
• Black marker pen

1 Peel the banana halfway down and cut or break off the peeled part. Cut the peel into eight strips and arrange them around the remaining upright half of the banana. Draw eyes and a mouth with a marker pen.

PEAR PEACOCK

you will need
• Half a pear (canned or fresh)
• Green grapes
• Blueberries
• Carrot sticks
• 1 raisin
• Butter knife

1 Place the pear half near the bottom of the plate, leaving space for the legs, and arrange the grapes and blueberries around the pear to make the tail.

2 Cut a corner off one of the carrot sticks with a butter knife to make the beak and cut the rest of the carrot stick in half to make legs. Cut a raisin in half for the eyes.

DONE!

117 INVITE FRIENDS TO A PICNIC

What better way to spend a gloriously sunny afternoon than with friends on a picnic? Plan ahead so you don't forget anything!

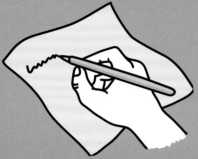

1 Decide on a beautiful picnic spot — it might be in your local park, on the beach, or in your own garden. Then write invitations to your friends. Don't forget to say where, when, and what to bring.

2 Make a list of who's coming and the food to prepare. Think carefully about what everyone likes to eat. Sandwiches or wraps and fruit are good starting points. List items that your friends have promised to bring so that you can work out whether there will be enough to go around. An adult can help you to do this as well as to go shopping.

3 Set out with at least one friend, and make sure that an adult knows where you're going. Get there a little early so you're there before your other guests. Lay out the picnic blanket, eat, relax, talk, and throw a Frisbee! Don't forget to take all of your trash home with you.

Why Not?
Try a winter picnic with flasks of hot chocolate or soup. Wrap up warm, and take blankets to cozy up in!

DONE!

118 PLAY THE MENU GAME

All you need to play this game is a coin and two players, but be warned. It might make you feel hungry or even put you off eating!

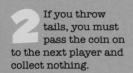

1 The idea is to collect food for your travel meal tray from the list on the right by tossing a coin. You can only collect food if you throw heads.

2 If you throw tails, you must pass the coin on to the next player and collect nothing.

3 Keep a note of the food choices you collect. Once you've collected something, another player can't have it. Toward the end of the game, you may have some yucky-sounding choices to make! You need to collect eight different foods to win.

Food List

- Burger
- Milkshake
- Curly fries
- Banana
- Muffin
- Ice-cream cone
- Pizza slice
- Spaghetti
- Fish stew
- Sheep's eye
- Chicken foot
- Sea slug
- Moldy sandwich
- Super-hot curry
- Bowl of air
- Fried locusts

DONE!

119 BAKE FARMYARD CUPCAKES

You'll have as much fun decorating these cupcakes as eating them.

you will need
- A cupcake or muffin tin
- Paper cupcake liners
- 7 tablespoons softened butter
- ½ cup (115 g) granulated sugar
- 2 eggs
- 1 cup (120g) self-raising flour sifted with 1 level teaspoon baking powder
- 2 cups (220g) sifted confectioners' sugar
- Food coloring
- To decorate: pink and white mini marshmallows, jelly beans, chocolate chips, or mini chocolate sweets

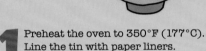

1 Preheat the oven to 350°F (177°C). Line the tin with paper liners.

2 Beat the butter, sugar, eggs, flour, and baking powder together for 2-3 minutes until well mixed.

3 Spoon the mixture into the cases and bake for 20 minutes, until golden brown. Ask an adult to check that they are cooked and take them out of the oven. Cool on a wire rack.

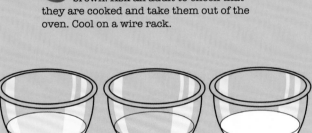

4 Put the powdered sugar in a bowl and gradually mix in 2-3 tablespoons of warm water until you have a fairly stiff icing. Color a third pink in a separate bowl and a third yellow.

5 Frost a third of the cupcakes with white icing, a third with pink, and a third with yellow, and allow the icing to harden.

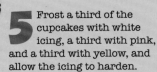

NOW GET DECORATING!

Use the pink marshmallows to make the pigs' snouts and cut pink marshmallows in half for their ears. Use chocolate chips or sweets for their eyes.

Use white marshmallows to make the sheep's faces and give them chocolate eyes and noses.

Use red jelly beans to make the chickens' combs and orange jelly beans for the beaks. Give them each a pair of chocolate eyes.

DONE!

Safety First!
Ask an adult to help you to use the oven and take the baked cupcakes out.

4 HANDY

The maker movement inspires everyone to build, design, and create. Get busy with cool projects you can do yourself, from macaroni monsters to marble runs. Follow the instructions, or hack the rules to make your very own inventive inventions. Get hands-on and be handy!

120 CONSTRUCT A PIÑATA

Making a piñata can be as much fun as breaking one, and if you use a paper bag as the base, you can spend all your time on decorating.

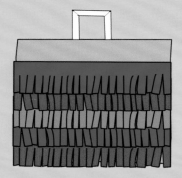

1 Cut the colored paper into long strips, then carefully cut the strips halfway through from the bottom to make a fringe.

Why Not?
Print out a picture of a cartoon character or superhero from the Internet to decorate your piñata.

2 Starting from the bottom, glue the strips of paper onto the bag in layers until you reach the top. Decorate the base, as well.

you will need
- Strong paper carrier bag
- Colored tissue or crepe paper (or paper streamers)
- Scissors
- Glue
- Sweets and/or small toys
- Balls of scrunched-up newspaper
- Packing tape, if necessary

3 Load the bag with goodies and fill any extra space with balls of newspaper. Glue the top of the bag together and use packing tape to strengthen the handles if necessary, then hang the piñata up and let the fun begin!

DONE!

121 FASHION A PAPER BOUQUET

This beautiful bouquet of paper roses would make a great gift for a birthday or Mother's Day. They don't need water and they'll never wilt.

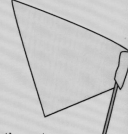

you will need
- Wooden sticks, such as kebab skewers, painted green or wrapped in green tape.
- Crêpe paper
- Scissors
- Green garden tape, or clear sticky tape
- Ribbon or wrapping paper

1 Make the center of the rose by cutting a square of paper and folding it into a triangle. Attach one corner to the stick with tape, then roll it around the stick and use tape to hold it in place.

2 Cut petal shapes from the crepe paper. If you fold the paper up, you can cut several at the same time. You'll need about 16 for each rose.

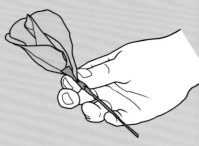

3 Wrap the petals around the bud and stick them in place. When you have enough roses to make a bouquet, tie them together with ribbon or wrap them in paper.

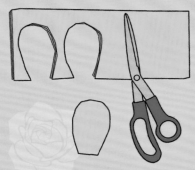

DONE!

122 MAKE A SAMURAI WARRIOR'S HELMET

It's so quick and easy to make this samurai helmet, you could make some for your friends and start your own warrior clan.

you will need
- Piece of paper about 20 inches (50cm) square
- Scissors
- Paints, markers, or crayons

1 Fold the paper in half diagonally to make a triangle with the fold at the top, then fold both the top corners of the triangle over so they touch the bottom corner.

2 Fold both the bottom tips up so they touch the top corner.

3 Now fold the tips outwards as shown.

4 Fold the upper large triangle at the bottom upward to cover most of the top of the helmet, then fold the remaining strip at the bottom up and over the helmet.

5 Tuck the other large triangle up inside the helmet.

6 Decorate your helmet with paint, markers, or crayons.

Did You Know?

- The word *samurai* means "one who serves."
- Children were trained to be samurai from the age of five.
- Up to one third of samurai warriors were women.
- Samurai named their swords because they believed that they contained their warrior spirit.
- Darth Vader's costume in *Star Wars* was inspired by samurai armor.

DONE!

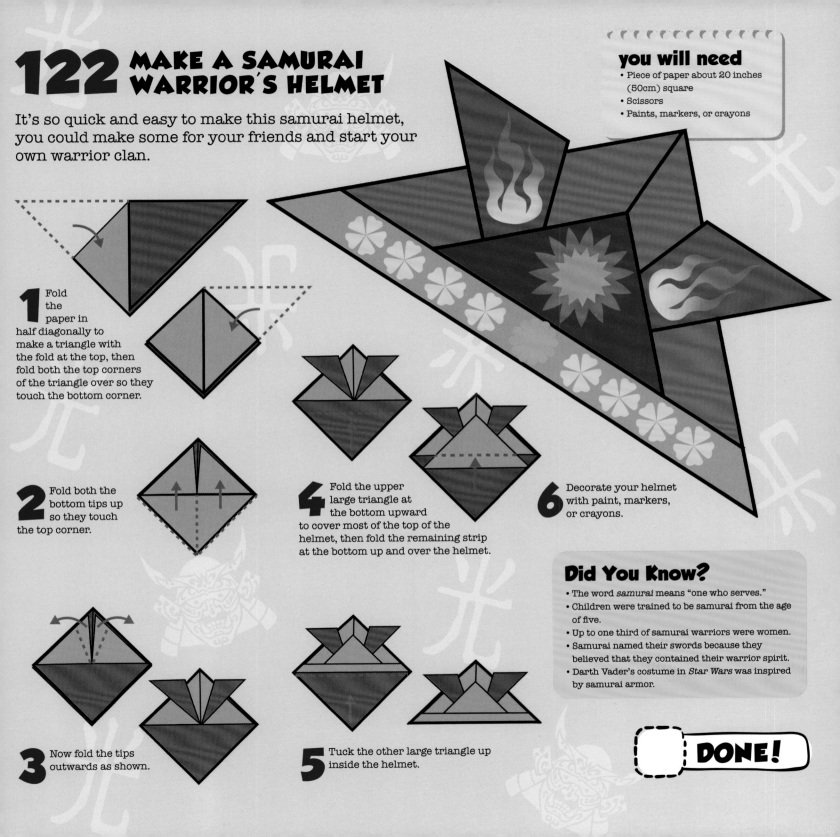

123 BUILD A PERISCOPE

Have you ever wished you could see over a tall fence or peek around a corner without being seen? If so, this periscope is your perfect spying tool.

you will need
- 2 tall juice or milk cartons
- Craft knife
- Ruler
- Pencil or pen
- 2 small flat mirrors
- Masking tape

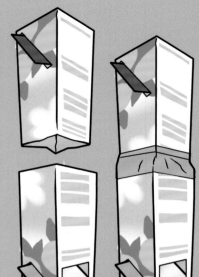

Safety First!
Ask an adult to help you cut the carton.

3 Starting at the corner, ask an adult to make a cut the length of one side of your mirror along the diagonal line.

5 Stand one carton up with the hole facing you, then place the other carton upside-down on top, with the hole facing away from you.

1 Ask an adult to cut the tops off both cartons with a craft knife and cut a window at the bottom of each, leaving about .25 inch (7mm) around the sides of the hole. Then wash them out.

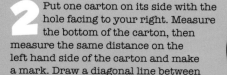

2 Put one carton on its side with the hole facing to your right. Measure the bottom of the carton, then measure the same distance on the left hand side of the carton and make a mark. Draw a diagonal line between the mark and the bottom-right corner.

4 Slide the mirror into the slot so you can see it through the hole in the front. You should be able to see the ceiling through the top of the carton. When it's in the right position, tape it securely into place. Repeat steps 2–4 with the other carton.

Top Tip
If you turn your periscope upside down you can look under tables (or into the bottom bunk), too.

6 Squeeze the bottom of the upside-down carton so it slides a little way inside the bottom carton, then tape the two together.

DONE!

124 MAKE A PHOTO BOX

This is a clever way to keep your photos safe and ready to display. It would make a great gift for a friend or grandparent, too.

you will need
- Round potato chip tube with a lid
- Pencil or pen
- Craft knife
- Thin card
- Scissors
- Ribbon
- Stapler (optional)
- Glue
- Photos
- Tape
- Paint or markers

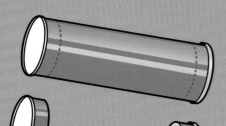

1 Measure 1 inch (3cm) from each end of the carton and draw a line all the way around. Ask an adult to cut around the box using a craft knife, so you have two separate ends.

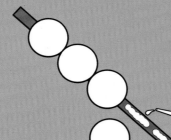

2 Cut out discs of card that are a little smaller than the inside of the carton (you could use a compass or find a glass or lid to draw around). You might want help with this. You'll need one disc for each photo. Glue or staple the discs to the ribbon.

Why Not?
Cut out an extra photo to stick to the lid of your photo box.

3 Using the same guide, cut out your photos and stick them to the card discs. Glue one end of the photo chain inside the bottom half of the carton and the other end inside the lid. If you have lots of photos, you could stick some to the backs of the discs, as well.

4 Tape the two ends of the carton together, then cut a strip of card 2 inches (5cm) wide and long enough to wrap around the carton. Decorate it using a theme to represent the photos in your box, e.g. holidays, a birthday, or Christmas.

5 Glue the strip of card around the photo box.

Safety First!
Ask an adult to help you cut the tube.

6 To display your photos, just take the lid off the box and gently pull them out.

DONE!

125 FORM PASTA MONSTERS

Pasta's not just for eating—it's a great craft material, too. Try gluing the pasta shapes to a magnet or a name badge to make a monster fridge magnet or badge.

you will need
- Plastic ziplock sandwich bags
- Vinegar
- Food coloring
- Pasta shapes, e.g. macaroni, penne, fusilli
- Paper towels or newspaper
- Strong glue
- Googly eyes
- Name badges or fridge magnets (optional)

1 Put the pasta into plastic bags, using a different bag for each color. Add three or four tablespoons of vinegar and several drops of food coloring, then close the bag and shake it until the pasta is evenly colored.

2 Open the bag a little and pour the liquid away. Lay the pasta on layers of paper towels or newspapers to dry.

3 Glue the pasta together to make monster shapes and attach the eyes.

DONE!

126 FASHION AN INDOOR TEEPEE

Camping outdoors is fun, but when it's cold outside, an indoor tent is much cozier.

you will need
- 6 tall bamboo canes
- String
- Blankets or sheets
- 12 clothespins
- Cushions, rugs, and pillows

Top Tip
Arrange some pillows around the outside of your teepee to keep the canes in place.

1 Tie the canes together with string, about 8 inches (20cm) from the top.

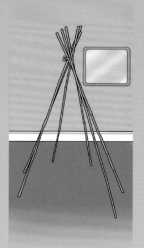

2 Rest the bottoms of the canes on the floor and pull them out to make a teepee shape. This is easier if you have someone to help.

3 Drape blankets or sheets around the canes and pin them in place at the top and bottom, then fill your teepee with pillows, rugs, and cushions.

DONE!

127 BUILD A SOLAR SYSTEM MOBILE

This model of the solar system will help you to learn the positions of the planets. If you forget, here's a handy phrase to remind you of their initial letters (from the Sun outwards): My Violent Evil Monster Just Served Us Nuts.

you will need
- Round piece of cardboard about 11 inches (30cm) across (e.g. from a frozen pizza)
- Hole punch
- Ruler
- Compass
- Pencil, crayons, or markers
- Different-colored card
- Scissors
- String

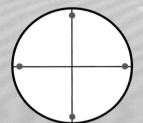 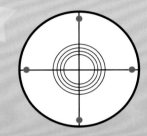  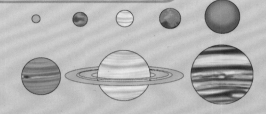

1 Use the ruler to find the center of the circle of card and draw lines across the middle, from top to bottom and left to right. Then use the hole punch to make four holes through the lines, near the edge of the circle.

2 Using the compass, draw a circle 1.5 inches (4cm) from the center, then draw 3 circles 0.5 inch (1.3cm) apart. These four circles are the orbits of the rocky planets: Mercury, Venus, Earth, and Mars.

3 Leave a gap of 1 inch (3cm). This is the asteroid belt. Then draw 4 more circles each 0.5 inch (1.3cm) apart. These 4 circles are the orbits of the gas giants Jupiter and Saturn and the ice giants Uranus and Neptune.

4 Cut circles of colored card for the Sun and the planets. The Sun is huge, so make this the biggest. The planets in order of size from the smallest are Mercury, Mars, Venus, Earth, Neptune, Uranus, Saturn, and Jupiter. Make a hole in the top of each circle with the hole punch.

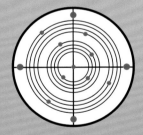  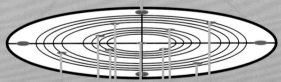

5 Make a hole with the compass point in the center of the circle and somewhere in each of the orbits, so the planets will be well spaced.

6 Tie string through the hole in the Sun and thread the other end through the hole in the center of the circle, then tie a knot. Do the same with the planets, attaching them to their matching orbits.

7 Cut four pieces of string about 8 inches (20cm) long and tie a piece through each of the four holes at the edge of the cardboard circle. Tie the ends together at the top of the circle so it is evenly balanced and hang up your mobile.

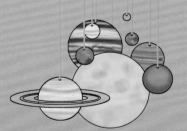 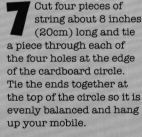

Safety First!
Ask an adult to help you make the holes.

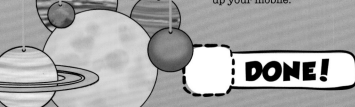

DONE!

128 GET ORGANIZED

Upcycle your family's old jeans to make this cool wall organizer.

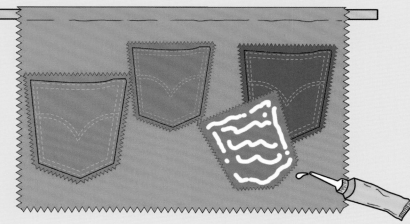

1 Carefully cut around the pockets of the jeans. If you use pinking shears, you'll get a funky zigzag edge that won't fray. Denim is thick and hard to cut, so ask an adult to help.

you will need
- Piece of strong fabric, large enough to fit all your pockets, with a border of 4 inches (10cm) at the bottom and sides and 8 inches (20cm) at the top
- Several pairs of old jeans
- Strong fabric glue
- Pinking shears or scissors
- Pole (e.g. a cane, broom handle, or curtain pole) at least 8 inches (20cm) wider than the fabric
- String or cord

3 Now arrange the pockets on the fabric. Spread glue all over the backs and stick them down.

4 Give the glue time to dry, then tie string to the ends of the pole and hang the organizer up.

2 Cut around the edges of the large piece of fabric with pinking shears (or turn over the edges at the sides and bottom and glue them down). Fold the top edge of the fabric over the pole and glue it in place.

Top Tip
The pockets are a perfect size for keeping your phone, remote controls, and sunglasses safe.

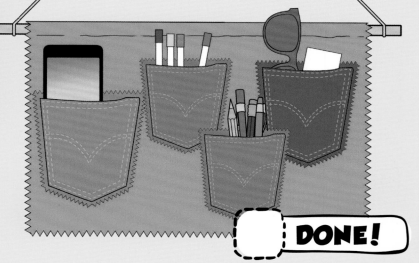

DONE!

129 SEW CARDS

Sewing is a useful skill that's fun to learn. Sewing cards make great handmade greeting cards, too.

Safety First!
Be careful not to prick yourself with the compass point or needle.

1 Lay your shape on the card and place it on top of something to protect the work surface. Prick evenly spaced holes around the outline with the point of the compass.

2 Thread the yarn through the needle and tie a knot in the end. Put your needle through one of the holes, with the knot at the back, then stitch around the shape, as shown.

3 You can sew across the shape as well, to fill it in.

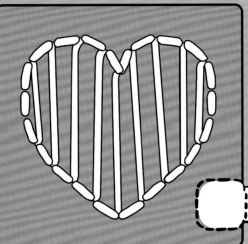

DONE!

130 UPCYCLE YOUR TOYS

Turn your trash into treasure by transforming the old and broken plastic toys lurking in your cupboards into an awesome work of art.

you will need
- A base, e.g., an old tray or large toy
- A big pile of plastic toys
- Glue for sticking plastic, such as clear model glue

1 Lay the toys on your base and make sure you're happy with the arrangement.

2 Ask an adult to help you stick the toys down, then leave the glue to set overnight. Hang the tray on the wall like a picture.

Top Tip
It's a good idea to give the toys a wash to make sure the glue sticks well. Leave them to dry overnight.

3 Try working with a 3-D shape. It will be more difficult! You'll need to stick the toys on in stages and leave the glue to set in between.

Safety First!
Ask an adult to help you use the glue.

DONE!

131 CATAPULT A MARSHMALLOW

You only need five marshmallows to make this catapult — which leaves lots for eating!

Top Tip
It's easy to tear the marshmallows at first, but if you leave the catapult overnight, they will harden up.

you will need
- 7 wooden kebab skewers
- At least 5 large marshmallows
- Plastic spoon
- Masking tape
- Thin elastic band

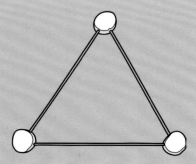

1 Make a triangle by sticking the ends of three skewers into three marshmallows.

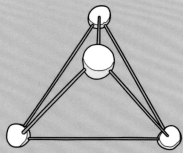

2 Use three more skewers and another marshmallow to make a pyramid.

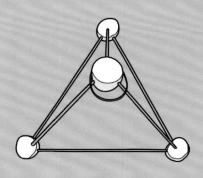

3 Tape the plastic spoon firmly onto another skewer.

4 Loop the elastic band over the top marshmallow.

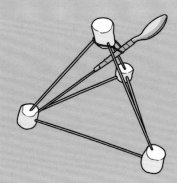

5 Slide the skewer holding the spoon through the elastic band and stick the end into the marshmallow opposite, at the base.

6 Place the last marshmallow on the spoon and pull it back gently, then let go. You may need to hold onto the base at the opposite side until the marshmallows have hardened up. Why not draw a target to aim at?

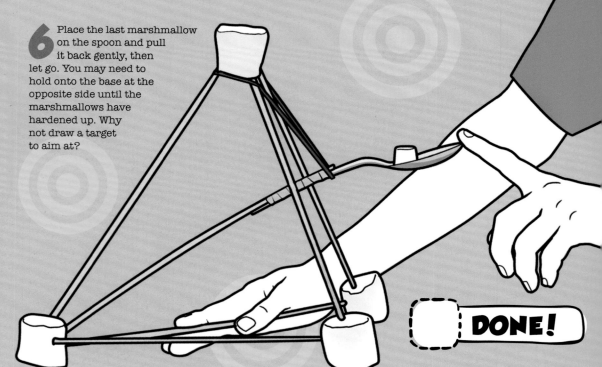

DONE!

132 MAKE AN ORIGAMI BOOKMARK

You'll never lose your place if you make this mini-monster bookmark.

you will need

- Piece of paper, about 5-inch (13-cm) square
- Pens, paints, and/or markers
- Decorations, such as googly eyes, white card, and yarn

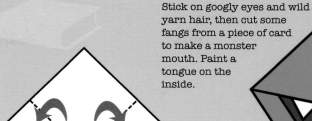

Stick on googly eyes and wild yarn hair, then cut some fangs from a piece of card to make a monster mouth. Paint a tongue on the inside.

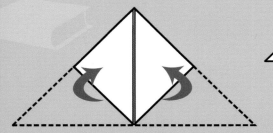

1 Fold the paper in two diagonally, with the fold at the bottom, then fold the outer corners up to the top of the triangle.

2 Unfold the corners to make a triangle again, then fold the top side of the paper triangle down to the bottom edge.

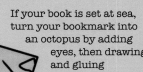

If your book is set at sea, turn your bookmark into an octopus by adding eyes, then drawing and gluing tentacles on the square side.

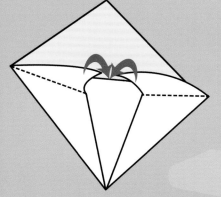

3 Tuck the two outer corners inside the bottom half of the bookmark.

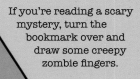

4 Think up some fun ways to decorate your bookmark. Maybe the book you're reading will give you an idea.

If you're reading a scary mystery, turn the bookmark over and draw some creepy zombie fingers.

DONE!

133 PIN YOUR PHOTOS

String this fab photo holder across a wall. It's perfect for displaying greetings cards and keeping important papers safe, too.

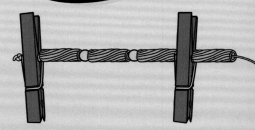

1 To color the clothespins, soak them overnight in a bowl of water mixed with food coloring. Dry the pin on a baking tray, or something that won't stain.

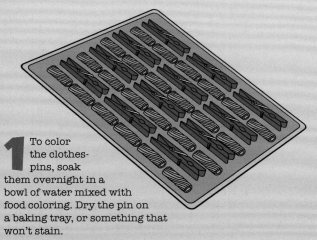

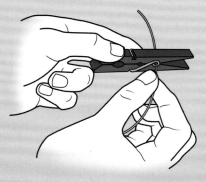

2 Measure about 12 inches (30cm) from one end of the string and tie a double knot. Thread the other end of the string through the hole in the metal spring of the first clothespin.

3 Add pasta and/or bead spacers, then add pins and spacers until you get to the last pin.

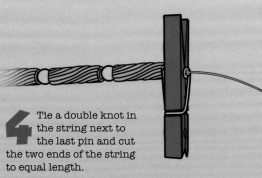

you will need
- 10 wooden clothespins
- Food coloring and/or 4 inches (10mm) washi tape
- Beads and/or pasta shapes with a hole through the middle, such as rigatoni, macaroni, or penne
- Piece of string about 39 inches (1m) long

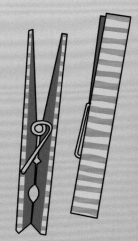

4 Tie a double knot in the string next to the last pin and cut the two ends of the string to equal length.

5 You could decorate the pins with washi tape.

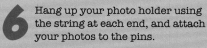

6 Hang up your photo holder using the string at each end, and attach your photos to the pins.

DONE!

134 BUILD A HELICOPTER

Launch your helicopter by holding the rectangle of paper below the blades and letting go very quickly.

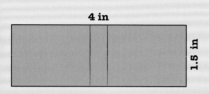

4 in

1.5 in

1 Draw two vertical lines 2 inches (5cm) from each end of the paper.

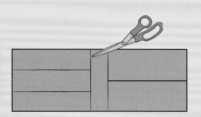

2 Draw a line across the center of the right-hand side and cut along it. Draw lines to divide the left-hand side into three.

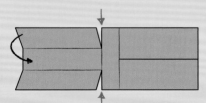

3 Following the red arrows, cut one third in from the edges of the paper on each side. Fold the sides over into the center to make one central strip.

4 Fold up the bottom quarter of the central strip and hold it in place with a paper clip. Fold one of the top flaps forward and the other backward. Now release your helicopter and watch it spin.

DONE!

---

135 CATCH THE SUN

Save colored cellophane candy wrappers to make this stained-glass-style sun catcher (but don't use it as an excuse to eat more candy!).

1 Cut the candy wrappers into triangle shapes and arrange them on the clear cellophane. Apply glue to the colored triangles and stick them down. Leave to dry overnight with a weight (e.g. a heavy book) on top.

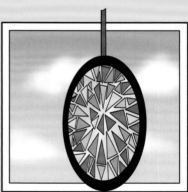

2 Cut two circular frames from the black card — use a compass, or draw around a smaller and larger dish or plate. Glue the cellophane to the bottom frame. Trim off the cellophane around the edges and stick some ribbon to the top of the lower frame.

3 Stick the second frame to the other side of the cellophane. Hang your sun catcher against a window to give your room a colorful glow.

Safety First!
Ask an adult to help you cut the frames.

DONE!

136 RACE IN A REGATTA

Once you've mastered the folding techniques, you can make these boats really quickly, so it won't take long to build up a fleet. Why not decorate your boats with little flags attached to toothpicks?

you will need
- Sheets of paper
- Wax crayons (optional)
- Toothpicks, markers, or paints (optional)
- Bathtub

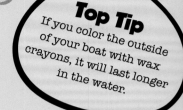

Top Tip
If you color the outside of your boat with wax crayons, it will last longer in the water.

1 Fold the paper in half across the middle and then fold the top corners in, so they meet in the center.

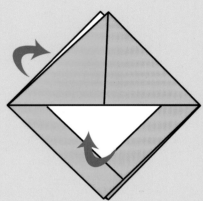

4 Fold the two bottom corners up to the top to form a triangle then push the two sides together again to form a square.

5 Pull the side flaps apart and a boat shape will appear. Put your fingers inside the triangle in the center and gently pull it apart so the boat stands up.

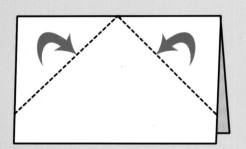

2 Fold the top of the oblong flap at the bottom up over the triangle above, then turn the paper over and do the same on the other side.

6 Decorate your boats, then put a small amount of cold water in the bath and see how well they float. Try creating a breeze by flapping a newspaper at one end of the bath to speed them along.

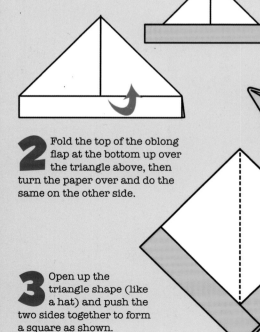

3 Open up the triangle shape (like a hat) and push the two sides together to form a square as shown.

DONE!

137 MAKE A PIGGY BANK

Allow a couple of days for this project, because each layer of papier-mâché needs to dry. You'll have to break your piggy bank to get at the money, so make sure you won't need it in a hurry!

you will need
- Balloon
- Egg carton
- Masking tape
- Newspaper torn into strips about 0.5 inch (1.3cm) wide
- Wallpaper paste (or flour and water mixed to a paste)
- Paints and paintbrushes
- Pipe cleaner (optional)

Why Not? Give your piggy a curly pipe-cleaner tail.

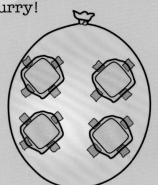

1 Blow up the balloon to about 5 inches (13cm) wide.

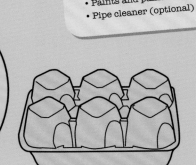

2 Cut the cups out of the egg carton. Tape four to the bottom of the balloon to make the legs.

3 Tape one of the remaining cups to the front to form the snout, then cut two ears from the other and tape them in place.

4 Dip the strips of paper into the paste and wrap them around the balloon, legs, snout, and ears until they are completely covered. Leave to dry. Repeat three times.

5 Ask an adult to help you cut a slot at the top of the piggy bank and pop the balloon inside.

6 Paint your pig and start saving!

DONE!

138 MAKE A FLICK BOOK

A flick book is an animation you can keep in your pocket. If you don't have sticky notes, you can use a notebook or even the corner of an old book. Thin paper is best for flicking.

Why Not?
Add moving arms, legs, and a head to your ball and turn it into a jumping man.

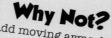

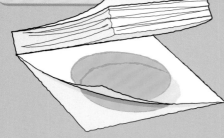

1 Start with a simple subject, such as a bouncing ball. Draw in pencil first and begin at the back of the book so you can see the previous drawing through the paper.

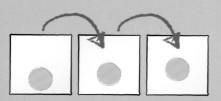

3 Put a binder clip at the top of the pad to stop it coming apart, or hold it tightly at the top, and start flicking!

2 Draw the object in a slightly different position on each page. Go over the drawings with marker pen when you're happy with them.

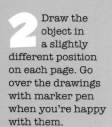

DONE!

---

139 RUN YOUR MARBLES

This recycling project is a great way to use all your old cardboard tubes and plastic bottles.

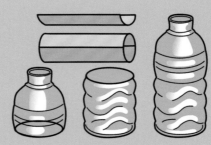

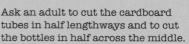

1 Ask an adult to cut the cardboard tubes in half lengthways and to cut the bottles in half across the middle.

Top Tip
If you don't have any marbles, use balls of rolled-up aluminum foil.

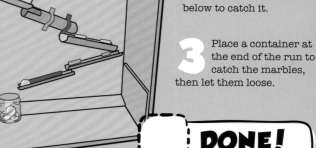

2 Starting at the top, tape the tubes and bottles to the back of the box (or to a door that won't be damaged by the tape). Make sure they slope downward and that when a marble drops, there's a tube or bottle below to catch it.

3 Place a container at the end of the run to catch the marbles, then let them loose.

DONE!

140 MAKE MUSIC

It's always fun to make music, and it's even better if you make your own instruments, too.

DRUM

Cut the end off a balloon and stretch it across the top of the can. Secure it with an elastic band.

you will need
- Large, clean cans with a smooth edge
- Balloons
- Elastic bands
- Drumsticks (e.g. chopsticks)

TAMBOURINE

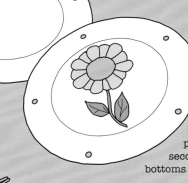

you will need
- 2 paper plates
- Hole punch
- 5 jingle bells
- Twist ties
- Paints, stickers, ribbons etc. (optional)

1 Punch five evenly spaced holes around the edge of one plate. Lay it on top of the other, and mark the position of the holes on the bottom plate with a pencil. Punch holes in the second plate. Decorate the bottoms of the plates if you like.

2 Thread the bells onto the twist ties. Put the tops of the plates face-to-face and use the twist ties to hold them together. You could tie ribbons through the holes as well.

WATER XYLOPHONE

Pour different amounts of water into each bottle or jar and tap them with a spoon. Arrange them in order, from the highest note to the lowest. You could color the water with food coloring or paint.

you will need
- 5-8 glass bottles or jars with flat bottoms
- Water
- Spoon
- Food coloring or paint (optional)

you will need
- 2 small plastic drink bottles
- Dried beans
- Materials for decorating the bottles (optional)

MARACAS

Put some beans into each bottle and screw the lids back on. Hold the bottles by the tops and shake in time with the beat.

DONE!

141 MAKE GLOVE MONSTERS

Don't throw away your old or single woolen gloves — make these lovable monsters instead.

fill with stuffing

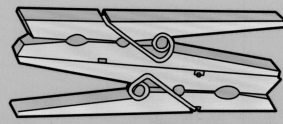

you will need
- Woolen gloves
- Polyester stuffing
- Fabric glue or a needle and thread
- Scissors
- Buttons
- Scraps of felt and yarn

1 To make four-legged monsters, push stuffing into the fingers, then push the thumb inside the glove.

2 Fill the rest of the glove with stuffing and turn the cuff inside. Stick or sew in place.

Top Tip
If there are holes in some of the fingers, push them inside and make an upside-down monster with horns instead.

3 Decorate your monsters with buttons, felt, and pieces of yarn.

DONE!

142 HOLD YOUR EARPHONES

This handy earphone holder will solve the problem of tangled cables. It would make a really useful gift, too.

Top Tip
Make sure you don't pinch any wires when you clip your cables into the pins.

you will need
- Newspaper
- Strong glue
- 2 wooden clothespins
- Acrylic paints and a brush and/or 10mm washi tape

1 Cover your work surface with newspaper. Apply glue to the side of one clothespin and lay the other on top, facing in the opposite direction. Leave to dry.

2 Paint the clothespins and leave to dry (they may need more than one coat) or decorate them with washi tape.

3 Clip one end of the earphones inside one pin, wind the cable round and clip the other end inside the other pin.

DONE!

143 MAKE AN ICE MOBILE

Make the most of a winter's day by making this sparkling ice mobile. If it's really cold, you could leave the tray outside to freeze overnight.

you will need
- Colorful berries
- Glitter
- Mini muffin (or cupcake) pan
- Ribbon
- Jug

1 Put some berries and glitter into the pan and drape a ribbon across it, so it dangles into each mould. There should be at least 12 inches (30cm) of ribbon free at one end.

2 Fill the jug with water and pour some into each mould so the ribbon is covered. Ask an adult to put the pan in the freezer for several hours or overnight.

3 When the water has frozen, dip the pan in warm water to loosen the ice, then hang the mobile outside in front of a window.

Safety First!
Some berries you find outside are poisonous, so never eat them without checking with an adult.

DONE!

144 FRAME YOUR DAY

When you next go the beach, take along a camera and snap a few selfies. If your beach allows it, collect shells, pebbles, and other interesting things to take home with you.

you will need
- Shells and pebbles collected from the beach
- Flat picture frame
- Craft glue

1 When you get home, lay your treasures on the ground outside to see what you've found. You might need to brush off the sand and wash them down before you use them. Pick out the best bits.

2 Arrange your treasures onto the picture frame. Play around with the design until it's exactly how you want it, then glue everything onto the frame with craft glue.

3 Print your best selfie and put it in the frame. What better way to remember a fun day at the beach? It could make a great present, too!

DONE!

145 STORE IN A ROBOT

This robot might not be able to tidy up for you, but it will store your stationery and craft materials neatly in one place.

Top Tip
Tall containers are great for storing your pencils or paintbrushes!

Some ideas for decorating your robot

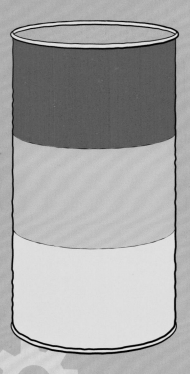

1 Wipe out the insides of the container to get rid of any grease or salt. Cover the outside of the cartons with paper.

you will need
- 1 tall chip container with plastic lid
- Colored or metallic paper
- Scissors
- Strong glue
- White paper
- Marker pens
- Thin card
- Metallic stickers and/or small metal objects, such as bottle tops, buttons, bolts, washers, nuts, springs, pieces from broken toys, etc.

2 Cut out a square of white paper that will fit on the container and draw a control panel, including circuits, cogs, and dials. You could include stickers and pieces of recycled metal. Glue the panel onto the container.

3 Use recycled materials to make a face and arms for your robot (or make them from card). If you have some wheels from an old toy, you could glue these near the bottom of the container.

 **DONE!**

146 MAKE AN OUTDOOR PHOTO BOOTH

Don't be shy! Step right up! Everyone loves taking silly pictures. This simple booth will allow you and your friends to have hours of fun and lots of memorable snaps.

you will need
- Large picture frame
- Sturdy tree branch
- Fishing line
- Dress-up clothes or props
- Mobile phone or camera

1 Find a large picture frame. It needs to be at least big enough to fit your head into. If you don't have something at home, hunt one down in a local thrift store.

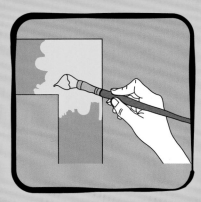

2 Remove the backing and everything in the frame. You might need an adult to help you to do this. Repaint or decorate the frame if you want to.

3 Find a tree with a sturdy branch in a nice setting for a photo. Ask an adult to help you to hang the frame from the branch with fishing line. You could also hang it from a post or hook.

4 Try out different heights and positions, for example, an oval frame might be nice on its side so that two people can fit into it. Make sure the frame isn't too high to reach! It needs to be at eye level.

5 Put a few props or an entire dress-up box on the ground near the frame.

6 Invite your friends over, ask them to stand behind the frame, and take their portrait! Encourage them to get inventive with the props.

DONE!

147 LAUNCH A PARACHUTE

Have you ever dreamed of making a parachute jump?
Maybe you should let your toy action figure have a go first . . .

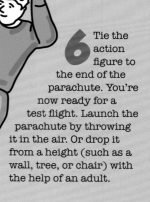

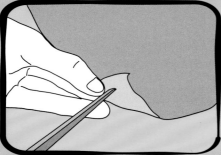

1 Fold over one corner of the fabric and snip a small hole with the scissors. Repeat on the other three sides.

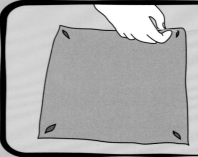

2 Take one of your threads. Tie one end to the corner of the fabric.

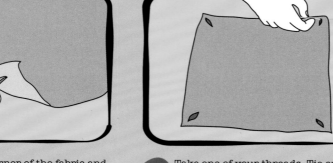

3 Take the other end of the thread through one button hole then through the diagonally opposite button hole.

4 Pull the thread until the button is in the middle and tie the loose end to the opposite corner of the fabric. Repeat with the other thread and corners.

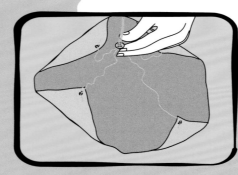

5 Hold the threads from the top of the button. Slide the button down about two-thirds of the thread and tie a knot.

6 Tie the action figure to the end of the parachute. You're now ready for a test flight. Launch the parachute by throwing it in the air. Or drop it from a height (such as a wall, tree, or chair) with the help of an adult.

you will need
- 10-inch (26-cm) square piece of lightweight fabric
- Scissors
- Button with 4 holes
- 2 lengths of 35-inch (90-cm) thread
- Small plastic action figure

DONE!

148 MAKE A STRING TELEPHONE

The way that a string telephone works isn't so different from how an old-fashioned telephone worked, except that string is used instead of an electric current. Try different lengths of string to see how far away it will work.

you will need
- 2 paper cups
- Non-stretchable thread (for example, kite string or fishing line)
- Measuring tape or ruler
- Sewing needle
- Friend

1 Cut a long length of string, between 65–98 feet (20–30m) long. Ask an adult to help you make holes in the bottom of your cups with a sewing needle. Thread the string through each cup and tie a knot at each end, inside the cups.

How it Works

When you talk into your cup, the bottom vibrates back and forth with sound waves. The vibrations travel along the string and are converted back into sound waves at the other end so your friend can hear what you said. Sound waves travel better through solids (such as your cup and string) than through air, letting you hear sounds that are much farther away.

2 Take one of the cups each, and spread apart until the string is tight. One of you should talk into the cup while the other one listens. Can you hear what the other person is saying?

DONE!

149 LIGHT UP A LAVA LAMP

Those cool blobs you see in a lava lamp are simple to re-create. And you can make them glow, too!

you will need
- Clean plastic bottle with cap (1.5L)
- Cooking oil
- Water
- Food coloring
- Indigestion tablet (broken into small bits) or rock salt
- Flashlight

1 Fill one quarter of the bottle with water and the remaining three quarters with oil. Add about 10 drops of food coloring.

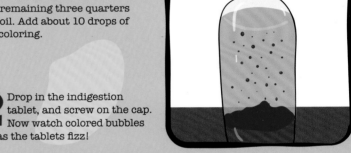

2 Drop in the indigestion tablet, and screw on the cap. Now watch colored bubbles rise as the tablets fizz!

3 Turn out the lights and shine a flashlight under the bottom of the bottle. You made that cool special effect. Way to go!

DONE!

150 MAKE A HAMMOCK

Have a lazy outdoor day, gently swinging in a hammock. If you don't already have one, make your own! All you need is a sheet, some climbing rope, and an adult to hang it up for you.

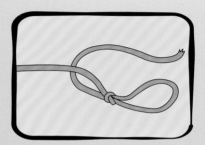

1 Take one piece of cord and make a loop at the end. Secure with a double knot. Leave a 4-inch (10-cm) "tail."

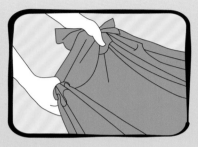

2 Loosely zigzag fold or gather your sheet lengthways. Then fold over one of the width ends at about 8 inches (20cm).

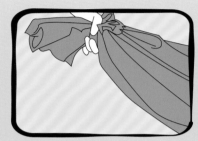

3 Gather the fabric from both sides about 4 inches (10cm) in from the edge. Hold with your fist.

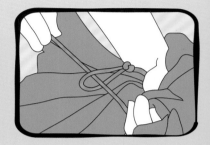

4 Wrap the cord around the sheet where your fist is, and then thread the cord through the loop.

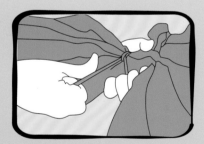

5 Pull the cord until the loop is tight to the sheet. Wrap the cord tightly around the sheet 5 or 6 times, and tie the two ends together with a secure double knot.

you will need

- 2 pieces of 2-foot (60-cm) utility cord (available from climbing shops and hardware stores)
- 1 large bed sheet (not too old and worn)
- 2 pieces of 3-foot (1m) webbing (available from climbing shops and hardware stores)
- Adult help

6 Thread one piece of webbing through the end of your sheet. Tie a secure knot in your webbing. Repeat these steps on the other side.

7 Your hammock is now ready for an adult to hang up for you. Ask him or her to check that your knots are secure first and to tighten them if necessary.

DONE!

PRESS FLOWERS

Keep summer alive forever! Pressed flowers are perfect for framing, decorating, or even placing inside a locket. There are lots of ways to press them, but here is the simplest way.

1 Find a heavy book. Encyclopedias or dictionaries are ideal. The moisture from the flowers might wrinkle the pages, so make sure the book isn't precious to someone!

2 Lay the book open somewhere near the middle. Line it with two sheets of paper on either side. Cut the paper to fit if you need to. The outer two sheets are your "blotters."

3 For best results, pick your flowers when they're at the height of their bloom, when their color is at its brightest. Choose flowers with fresh petals that haven't started to droop or die and that aren't damaged by insects.

4 Ideally, pick flowers when they are dry. If you pick flowers that are still wet with dew or rain, allow them to dry completely before you press them. Dab them gently with kitchen paper to speed up the drying process.

5 Lay your flowers on one side of the book. Arrange them with spaces in between, and not too close to the paper edge. Do not overlap, unless you want your finished pressed flowers to do so.

6 To press flowers with a conical shape (like tulips or roses), cut them in half lengthways, or press individual petals.

7 If you have a lot of flowers, line other pages of your book with four sheets of paper, and use those, too. But make sure that you leave about 0.5 inch (1.3cm) between the different pages that you're using to press the flowers.

8 Close the book very carefully, without disturbing your flower arrangement or the paper alignment. Pile more heavy books on top of the pressing book. Leave in a dry place in your home.

9 Change the paper sheets every few days. Do this very carefully so you don't disturb the delicate flowers. After a couple of weeks, the flowers will be completely dry. Remove carefully with your fingers or a pair of tweezers.

DONE!

152 MAKE A WIND CHIME

You can't beat the soft jingle of a wind chime blowing in the breeze. You can use all sorts of bits and pieces to make one. Use your imagination!

Safety First!
Ask an adult to help you cut the fishing line.

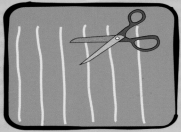

1 Measure and cut six pieces of fishing line, about 30 inches (75cm) long. Gather together all of your found bits and pieces.

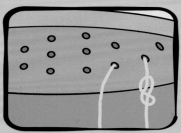

2 Thread one piece of fishing line through two holes just above the circular rim of your colander. Pull through until you have half the length hanging from each hole. Tie knots in the middle of the fishing line to fix it securely. The two threads should dangle down.

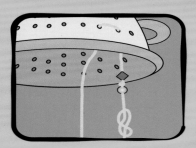

3 Thread or tie your treasures onto each side of the fishing line, one at a time. Each time you slide a bead or button onto the string, tie a knot beneath it. Make sure that the knot is big enough to stop them from sliding down.

you will need
- Fishing line (ideally) or string
- Colander (or any other plastic or metal object with holes, for example, a cheese grater)
- Bits and pieces that you can thread or tie, such as beads, keys, shells, buttons, pine cones, paper clips — whatever you like!

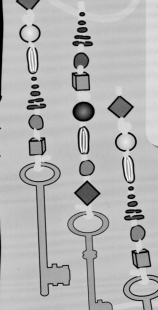

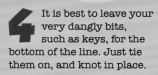

4 It is best to leave your very dangly bits, such as keys, for the bottom of the line. Just tie them on, and knot in place.

5 Put one piece of line to the side. Thread and decorate the rest as in steps 2 to 4. Space them out evenly around the colander.

Why Not?
Ask an adult to help you to hang your wind chime outside near your bedroom window.

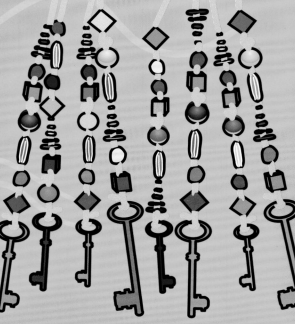

6 Take the last piece of fishing line and tie each end to the handles of the colander. This is for hanging it up. Now just wait for a soft breeze to work its magic.

DONE!

153 HANG A WREATH

Welcome visitors to your door by hanging a wreath! Use leaves and stems collected from your garden or local area at any time of the year. Berries and flowers add a great splash of color.

you will need
• Foliage, for example, sprigs of fir, holly, ivy, mistletoe, rosemary, lavender, flowers, berries — anything that you can find with a stem!
• Florist foam ring with a plastic bottom
• Ribbon
• Scissors

1 Collect foliage. Sprigs of fir, holly, and berried ivy all work well. But anything with a stem will work! Use scissors to cut stems about 4 inches (10cm) long. Ask permission before you pick anything!

2 Remove 1 inch (3cm) of leaves or needles from each sprig so that you have stems to press into the foam. Either trim with scissors or remove them with your fingers. Watch out! They can be prickly!

3 Float the foam ring face down into a bowl or basin of water and allow it to sink naturally. Do not force it under. After about a minute it will turn dark green. Take it out.

4 Insert sprigs of one plant into your foam at regular intervals. Angle the sprigs to follow the shape of the wreath.

5 Insert leaves or sprigs of different plants at different angles, still following the wreath's outline. Make sure you cover all parts of the foam equally. Keep going until you have filled all the gaps in the wreath.

6 Thread the ribbon through the center of the wreath. Tie a knot at the top so that you can hang it. If you want to, tie a bow instead of a knot. Hang on your door to welcome all your visitors!

DONE!

154 MAKE TWO NATURAL INSTRUMENTS

The best music comes from outdoors, like birds chirping or insects buzzing. Make these two instruments to get back to nature!

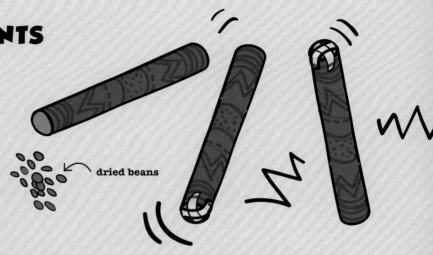

dried beans

you will need

- Cardboard tube
- Paint or colored markers
- Sticky tape
- Paper
- Plastic or wooden toothpicks
- Scissors
- Dried beans

RAIN STICK

An instrument from South America, usually made from the wooden skeleton of a cactus. Your rain stick will be a little different, but it should produce the same effect.

3 Drop a handful of dried beans inside. Then tape another circle of paper over the open end. Tip your stick gently back and forth to hear the soft sound of rain.

cardboard tube

1 Take a cardboard tube (a paper towel or wrapping paper tube works well) and decorate the outside with paint, markers, etc. Tape a circle of paper over one end.

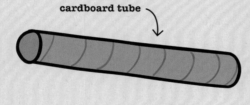

toothpicks

2 Poke some wooden or plastic toothpicks into the tube, following a downward spiral pattern. You should end up with something a lot like the image below. Secure the ends of the sticks with tape.

GRASS TRUMPET

Make a funny, high-pitched squeal to, erm, DELIGHT your friends with just a blade of grass and your hands!

1 Find a wide blade of grass. Hold up your left hand in a loose fist with your thumbnail pointing toward you. Then put your right hand up next to your left hand with the blade of grass flat between your thumbs.

2 Hold the grass between your thumbs. Move the grass so that it is stretched tightly in the gap between your thumbs — and then move the gap against your lips.

3 Pucker your lips as if you were going to blow out a candle and blow hard into the gap. If you do it correctly, you will hear the grass make a loud, squeaky sound.

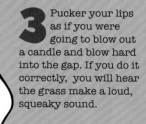

DONE!

155 BUILD A BOX CITY

Find everything it takes to make an entire city, using just the cardboard boxes you usually put in the recycling bin!

1 Get a bunch of boxes. You want different sizes and widths. Best bets: cereal boxes, shoe boxes, smaller snack boxes, juice boxes, cardboard tubes, and spaghetti boxes (for skyscrapers, of course!). Wrap each box in paper.

Why Not?
Make part of your town look like a famous building, such as the Empire State Building!

2 Design and color in your buildings using crayons, markers, and paint. Draw windows, doors, bricks, tiles, and whatever else you'd see on a building. How about plants, balconies or a teeny photo of you inside one of the windows?

3 Place your buildings in an area together to make a town. Once all the buildings are in place, you can add even more details, such as streets or a park. This city is only limited by your imagination!

DONE!

156 MAKE A SNOW GLOBE

Snow globes show a miniature scene with "snow" falling around it. Have a go at making your own!

1 Take a small jar with a lid (a jam jar is perfect). Clean out the inside and remove all labels.

2 On the inside of the lid, glue down small objects like figurines or old board game pieces. Use strong glue so that nothing will come loose inside the jar.

3 Fill the jar with water almost to the top and add a drop or two of glycerine (you can find this in the baking aisle at the supermarket). Now pour in a spoonful of glitter.

4 Carefully put the lid back on the filled jar and screw it shut tight. Then flip over and shake!

DONE!

157 BE A REAL "SEW" OFF

First, thread a needle — now, get useful! Sew a button and a patch. Whoa, you are "sew" awesome!

SEW ON A BUTTON

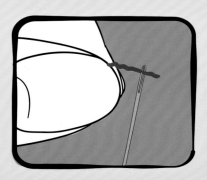

1 Cut 12 inches (30cm) of thread the same color as the fabric you're sewing onto. Then thread the end through the "eye" of your needle. Careful! Needles are sharp.

2 Take your button and place it where you want it to go. Poke the needle through the back of your fabric and one buttonhole, then down through the hole which is diagonal to it. Repeat this step with the other holes. Do this a total of at least six times, forming an X across the button holes.

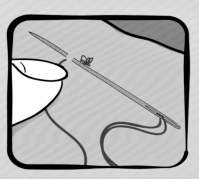

3 Once the button feels firm, sew a few small stitches in the back of the fabric, behind your button, to finish off. Watch where you're sticking the needle — you don't want to stick it into your finger!

PATCH-UP JEANS

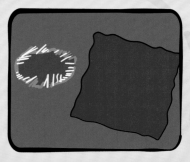 

1 First, cut a square of fabric that is 1.5 inches (4cm) bigger than the hole around each side.

2 Carefully fold the edges of your patch inward and pin in place on top of the hole.

3 Sew small stitches about .25 inch (0.6cm) from the edge of your patch and the fabric to keep it secure. Be sure to watch your fingers!

Why Not?
Choose crazy fabric to make your jeans stand out from the crowd!

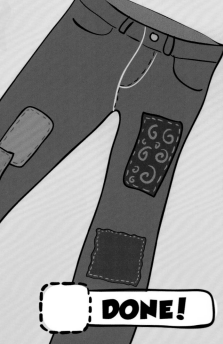

DONE!

158 MAKE PAPER-CUP SPEAKERS

Make your own handy pair of paper-cup speakers for your smartphone!

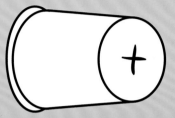

1 Use the toothpicks to carefully make a small, cross-shaped slit in the base of the two cups that will be the speakers.

2 Insert the earbuds all the way through the holes, until only the wire is left outside the cup.

3 Turn the remaining cups upside down, then place your "speakers" sideways on top. Tape the sides to secure them into place. Plug the earbuds into your smartphone and play some tunes!

DONE!

159 TELL THE TIME WITHOUT A CLOCK

A sundial uses the sun to measure the passing of time by casting a shadow over numbers. How cool!

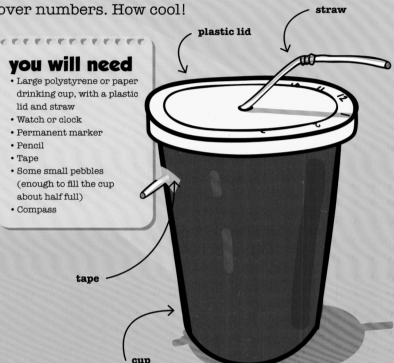

straw

plastic lid

tape

cup

1 Use the pencil to poke a hole in the side of the cup, approximately 2 inches (5cm) below the top. Put the pebbles in the cup so it doesn't tip over. Put the lid on the cup.

2 Put the straw through the hole in the lid and the hole in the side of the cup. Let it stick out about 0.75 inch (2cm) from the side and tape the straw to the cup.

3 Find a sunny spot and place the cup on a level surface. Use a compass to find north and point the straw in that direction. Make sure that the sun shines right on the straw!

4 At 10 A.M., mark where the shadow from the straw falls on the lid of the cup. Repeat this every hour until 3 P.M. The next day, you'll be able to tell the time without a clock!

DONE!

160 MAKE A NO-SEW BAG

Find a colorful old T-shirt and give it a new life as a bag for storing what you need to make any outing fun.

you will need
- Old clean T-shirt — an adult-sized T-shirt for women would be the best size
- Sharp fabric scissors
- Measuring tape
- Ballpoint or fabric pen

Safety First!
Ask an adult to help you cut the T-shirt.

1 Lay the T-shirt flat and ask an adult to help you carefully cut around the sleeves.

2 Turn the T-shirt inside out and lay it flat again. Now cut around the neck. You could use a bowl to help you get a good rounded shape. Draw around the bowl with a ballpoint or fabric pen and cut along the line.

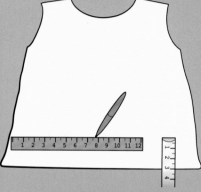

3 Use a tape measure to mark 3 inches (8cm) up from the bottom of the T-shirt, on both sides. You need to draw a line across the bottom between the two sides.

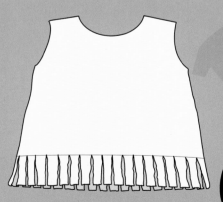

4 Cut through the double layer of T-shirt up to the line you drew. Make the strips roughly the width of a thumb. This will make the fringe.

5 Knot each front fringe piece to the back fringe piece behind it. Tie them tightly.

6 Turn the T-shirt back the right way round. Your bag will appear! Knot the top of the handles if you like.

Why Not?
Use fabric pens to decorate your new T-shirt travel bag.

DONE!

161 HOLD YOUR PENCILS

Make a handy pen and pencil holder that you can roll up, tie up, and carry on a trip.

1 Fold the cloth in half widthways. Snip some 0.5 inch (1.3cm) slots along the fold. Leave about 2 inches (5cm) at either end.

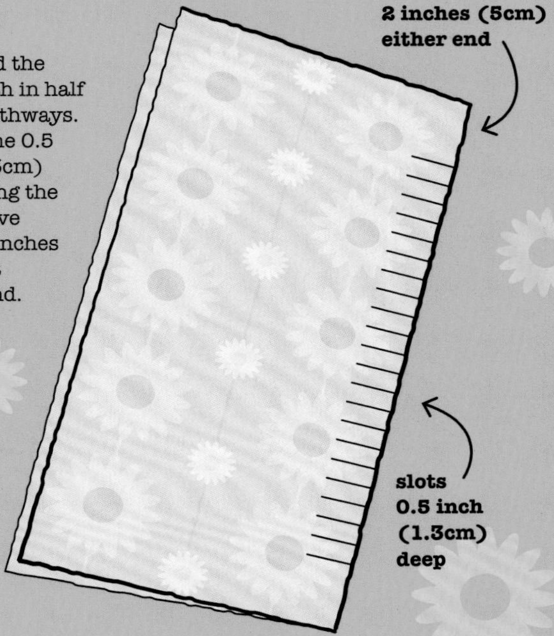

2 inches (5cm) either end

slots 0.5 inch (1.3cm) deep

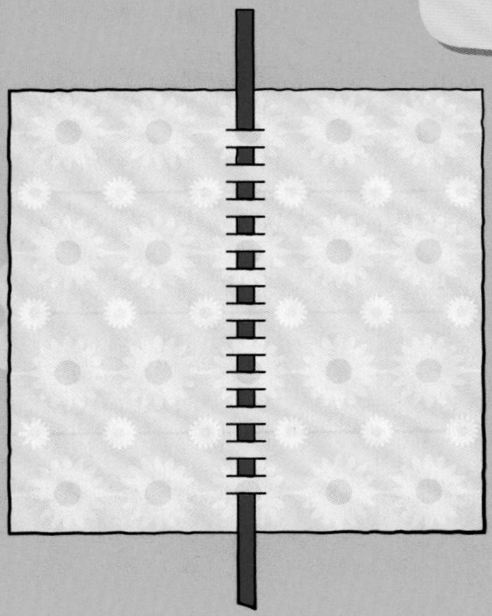

2 Open up the cloth again and weave the thin strip through the slots as shown.

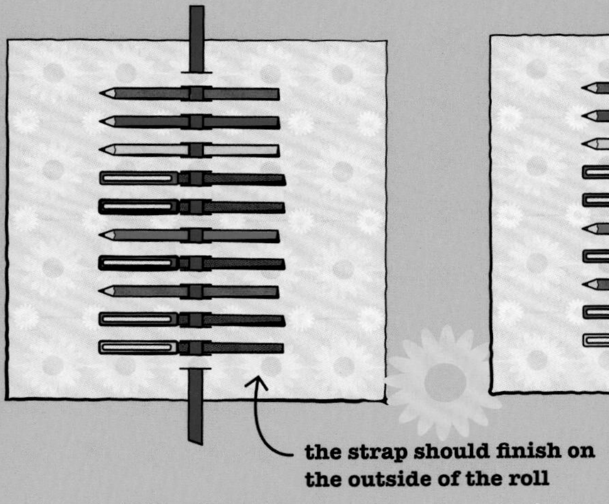

3 Fit some pens through the little pockets you have made, making sure the strap is not too loose.

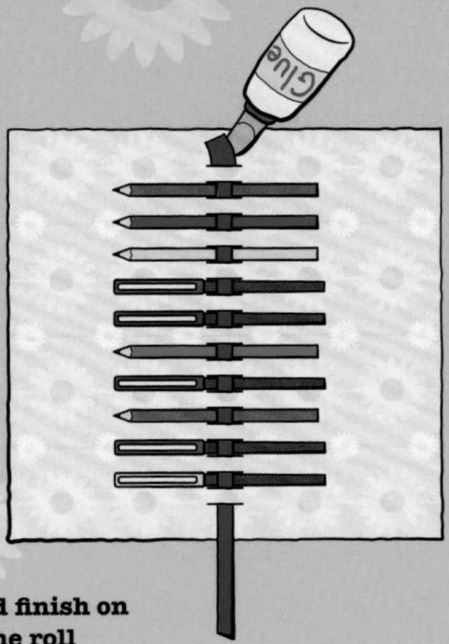

the strap should finish on the outside of the roll

4 Now glue one end of the strap to the inside of the cloth as shown.

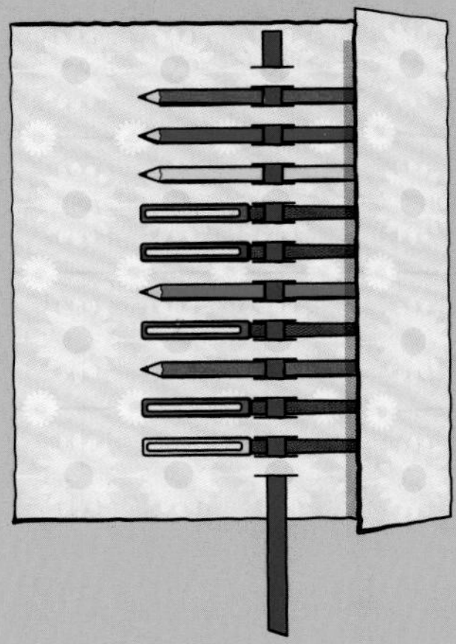

Glue

5 Fold down one long edge of the cloth and glue the edges to make a pocket.

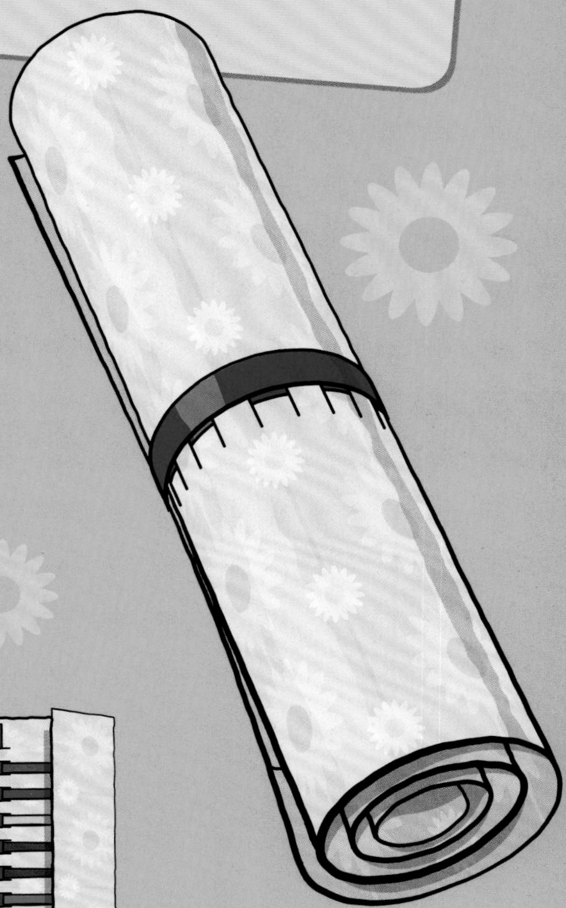

6 Fold over the top, roll up your roll, and tie the strap back on itself to keep it secure.

DONE!

162 MAKE A FINGER BUNNY

Use a paper napkin and a paper clip or tape to make a funny finger puppet bunny.

you will need
- Square paper napkin
- Paper clip or some tape

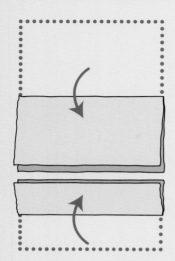

1 Fold the napkin in half widthways, then fold it down in half again to make a narrow strip.

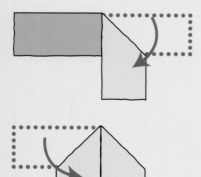

2 Fold down the right-hand top corner as shown. Now do the same on the left-hand side. You end up with a house shape.

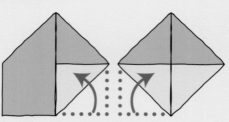

3 Fold the bottom corners up as shown. You get a square shape.

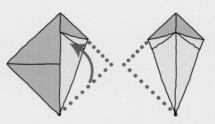

4 Fold the left- and right-hand corners into the middle as shown. You get a kite shape.

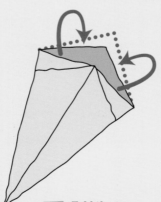

5 Fold the top backward as shown. You end up with a triangle shape.

fix down with tape

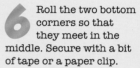

6 Roll the two bottom corners so that they meet in the middle. Secure with a bit of tape or a paper clip.

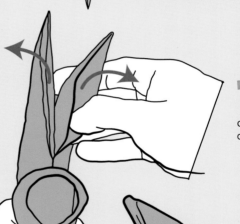

7 Turn the napkin over and open out the face on the other side. Then open out the ears.

Why Not? Draw a face on your bunny finger puppet.

DONE!

163 MAKE AN OUTDOOR SILHOUETTE THEATER

Dusk and dark can be magical times outdoors. What better time to put on a shadow show for your family and friends? It can be quite simple . . . or simply epic!

1 First, decide on the story that you are going to perform. Is it a well-known story, like a fairy tale? Or is it something you've made up yourself? Sketch the characters and props that you need.

2 Make your shadow puppets. For each character, draw a head and body onto the black card with the pencil or crayon. Include details, such as eyes, hair, and mouth.

3 Add limbs. Cut out arms and legs, and join them to your character's body with brads (split pins). This will mean that you can move them in the show.

4 Attach the skewers to the main body and the limbs. Fix in place with the masking tape. You will hold the skewers to move the characters and their joints.

you will need
- Old sheet
- Big flashlight or outdoor lamp
- Sketch book and pencil
- Black card
- Scissors
- Brads (split pins)
- Wooden skewers or a thin garden cane
- Masking tape
- Light-colored pencil or crayon
- Your imagination!

5 Hang the sheet up outside — you could tie it to the branches of a tree or between two posts. You will need space in front for the audience and behind for you to sit with the puppets. If you have nowhere to hang it, a couple of friends could hold the sheet for you.

6 Fix the light source. You could fix a big flashlight or outdoor lamp onto a tree or a post, or ask another friend to hold it for you.

7 Now invite your friends, wait until dark, and put on your show!

DONE!

5

BRAINY

Want to train your brain? Engage in activities that make you smarter? Convince ever yone of your true genius? Then use your noggin on these brilliant, brain-boosting, boredom-busting projects and activities. Why not think outside the box?

164 CHALLENGE YOUR MEMORY

You'll need concentration for this classic pairs game. Play with friends or test your memory by playing on your own.

you will need
- Pack of playing cards, including one joker if you're playing with others
- Space to lay them all out

1 Shuffle the cards and lay them face down, without touching.

2 The first player turns over two cards. If they are a pair the player takes the cards and has another go. If not, they are flipped back over and the next player takes a turn.

3 If a player turns over the joker, he/she must miss a turn. The game continues until all cards (except the joker) have been matched. The player with most pairs wins the game.

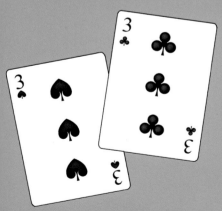

4 To make the game harder, add the rule that the cards must match in color too.

165 WRITE A MINI-MYSTERY

Everyone loves a good mystery story, so why not write your own to entertain your friends and family?

1 It's best to start with a main character and setting that you know well. You could base the hero or heroine on yourself or your best friend, for example, and set your mystery in a school.

2 Sketch out the plot. Perhaps the head teacher is suddenly acting strangely, or something odd has been found in the playground. Someone or something could have disappeared without any explanation.

3 Try to build up tension and end each chapter with a cliffhanger. The main character could get trapped somewhere, or suddenly come face-to-face with the villain. You'll need to plan their escape from any sticky situations, too.

4 Your story needs a satisfying and convincing ending. Perhaps there was a perfectly logical explanation to all the strange things that had been happening, or maybe the head teacher really was abducted by aliens. The characters are in your hands and it's up to you to decide their fate.

DONE!

166 MAKE A SPECTROMETER

Spectrometers split light into its separate colors — white light from the sun is made up of all the colors of the rainbow, for example. Try comparing the colors of light from different types of bulbs.

1 Ask an adult to cut a 1.5-inch- (4-cm-) wide hole at the bottom of the box.

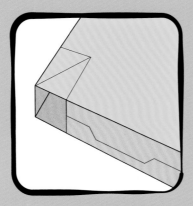

2 Draw a rectangle 1.5 inches (4cm) wide and 2.5 inches (6cm) tall on the front of the box, next to the hole. Draw a diagonal line from the corner of the box to the top of the rectangle. Turn the box over and do the same on the back.

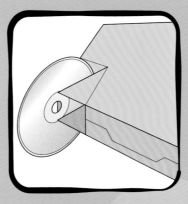

3 Ask an adult to cut along the diagonal lines, then slide the CD into the groove.

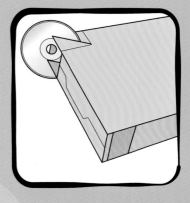

4 Turn the box around and draw lines on the side panel opposite the CD, 0.5 inch (1.3cm) and 1.5 inches (4cm) from the corner. Ask an adult to cut along these lines and the edges of the side panel to make a 1-inch- (3-cm-) wide hole.

5 Cut two 4-inch (10-cm) squares of foil and fold them in half. Position them over the hole, with the folded edges in the middle, leaving a 1/16-inch (1.5mm) gap between them, then tape them in place.

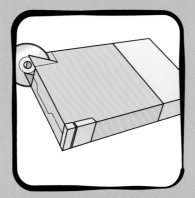

6 Cover the top third of the box with a large piece of foil to block out extra light and secure it in place with tape.

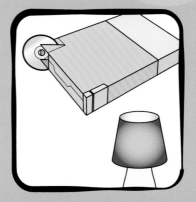

7 Point the thin gap between the two pieces of foil at a lamp. Look at the surface of the CD inside the box through the hole in the bottom of the box. What colors can you see?

you will need
- Cereal box
- Ruler
- Pen
- Craft knife
- Old or damaged CD (or DVD)
- Aluminum foil
- Tape

DONE!

167 MAKE A DINORAMA

If you want your diorama to be accurate, make sure your dinos lived during the same period. Jurassic dinos included Stegosaurus and Diplodocus, while T. rex and Triceratops lived in the Cretaceous period.

you will need
• Box with a lid, e.g. a shoebox
• White card
• Markers, pencils and paints
• Paintbrush
• Glue
• Scissors
• Model plants and trees, small stones (optional)

1 Paint the insides of the two short sides and one long side of the box blue, then paint a background scene on a piece of card the size of the base of the box. Include the sky, some trees, and a volcano.

2 When the paint is dry, glue the background scene to the base of the box and glue the box inside the upturned lid, as shown.

3 Paint the inside of the lid and the bottom side of the box green and add a little stream running through it.

4 Draw, trace, or photocopy the dinosaurs you want to include onto card, then paint them and cut them out.

5 Cut out card stands and fold them into an L-shape. Glue one side to the dinos' legs and the other side to the ground so the dinosaurs stand up. Dab some paint on the tabs so they blend in with the ground.

6 Complete your dinorama by adding plants, trees, and some real pebbles, if you like.

DONE!

168 OUTLINE YOUR FAMILY TREE

Families come in all shapes and sizes (and they can get complicated), so to make a family tree it's best to begin with a draft version while you work out who belongs where.

you will need
• Large piece of paper or several sheets taped together
• Sticky notes
• Colored pens

James
(Father)
Born 03.09.1979

Rosie
(Half-sister)
Born 07.21.2012

1 Write the names of your family members on sticky notes so you can move them around easily. Leave space at the bottom to fill in their relationship to you, date of birth (and death, if necessary).

Amy
(Mother)
Born 05.05.1980

ME
Born 04.15.2007

Lucas
(Brother)
Born 01.30.2005

2 Start by putting yourself in the middle of the paper, at the bottom, and add any brothers and/or sisters alongside.

Oliver
(Half-brother)
Born 12.10.2013

Top Tip
Ask the oldest person in your family to tell you about their relatives. This could add even more layers to your family tree.

3 If you have half- or step-siblings, include them in the row(s) above. Color coding helps to make relationships easier to understand. The next row up is for parents and the row above that is for grandparents.

Grandfather (father's side)	Grandmother (father's side)		Grandfather (mother's side)	Grandmother (mother's side)
Stepmother	Father		Mother	Stepfather
Stepbrother	Half sister		Half brother	Stepsister
	Brother	Me	Sister	

4 Here's one example of a family tree. Yours might look quite different.

5 Now you have the core of your family tree, extend it outward by adding aunts, uncles and cousins, and upwards by including great-grandparents. If you run out of space, just stick an extra sheet of paper to the sides and top.

Mary
(Great-aunt)
Born 10.12.1918
Died 02.13.1999

Harry
(Great-grandfather)
Born 03.09.1916
Died 08.20.1991

6 When you're happy with your draft, make a neat copy on a big piece of paper.

DONE!

169 REVAMP YOUR ROOM

Unleash your inner interior designer and create a mood board for your dream bedroom.

you will need

- Bulletin board or a strong piece of cardboard — the bigger, the better
- Sticky tack, tape, or thumbtacks
- Magazines, catalogs, pieces of fabric, paint charts or paints

1 First, decide on a theme. It could be your favorite band or football team, a tropical forest, under the sea, or even outer space.

2 Choose colors to suit your theme. Cut out some colors from the paint chart or paint them onto white paper and stick them to the board. Add pieces of fabric if you have them.

3 Cut out magazine or catalog pictures of things you would like in your dream room. If you can't find what you want, design and draw it yourself.

Top Tip
Add to your mood-board as you come across other pictures you like.

DONE!

170 WRITE A SEQUEL

Were you disappointed when your favorite book, film, or TV series came to an end? Would Harry Potter become headmaster of Hogwarts? What happens to Elsa at the end of *Frozen*? Why not write the sequel yourself?

1 Write a draft by taking up the story where it ended. Resolve any cliffhangers, and make sure your story has its own plot too. Otherwise, your readers will soon get bored.

2 You have the main characters, but you'll need to introduce some new ones to move the story forward. Think about their relationships with your existing characters.

Why Not?
Get together with some friends and all write sequels, then read them out.

3 Keep to the theme of the original story. If it was a romantic comedy, fans won't be pleased if the sequel features a zombie attack!

DONE!

171 DESIGN A BOARD GAME

Making your own board game is easier than you think — and you get to make up all the rules!

1 The aim of a board game is normally to travel from one end of the path to the other, so sketch the path on paper, starting in one corner. Have a round number of squares, e.g. 50 or 80.

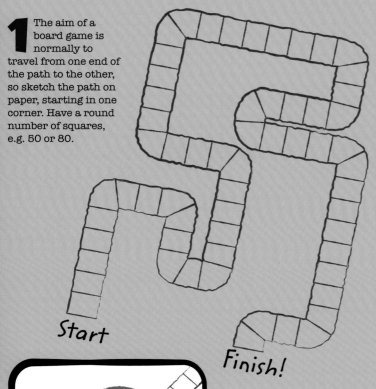

Start

Finish!

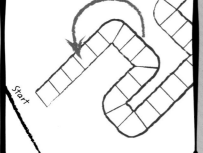

Start

2 You'll need some leaps forward and setbacks along the way, so add some arrows showing where players might jump ahead or go back.

Start   Finish!

3 Think of a theme — for example, some explorers are lost in the jungle and have to find their way out. This will help you to design the board and come up with rewards and forfeits to suit the story.

4 You could include cards for players to pick up. If so, add some "Pick up a card" squares and write the cards, such as "Tiger ahead! Hide and miss a turn."

you will need
- Large piece of paper (or 2 sheets stuck together)
- Colored pencils, pens, and paints
- Counters and a dice
- Piece of poster board for your finished game

35 36 37 38 3

33

32

Climb up a liana vine to 35

30

29 28 27 26 25

5 Write instructions in the squares where players have to move forwards and back, such as "Climb up a liana vine to 35."

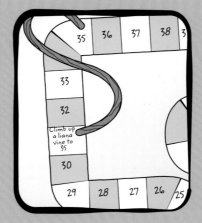

Start   Finish!

6 Test out your game by playing it with friends. If it works well, copy it onto a piece of board and design a cool background. Otherwise, make a few tweaks and try it out again.

DONE!

172 GROW CRAZY CRESS HEADS

Seeds can grow without soil, but they need light and water, so keep them in a sunny spot and don't let them dry out. If you don't have any eggshells, use yogurt containers to make your hairy family instead.

Why Not?
Make a mini greenhouse from a plastic bottle with the top cut off and put it over one eggshell. It should make the cress grow faster.

You will need
- Cress seeds
- 2 boiled or raw eggs
- Eggcups or egg cartons
- Paper towel
- Cotton balls
- Felt tips or paint
- Googly eyes (optional)

1 If you're using boiled eggs, eat the eggs first — they're delicious with toast. Otherwise, ask an adult to break off the top off the eggs and empty them out into a bowl.

2 Gently clean out the insides of the eggshells and draw faces on them, then put the eggs in eggcups or egg cartons.

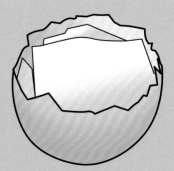

3 Wet a piece of paper towel and screw it up inside the shell. Then, wet a piece of cotton ball and put it on top.

4 Sprinkle a layer of cress seeds on the cotton ball and put the eggs on a sunny windowsill. Keep the cotton ball slightly moist but not wet.

5 In about a week the cress should be about 1.5 inches (4cm) tall. Now you can snip it off and put it on a salad or in a sandwich.

6 Save the shells and start again, or boil some eggs to add to your cress sandwich and use those shells to grow another crop.

DONE!

173 DEFY GRAVITY

You will amaze everyone with this gravity-defying trick. Don't use the best silverware because the prongs of the fork can get bent.

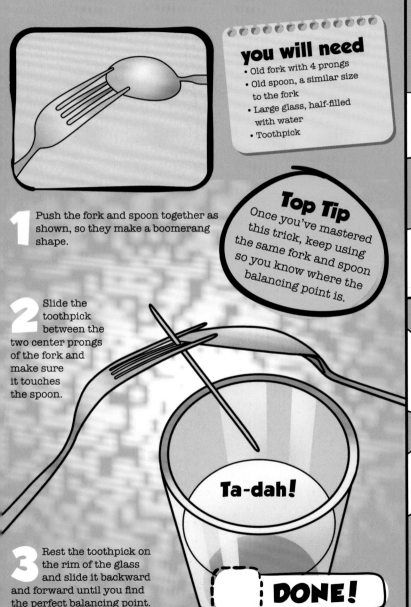

1 Push the fork and spoon together as shown, so they make a boomerang shape.

2 Slide the toothpick between the two center prongs of the fork and make sure it touches the spoon.

3 Rest the toothpick on the rim of the glass and slide it backward and forward until you find the perfect balancing point.

Top Tip
Once you've mastered this trick, keep using the same fork and spoon so you know where the balancing point is.

Ta-dah!

DONE!

174 TRY THE PENCIL TRICK

This trick should be performed quickly so spectators don't have time to try to work out how it's done. Practice in front of a mirror first.

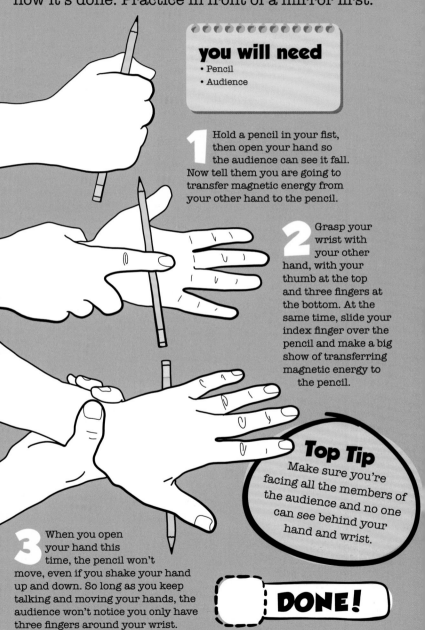

1 Hold a pencil in your fist, then open your hand so the audience can see it fall. Now tell them you are going to transfer magnetic energy from your other hand to the pencil.

2 Grasp your wrist with your other hand, with your thumb at the top and three fingers at the bottom. At the same time, slide your index finger over the pencil and make a big show of transferring magnetic energy to the pencil.

3 When you open your hand this time, the pencil won't move, even if you shake your hand up and down. So long as you keep talking and moving your hands, the audience won't notice you only have three fingers around your wrist.

Top Tip
Make sure you're facing all the members of the audience and no one can see behind your hand and wrist.

DONE!

175 MAKE A CODE WHEEL

If you're going to share coded messages with a friend, you'll need two copies of this code wheel. Why not make them together?

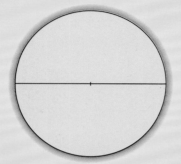

1 Find the widest point of one of the small paper plates and draw a line from one side to the other. Use your ruler to find the center of the line and make a mark.

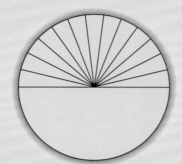

2 As there are 26 letters in the alphabet, you will need to divide each half of the plate into 13 sections using the protractor. Each section should measure just under 14°.

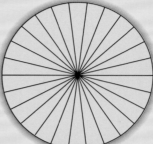

3 Now use the ruler to extend the lines across the plate so you have 26 sections. Use this plate as a guide to mark the 26 sections on the edge of the other small plate, then draw the lines on that one, too.

Top Tip
If you think someone may have cracked your code, just change the two matching letters.

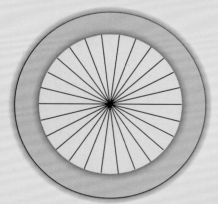

4 Ask an adult to make a hole in the center of all four plates. Push a paper fastener through one of the small plates, then through one of the large plates to join them together. Repeat with the other two plates.

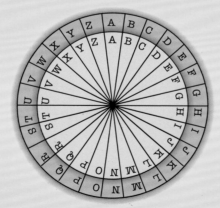

5 Use the small plate as a guide to mark the sections on the large plate and write a letter of the alphabet in each section on all four plates.

6 To use your code wheel, decide which two letters you want to match up. You could use the first letters of your name and your friend's name, e.g. "H" and "M." To write your message, replace the letter on the outside of the wheel with the letter on the inside.

Can you work out what this message says?

HZZO HZ
VAOZM
NXCJJG

Answer:
MEET ME AFTER SCHOOL.

DONE!

176 MAKE QUICKSAND

Quicksand is sand that contains so much water it reduces the friction between the grains. The mushy mix can't suck you down, but the more you struggle, the more you will sink. This experiment shows how it works.

you will need
- 3¼ cups (450g) cornstarch
- 2 cups (475ml) water
- Large mixing bowl
- Spoon

1 Mix the cornstarch and water together in the bowl. Stir it slowly and drip it from the spoon to prove it is a liquid.

2 Try punching the mixture, making sure you pull your fist back quickly. You would expect it to splash, but in fact it turns hard because your fist makes the water flow away, leaving a solid patch of cornstarch.

3 Scoop some of the mix into your hand and roll it into a ball. As long as you're pressing on it, the ball will stay solid, but when you stop, it will trickle back into the bowl as a liquid.

DONE!

177 BUILD A MINI-MUSEUM

If you have a collection of tiny treasures, why not become a museum curator and put on a display for other people to enjoy?

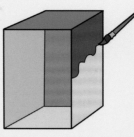 

1 Paint the inside and outside of the box, or cover the outside with paper. You could choose a theme related to your display.

2 Turn the box on its side and stick cartons or lids at the back to raise items up for easy viewing. Arrange your exhibits inside and hold them in place with sticky tack.

you will need
- Box, such as a shoe box
- Paints or paper to decorate the box
- Tape or glue
- Small lids or cartons
- Sticky tack
- Exhibits
- Paper or card

1. Ammonite, at least 65 million years old, found on Seaview Beach.
2. Penny, 1966, dug up in garden.
3. Antique glass bottle stopper, dug up in garden.
4. Victorian military button, found in woods.

3 Give each item a number and make a list to go on top of the box, giving as much information about each exhibit as possible.

DONE!

178 CONSTRUCT A BAROMETER

A barometer measures air pressure and helps to predict the weather. When the pressure is high, the weather is usually fine. When it drops, bad weather may be on the way.

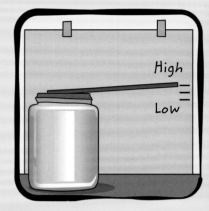

1 Blow the balloon up to stretch it, then cut it in half and stretch the top half tightly over the jar. Secure it with the rubber band.

2 Tape the straw to the top of the jar so two thirds is hanging over the edge. Put the jar near a wall, out of the sun, and away from any source of heat.

3 Draw three lines about .25 inch (0.6cm) apart on the piece of card stock and label the top and bottom one "High" and "Low." Tape the card against a wall behind the jar so that the straw points to the mark in the middle.

4 If the air pressure rises, it will push the balloon into the jar and the straw will move up. If you know from the weather forecast that pressure is high and your straw doesn't point to the top marker, move the card so it does.

You will need
- Balloon
- Scissors
- Large jar
- Rubber band
- Sticky tape
- Straw
- Piece of card stock
- Marker pen

5 If the pressure falls, the air in the jar will expand, pushing the balloon up, so the straw will move down.

WEATHER CHART

	Pressure	°F/°C	Weather	Wind
Mon	Low	46°/8°	S	Strong
Tue	Mod.	57°/14°	C	Light
Wed	High	68°/20°	A	None
Thu	Mod.	59°/15°	P	Light
Fri	Low	50°/10°	S	Light
Sat	Low	48°/9°	U	Strong
Sun	Mod.	55°/13°	C	Light

Top Tip
Make sure the balloon stays tightly sealed and there are no holes in it during your experiment.

6 Try to check your barometer at the same time each day and keep a diary of your readings and the weather. Can you see any pattern?

DONE!

179 CALCULATE STORM DISTANCE

If you like storms, you'll love this! But remember to stay safe. If the storm is overhead, enjoy it from a safe place indoors.

1 On a stormy day, watch out for a flash of lightning in the sky.

2 As soon as you see a flash of lightning, start counting the number of seconds until you hear the thunder. To be really precise, use a stopwatch. Or be as accurate as you can count like this: one-one thousand, two-one thousand, three-one thousand, etc.

3 For every 3 seconds that pass, the storm is a half a mile (0.8km) away, or for every 5 seconds, the storm is 1 mile (1.6km) away. Divide the number of seconds you count to work out the distance.

How it Works
Thunder and lightning happen at the same time, but light travels more quickly than sound. The light of the lightning flash travels more quickly than the sound of the thunder.

DONE!

180 TALK BY FLASHLIGHT

Before satellites, Morse code was used by almost everyone needing to send messages over long distances. It helped to save lives and to win wars. Get together with a friend and give it a try with a flashlight. It might take longer than texting, but it's a lot of fun!

1 Before dark, you should both practice without the flashlight. Write messages in dots and dashes on paper, and pass them to each other to decipher. Use the chart below to work out each letter. Keep the messages short and snappy.

For example:

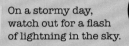
H E L L O

INTERNATIONAL MORSE CODE ALPHABET

a •-	j •---	s •••	1 •----
b -•••	k -•-	t -	2 ••---
c -•-•	l •-••	u ••-	3 •••--
d -••	m --	v •••-	4 ••••-
e •	n -•	w •--	5 •••••
f ••-•	o ---	x -••-	6 -••••
g --•	p •--•	y -•--	7 --•••
h ••••	q --•-	z --••	8 ---••
i ••	r •-•		9 ----•
			0 -----

2 After dark, send messages with your flashlight. Stand at either end of a garden or path, and use long flashes for the dashes and short flashes for the dots. If you're receiving the message, write down the dots and dashes on paper so that you can decipher them with the international Morse code alphabet.

DONE!

181 SEND A SEMAPHORE

The semaphore flag system was designed more than 150 years ago, and it is still used today. Make yourself a semaphore flag and try signaling a message to your friends from the other side of a football field (or from the end of your backyard).

1 Draw a diagonal line from the top right-hand corner to the bottom left-hand corner of each yellow sheet of paper. Cut along the lines. Glue each triangle onto the backs and fronts of the red papers, making sure that the red triangles are always at the top.

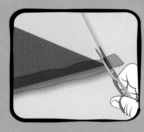

2 Place the adhesive tape along the left-hand edge of each flag, half on the paper, half off.

you will need
- 2 sheets of thick yellow paper
- 2 sheets of thick red paper
- White glue
- Ruler
- Pencil
- 2 dowels or flower sticks
- Adhesive tape
- Notebook and pen (for the person receiving your signals)

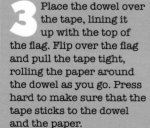

3 Place the dowel over the tape, lining it up with the top of the flag. Flip over the flag and pull the tape tight, rolling the paper around the dowel as you go. Press hard to make sure that the tape sticks to the dowel and the paper.

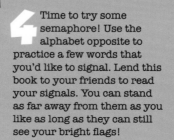

4 Time to try some semaphore! Use the alphabet opposite to practice a few words that you'd like to signal. Lend this book to your friends to read your signals. You can stand as far away from them as you like as long as they can still see your bright flags!

 A and 1
 B and 2
 C and 3
 D and 4
 E and 5

 F and 6
 G and 7
 H and 8
 I and 9
 J

 K and 0
 L
 M
 N
 O

 P
 Q
 R
 S
 T

 U
 V
 W
 X
 Y

 Z
 Error

THE SEMAPHORE ALPHABET

 DONE!

182 FORECAST THE WEATHER

Pine cones naturally close when it is wet and open up when it is dry, so they are great weather indicators. Use one to make your very own weather-predicting hygroscope!

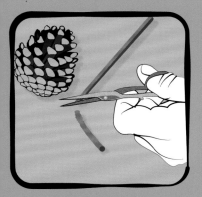

1 Cut off the top of a flexible straw at the top where it bends.

2 Position the tip of the straw on top of an open scale of the pine cone. Glue into place.

3 Put your pine cone onto a windowsill. When the air is humid, the scales of the pine cone will close and the straw will rise. This means that it is likely to rain. When it is sunny, the scales open up and the straw bends down.

WET

DRY

DONE!

183 MAKE A BALLOON ROCKET

Real rockets need fuel to launch them into space, but you can send yours whizzing across the garden using just escaping air!

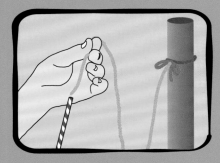

1 Tie one end of the string to a post or tree. Thread the loose end of the string through the straw. Pull the string tight before fixing it to the other post.

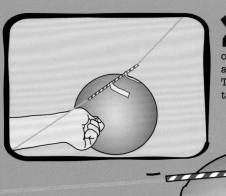

2 Blow up the balloon, but don't tie it off. Pinch the end and don't let go! Tape the balloon to the straw.

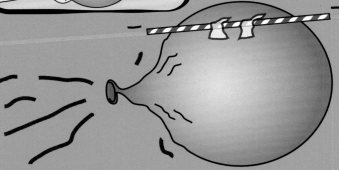

3 Pull the straw and balloon to one end of the string. Let go for blastoff! How quickly can it get to the end of the string?

DONE!

184 CREATE A GEYSER

If you like messy, dramatic experiments, this is one for you! With just a bottle of diet cola and a packet of Mentos, you can create a mighty geyser. Some people say theirs have been 29 feet (8.8m) tall! How high can you make yours?

1 Find an open space where you can make a mess. Go as far away as possible from anyone's nice clean windows or anything else you don't want to get sticky and yucky!

2 Stand the bottle of cola upright and unscrew the lid. If you have a funnel, put it into the top of the bottle.

3 Drop about half a packet of Mentos into the bottle through the funnel, and get out of the way! Stand far back to watch a mighty, bubbly geyser erupt from the bottle!

DONE!

185 FIND THE AGE OF A TREE

If a tree has been cut down, you can work out how old it was when it died by counting its rings. But if the tree is alive, there's another way to calculate its age.

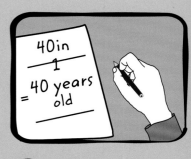

1 Decide on the tree whose age you want to find. Wrap your tape measure around the trunk, and measure its circumference, or girth.

2 The growth of an average tree girth per year is 1 inch, or 2.5 centimeters. If you have measured in inches, divide this figure by 1; if you've measured in centimeters, divide by 2.5. So a tree with a 16-inch (40-cm) girth will be approximately 16 years old.

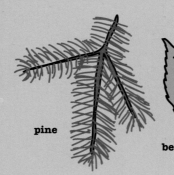
pine

beech

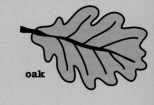
oak

sycamore

3 If you know the species of your tree, you can age it more accurately. For example, oaks and beeches grow approximately 0.7 inch (1.75cm) per year. Pine trees grow about 1 inch (3cm) per year, and sycamores grow around 1 inch (2.75cm) per year. Divide by these figures instead of 1 or 2.5.

DONE!

186 LAUNCH A VINEGAR ROCKET

Baking soda and vinegar make brilliant rocket fuel!
Try mixing them together in an empty water bottle
to launch your very own rocket.

1 Tape the pencils to the side of the bottle in a triangle to make fins. The bottom ends of the pencils should be facing upward. The ends should line up at the bottle top.

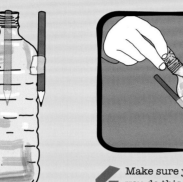

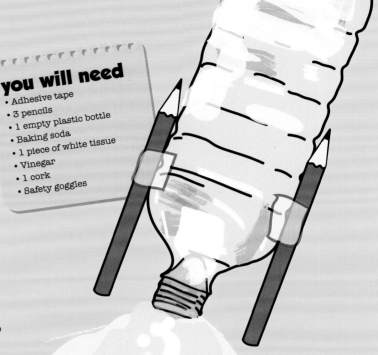

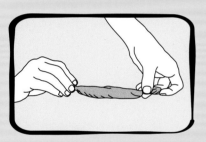

2 To make the baking soda packet, put two large spoonfuls of baking soda into the middle of the tissue. Fold the corners up and twist the wrap to hold the powder inside.

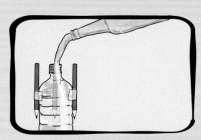

3 Fill the bottle about a third of the way up with vinegar. Any vinegar works, but white vinegar is less messy.

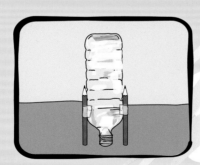

4 Make sure you are outside before you do this step. Carefully push the baking soda parcel into the top of the bottle. Ask an adult to help you to push the cork firmly into the bottle top.

5 Gently shake the bottle, making sure you keep it away from your face. Quickly stand the rocket up on its fins and move away.

6 Stand well back and wait for **LIFT-OFF!**

Safety First!
Always do this with an adult. Stay well away from the bottle. You MUST be outdoors in a large space.

How it Works
When the baking soda and vinegar react, carbon dioxide is released, creating pressure in the bottle. When the pressure gets high enough, it will push the cork out and the pressure will force all of the liquid and gas out of the bottle very fast, making it shoot upwards.

DONE!

187 MAKE A TIME CAPSULE

Making a time capsule is like building a cool treasure chest. Items are stored and sealed so that they can be rediscovered in the future!

clothes or accessories

most recent magazine or newspaper

date: NAME:

a letter or diary entry

photographs

coins

toys

YOUR CAPSULE

You can make your capsule from any type of box. Mark your container clearly with today's date and your name, then fill it with cool items from your time. Next, seal it and hide it somewhere safe, like the attic, basement, or garage. You can also ask an adult to help you bury it outside— just make sure to wrap it in plastic first!

Top Tip
Never include perishable stuff (like food) that will get moldy or attract animals.

DONE!

188 MAKE YOUR OWN COMPASS

A compass is a tool for navigation. It contains a magnetized needle that responds to our planet's magnetism and points north.

1 Magnetize your paper clip needle by rubbing it against the magnet about 20 times, in the same direction.

you will need
- Straightened paper clip to use as a needle
- Bar magnet (a straight rectangular magnet with a north and south pole on either side)
- Pliers
- Round piece of cork
- Small dish half-filled with water

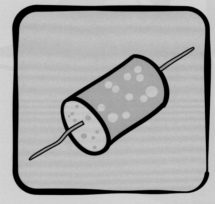

2 Using pliers, carefully push your needle through the cork. You need the same amount of needle showing on each side. Ask an adult to help.

3 Place the cork and needle on the water. The end of the needle that points toward the sun at midday is pointing south if you are in the northern hemisphere, and north if you are in the southern hemisphere.

DONE!

189 WRITE A SPOOKY STORY

You know how to write an essay for school, and diary entries are easy, but what do you know about writing a scary story? Here are four tips to make your next tale a real scream.

Start by scaring the pants off yourself. Face your fears head-on. What kind of story would make your toes curl? What do you see in your scariest dreams? Write about THAT.

What?
Choose a "what if" and go from there. What if you got locked out after dark? What if you faced a beast in the woods? What if your best friend was a vampire?

Where?
Choose a setting and add lots of scary details: fog, strange sounds, darkness and more. Maybe make it so cold you can see your breath. Brrr!

Who?
Identify the main character. Who is he/she? Why is he/she in this scary setting? Make up your villain. What does your villain look like? How does he/she act? Identify three moments of danger between your villain and your hero.

How?
Use the right words to scare your reader, such as "ghoulish," "terrifying," or "spooky." Take your time to present the details. Remember that half the work is creating tension! Tell the reader that bad things will happen — and then write them . . . eventually.

DONE!

190 COUNT TO TEN IN FIVE LANGUAGES

Thousands of languages are spoken across the globe. Impress your friends by counting to ten in five of them!

According to linguists (people who study languages) 6,909 languages are spoken in the world. Yikes! Study the numbers 1 to 10 in the chart below (how to pronounce them is in brackets). Impress your family and teachers with your linguistic skills!

	1	2	3	4	5	6	7	8	9	10
English	One	Two	Three	Four	Five	Six	Seven	Eight	Nine	Ten
French	Un (uh)	Deux (duhr)	Trois (twah)	Quatre (katr)	Cinq (sank)	Six (sees)	Sept (set)	Huit (weet)	Neuf (nurf)	Dix (dees)
Mandarin Chinese	Yi (eee)	Er (arr)	San (sahn)	Si (ssuh)	Wu (woo)	Liu (liou)	Qi (chee)	Ba (bah)	Jiu (Jeou)	Shi (shehr)
Spanish	Uno (oono)	Dos (dose)	Tres (tress)	Cuatro (kwah-tro)	Cinco (sink-oh)	Seis (sayss)	Siete (syet-tah)	Ocho (oh-cho)	Nueve (nwehv-ay)	Diez (dees)
Russian	Adin (ah-din)	Dva (dvah)	Tri (tree)	Chetyre (che-terr-ee-eh)	Pyat' (pyah-ts)	Shyest' (shey-st)	Cyem (siem)	Voysyem (vo-siem)	Dyevyet (dee-eviet)	Dyeset (de-ee-siet)

DONE!

191 GO STAR GAZING

Constellations are groups of stars in the night sky. There are at least 88 different constellations, each named after animals or characters from mythology.

WHERE ARE YOU?

The biggest constellation is called Orion, also known as the Great Hunter. How can you find it? Go outside in the evening and look at the southwest sky if you are in the northern hemisphere, or the northwestern sky if you are in the southern hemisphere. If you live on or near the equator, Orion is visible in the western sky.

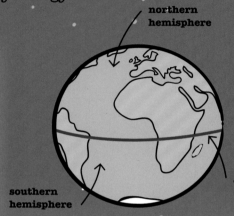

northern hemisphere

southern hemisphere

equator

ORION

Look for the pattern of stars shown here (turn this page upside down if you are looking from the southern hemisphere). Three bright stars close together in a line are easiest to spot first. These three stars represent Orion's belt. Two bright stars above this are Orion's shoulders. The two below are his knees.

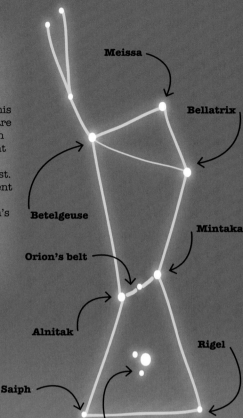

Meissa

Bellatrix

Betelgeuse

Mintaka

Orion's belt

Alnitak

Saiph

Rigel

Orion nebula
A cloud of dust and gas where stars are born.

Plough

URSA MAJOR

A famous constellation is Ursa Major, or the Great Bear. Inside Ursa Major is the Plough, also called the Big Dipper. But guess what? The Plough is NOT a constellation. It is actually called an "asterism," which is a grouping of stars within the larger constellation.

CANIS MINOR

Why Not?
Find out when you can see a meteor shower near you and spot a shooting star!

CANIS MAJOR

Near Orion you may be able to see Canis Major and Canis Minor, Orion's two hunting dog companions.

DONE!

192 INVENT A SUPERHERO

Flash! Zap! Pow! Use your very own superhero in a comic or for your next fancy dress costume. Here are five things every superhero needs.

1 Motivation! There can be no superhero without conflict. What motivates your superhero to dress up and fight evil?

2 An identity — or two! Give them a name that reflects their talents and strength. Then come up with a daytime disguise!

3 A costume to fit the identity. A helmet, horns, or an oversized mask? A cape? A super-cool symbol?

4 The villain! Someone to fight battles with — and launch a sneak attack to take over the world.

"Planet... rescued!"

Help!

5 A tragic flaw and a trademark! Their flaw is the one thing that can defeat them. The trademark could be something the hero says.

Why Not? Draw a comic strip about your new character.

DONE!

193 LEARN TO READ MUSIC

Reading music can be like reading a foreign language. Here are some basic tips to help you read notes and the speeds they are played.

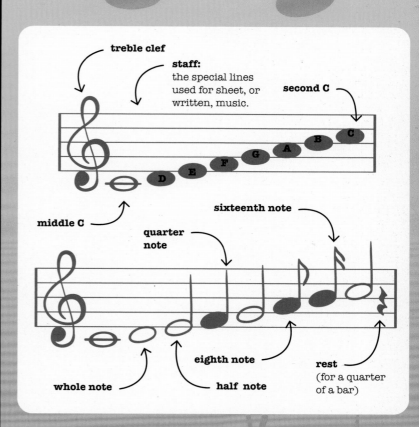

treble clef

staff: the special lines used for sheet, or written, music.

second C

middle C

quarter note

sixteenth note

whole note

half note

eighth note

rest (for a quarter of a bar)

Why Not? Learn to play a simple tune on an instrument like a recorder or piano.

DONE!

194 BOOST YOUR MEMORY

Remembering things can be tricky, especially if you are studying for a super-important test! Here are some great tips to help.

1 Take your time and concentrate when you study new material. Create a picture in your mind. Make visual associations to remember names and words. Make up a song or a rhyme with the details you need to recall.

I before E, except after C!

2 Create a story timeline to remember an order of events or items. For example if you need to remember sunglasses and flipflops for a trip, you could say, "It was a bright and sunny morning when Mark bumped his toe. . ."

3 Use a "mnemonic." This memory trick works like a clever word puzzle. It's a sentence where the first letter of each word corresponds to another word. For example:

Naughty **E**lephant **S**hoots **W**ater reminds us the directions on a compass in the order they appear, starting at the top: North, East, South, and West.

DONE!

195 CREATE THREE COOL CODES

You've been chosen as a spy for a secret mission. How do you plan to communicate? In code, of course!

MAKE A CODE STICK

1 Take a pencil and wrap a long, thin piece of paper around it. Then write a message on the piece of paper. Once the message is written, remove the paper from the pencil. Your code will be tough to piece together to the untrained eye!

MESSAGE IN THE MIRROR

2 Take a sheet of paper and write a message while looking in a mirror. The letters should all be backwards. Without a mirror, the message looks like gobbledygook. With a mirror, the code message is instantly revealed.

this is what mirror writing looks like. now you try it.

CODE WORD: CHAPTERS

3 Many codes substitute letters for other ones. The one below uses the word CHAPTERS for the first eight letters of the alphabet, then lists the remaining letters of the alphabet backwards. Swap the letters in your code from Row A to Row B!

C	H	A	P	T	E	R	S	Z	Y	X	W	V	U	Q	O	N	M	L	K	J	I	G	F	D	B	**Row A**
A	B	C	D	E	F	G	H	I	J	K	L	M	N	O	P	Q	R	S	T	U	V	W	X	Y	Z	**Row B**

Can you work out this message?

Z WQIT KQ MTCP!

(Answer: I love to read!)

DONE!

196 DEAL WITH AN EMERGENCY

Handling an emergency well starts with being prepared. Know where to seek help and to stay calm when you need to.

FIRST-AID KIT

Have a basic first-aid kit packed and ready at all times. You can buy a complete kit, but check that it contains these essential items.

Safety First!
If in doubt, call the emergency services. They will give you advice about what to do.

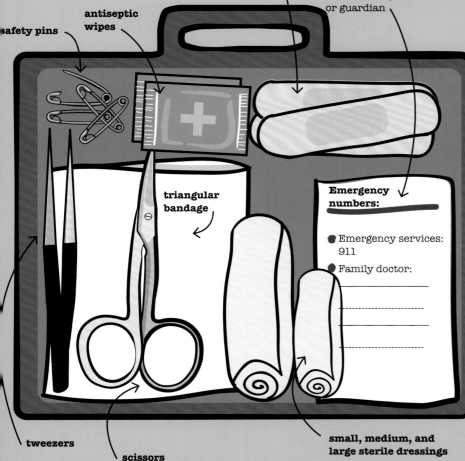

adhesive dressings

a list of important phone numbers such as your doctor, dentist, and parents or guardian

safety pins

antiseptic wipes

triangular bandage

Emergency numbers:

- Emergency services: 911
- Family doctor:
  _____
  _____
  _____

tweezers

scissors

small, medium, and large sterile dressings

WRAP AN ARM SLING

Arm or wrist injuries can be very painful. Make your patient more comfortable by wrapping their injured arm in a supportive sling. If the injury is serious, make sure they see a doctor or nurse as well.

1 Ask the person to sit down and support their injured arm, holding the wrist and hand slightly higher than the elbow.

2 Gently pull a triangle bandage between the arm and the chest so that one long end goes over the shoulder. Lift the lower part of the bandage over the arm and tie a knot beside the neck.

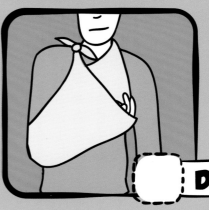

3 Bring the point of the sling by the elbow around the arm and secure it to the back of the bandage with a safety pin.

DONE!

197 PREPARE FOR DISASTER

Hurricane! Earthquake! Flood! What would you do if you found yourself in the middle of a disaster? Here are a few survival tips.

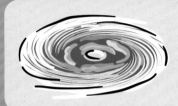

SURVIVAL KIT

Be prepared before disaster strikes. Keep an emergency first-aid kit and a store of nonperishable food (like cans of beans) and bottles of water so you have them in case the power goes off. Don't forget to keep batteries, a flashlight and a blanket with your first-aid kit, too.

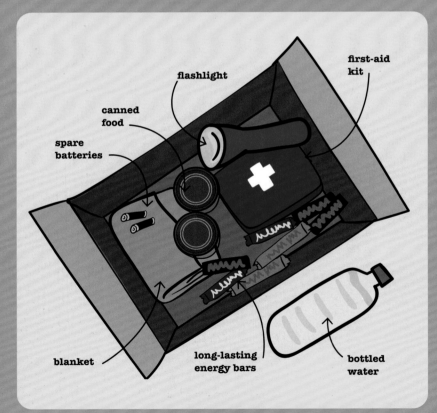

flashlight

first-aid kit

canned food

spare batteries

blanket

long-lasting energy bars

bottled water

GET READY

Many things can happen during a natural disaster that are beyond your control. The best thing you can do is know how to react when the time comes! Here are some top tips for specific disasters.

Hurricane

Fast winds may cause branches to break off the trees. Secure your windows and doors and move to a room inside your home as far away from windows as possible.

Flood

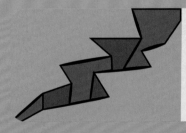

Heavy rains or storms can cause flooding in an area near water. Get as high up as possible in your home and listen to a local radio station for any evacuation orders.

Earthquake

An earthquake can loosen items inside in the home. Stay low, cover your head with your hands, and crawl under a sturdy table.

Tornado

Fast winds can cause havoc in a small area. If indoors, stay on the lowest floor or basement. If outdoors, lie in a ditch.

DONE!

The study of astrology believes we are born under one of twelve different zodiac signs. Does your star sign sound like you?

Why Not?
Look up your daily horoscope in a newspaper or magazine!

CAPRICORN

The goat
(December 22nd – January 19th)
Realistic, generous, and thoughtful.

ARIES

The ram
(March 21st – April 19th)
Loyal, loves to be challenged and works hard.

CANCER

The crab
(June 21st – July 22nd)
Patient, protective, and a little shy.

LIBRA

The scales
(September 23rd – October 22nd)
Great friend, artistic, but not good at making decisions!

AQUARIUS

The water-bearer
(January 20th – February 18th)
Peaceful, inventive, and often quiet.

TAURUS

The bull
(April 20th – May 20th)
Glamorous, dependable, but easily embarrassed!

LEO

The lion
(July 23rd – August 22nd)
Playful, ambitious, and loves being the center of attention.

SCORPIO

The scorpion
(October 23rd – November 21st)
Intense, trusting, and great at keeping secrets!

PISCES

The fish
(February 19th – March 20th)
Sympathetic, funny, and emotional.

GEMINI

The twins
(May 21st – June 20th)
Talkative, charming, and caring.

VIRGO

The maiden
(August 23rd – September 22nd)
Dedicated, organized, and a perfectionist.

SAGITTARIUS

The archer
(November 22nd – December 21st)
Gentle, good attitude, but impatient!

DONE!

199 MAKE A THAUMATROPE

Check out this cool trick, based on an invention called the thaumatrope. It plays a trick on your eyes to create one cool image!

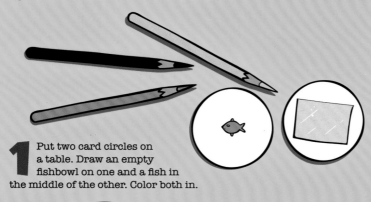

1 Put two card circles on a table. Draw an empty fishbowl on one and a fish in the middle of the other. Color both in.

2 Tape the two cards back to back with a pencil in the middle. Leave enough room at the bottom to place your palms over the pencil.

How it Works

The illusion works best when the pictures are continuously visible. If you spin very fast, your brain thinks the images are joined together. If you spin slowly, they just switch from one image to another.

3 Place the pencil between your palms and spin it quickly. The images on the cards should begin to blend together so you see the fish inside the fish tank!

DONE!

200 BE A MAD SCIENTIST

By mixing together ordinary items from the kitchen, you can change the color of liquids in a flash!

you will need

- Mixing bowl, ideally glass
- 7 clear plastic drinking cups
- Red cabbage
- Kitchen knife
- Approximately ½ cup (120ml) of the following 7 liquids:
- Lemon juice
- Vinegar
- Baking soda
- Clear or colored dish soap
- Ketchup
- Lemonade or cola
- Tap water

1 Carefully chop the cabbage and put small pieces into a bowl with ½ cup (250ml) of water, then mash it with a fork until the water turns bright purple. Pour 1-2 tablespoons of the liquid into each of the plastic cups.

2 Now add 1-2 tablespoons of your seven liquids to the cups individually, making a note of which liquid has been added where. The liquids in the cups should change color!

The Results

When the cabbage juice turns red, it means that your other liquid is **acidic**, like the lemon. When the juice goes blue, it means the substance is **alkaline**, like the baking soda. If the color doesn't change, it means your mixer is **neutral**.

DONE!

201 LEARN ABOUT THE SEVEN WONDERS OF THE ANCIENT WORLD

The most famous list of wonders consists of seven from ancient times. Only one landmark remains, while others have disappeared over time.

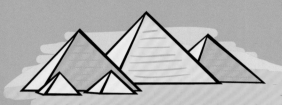

1. The Great Pyramids of Giza
- **When?** 2,500 BCE
- **What?** Stone tombs built 820 feet (250m) wide and 410 feet (125m) high, with more than 2 million blocks of stone.
- **Cool fact:** Each stone block weighs more than a car!

4. The Colossus of Rhodes
- **When?** 292 BCE
- **What?** Enormous 98-foot (30-m) tall statue of Helios, the patron god of Rhodes.
- **Cool fact:** After a battle, leftover armor was melted down to make this statue.

6. The Statue of Zeus at Olympia
- **When?** 5th century BCE
- **What?** Enormous throned figure of Zeus made from ivory, gold, wood, and other materials.
- **Cool fact:** The statue held a small sculpture of Nike, the goddess of victory, in his right hand.

2. The Hanging Gardens of Babylon
- **When?** Unknown
- **What?** Lush gardens with tree roots that grew into doorways and roads.
- **Cool fact:** There is no formal record of the garden, leading many to believe it was made up.

5. The Lighthouse of Alexandria
- **When?** 3rd century BCE
- **What?** The world's first lighthouse tower used to guide sailors at sea.
- **Cool fact:** It used mirrors to reflect sunlight during the day. At night, men burned fires to create a guiding light.

7. The Mausoleum at Halicarnassus, Turkey
- **When?** 4th century BCE
- **What?** Decorated with columns and sculpted carvings.
- **Cool fact:** Built for King Mausolus. The word "mausoleum," which means above-ground tomb, comes from his name.

3. The Temple of Artemis at Ephesus
- **When?** 6th century BCE
- **What?** Awesome towering temple built in honor of Artemis, the Greek goddess of hunting.
- **Cool fact:** The temple was destroyed by floods, earthquakes, and raids.

DONE!

202 UNDERSTAND CLOUDS

The clouds above your head aren't just there to look pretty, they can tell you a lot about the weather!

CIRRUS

Cirrus clouds are the thin wispy clouds often seen against a clear sky, formed by ice crystals. It should stay nice and dry for the time being!

ALTOCUMULUS

These clouds look like little clumps. Lots put together will create storm clouds.

CUMULUS

These are the big fluffy clouds that look like cotton balls and disappear before the sun goes down. Lots of them can mean showers later on!

CUMULONIMBUS

When it's gray outside, it's probably because a cumulonimbus cloud is covering the sky! It means that it's raining where you are, or nearby.

DONE!

203 LEARN MOON PHASES

As the moon travels around the earth, it seems to change shape. These shapes are called phases. What phase is the moon in tonight?

first quarter

waxing gibbous

SHAPE SHIFTER

waxing cresent

full moon

new moon

waning gibbous

last quarter

waning crescent

The moon looks like it's changing shape because the light from the sun hits it at different angles as it travels around the earth. It takes 29.5 days for the moon to travel once around the earth.

DONE!

204 SAY THANK-YOU TEN WAYS

Be the perfect guest wherever you are by learning how to say "thank you"!

"gracias"
Spanish

"merci"
French

"tak"
Danish

"spacibo"
Russian

"grazie"
Italian

"kiitos"
Finnish

"efharisto"
Greek

"dank je"
Dutch

"xie xie"
Mandarin
"syeh-syeh"

"arigatô"
Japanese

DONE!

205 TRICK YOUR BRAIN

These simple optical illusions seem straightforward, but some things are not always as they seem at first glance!

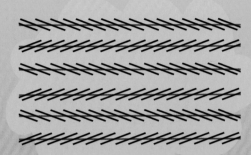

1 The red lines look like they're tilted, but are they?

In fact, they're perfectly straight! The illusion was discovered by German astrophysicist Johann Karl Friedrich Zöllner.

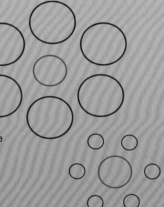

2 Which one of the red circles below is the biggest?

Think you've got it? Well, actually, they're both the same size, it's just that the small circles surrounding the one at the bottom make it look bigger.

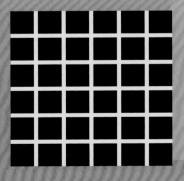

3 This grid is made of squares, but can you see spots?

This illusion is called a scintillating grid.

DONE!

206 WRITE WITH INVISIBLE INK

Want to send a secret message to your friend? Here's one sure-fire way to get the word out — without anyone seeing a thing!

1 Dip your paintbrush or cotton swab lightly in the lemon juice and write a message on white paper. Don't use too much; you want it to dry quickly.

2 As the paper dries, the message will disappear. Fold it up and give it to your friend.

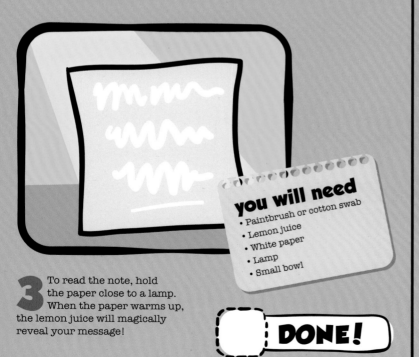

3 To read the note, hold the paper close to a lamp. When the paper warms up, the lemon juice will magically reveal your message!

you will need
- Paintbrush or cotton swab
- Lemon juice
- White paper
- Lamp
- Small bowl

DONE!

207 READ YOUR OWN PALM

For centuries, people have been telling the future by reading palms. Take a look at your own hand to see what's in store for *you*.

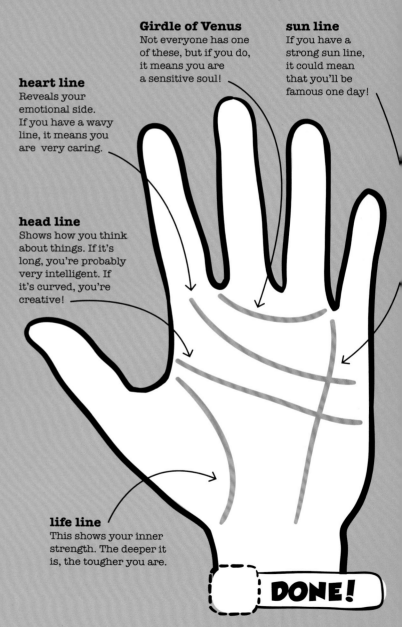

Girdle of Venus
Not everyone has one of these, but if you do, it means you are a sensitive soul!

sun line
If you have a strong sun line, it could mean that you'll be famous one day!

heart line
Reveals your emotional side. If you have a wavy line, it means you are very caring.

head line
Shows how you think about things. If it's long, you're probably very intelligent. If it's curved, you're creative!

life line
This shows your inner strength. The deeper it is, the tougher you are.

DONE!

208 MAKE A KITCHEN VOLCANO

Make your very own volcano with just a few items from your kitchen cabinet. Be sure to ask your parents, first!

Why Not?

Cover your baking tray with sand and add some toy dinosaurs for a prehistoric volcano scene!

Did You Know?

- The word "volcano" comes from the Roman god of fire, Vulcan.
- The largest known volcano in the universe is Olympus Mons, a volcano on the planet Mars. It measures 372 miles (598km) wide, which is as big as the entire country of Austria!
- One of Jupiter's moons is completely covered in volcanoes.

1 On a baking tray, shape the modeling clay around the plastic bottle to create a mountain shape. Leave the top of the bottle open and make sure nothing drops inside.

4 Carefully add six drops of the dish soap and the baking powder into the mountain, too.

2 Mix a few drops of food coloring with water until it turns a fiery shade of red.

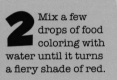

you will need
- Baking tray
- Modeling clay
- 33 ounce (1 L) plastic bottle with lid
- Red food coloring
- Warm water
- Plastic funnel
- Dish soap
- 2 tablespoons baking powder
- White vinegar

5 Now it's time for your volcano to erupt! Slowly pour your white vinegar through the funnel — you won't need much before the eruption begins!

3 Pour the red water into your "mountain" opening using the funnel.

DONE!

209 MAKE YOUR OWN NEWSPAPER

Making your own newspaper is a fun way to sharpen your writing skills and get your imagination going!

THE FRONT PAGE

Each **front page** shows one or two **headlines**. Words in headlines are large and need to catch the reader's attention.

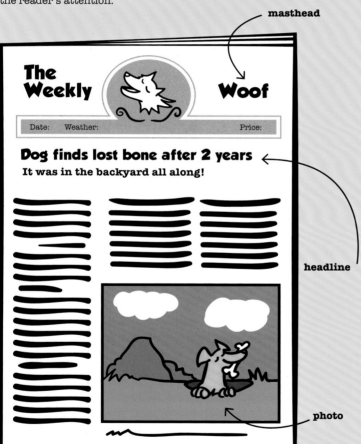

masthead

The Weekly Woof

Date: Weather: Price:

Dog finds lost bone after 2 years
It was in the backyard all along!

headline

photo

Name your newspaper and create a **masthead**. This will be the most noticeable part of your front page. Add on all the details you would find in a real paper: date, weather forecast, and price.

INSIDE YOUR NEWSPAPER

When you have made your **front page**, you can make the rest of your paper. Fill out the pages with smaller headlines, more articles, and more stories. When it's finished, staple it together — and it's ready for the newsstand!

Write your **article**. Your story can be about anything you like! It could be a made-up event or something that's really happened to you or your family.

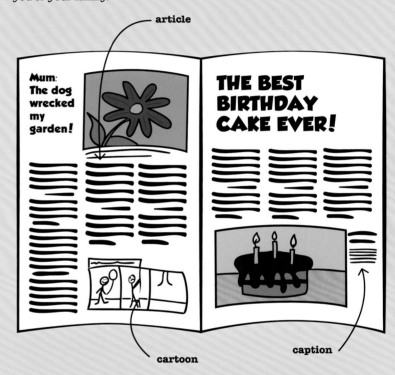

article

Mum: The dog wrecked my garden!

THE BEST BIRTHDAY CAKE EVER!

cartoon

caption

Include photographs or drawings with **captions**. Think of funny captions to go with your images and make sure each image relates to your story.

Why Not?
Make a newspaper all about your family! You could send it to relatives you don't see very often.

DONE!

210 MAKE GLOW-IN-THE-DARK GOO

Make a batch of crazy, glow-in-the-dark gloop!

1 Mix the cornstarch with water, a little at a time. Stir until the mixture becomes dough-like.

2 Add the glow-in-the-dark paint. Mix again until it's completely mixed together.

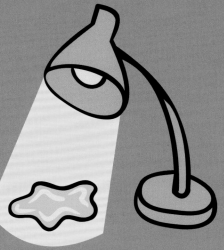

Top Tip
Don't forget to wash your hands when you are finished, and store any leftover slime in a sealed sandwich bag.

3 Once your slime is ready to handle, hold it close to a light to activate the glow in the dark magic.

DONE!

211 MEASURE RAINFALL

You don't need lots of expensive equipment to learn about the weather. Try making a simple rain gauge, and start keeping track of rainfall in your area.

1 Cut the top of an empty 67.7-ounce (2 L) bottle and weigh it down with some stones at the bottom. Flip the top section upside down and pop it back inside to make a funnel.

2 Mark a scale in inches on the side of your gauge using a waterproof marker and a ruler.

3 Write down the amount of rainfall you see on a graph, or a simple chart. Mark the days of the week along the bottom axis, and write the amount of rainfall along the side axis.

Why Not?
Ask a friend or relative to also keep track of rainfall where they live and then compare notes!

DONE!

212 FIND YOUR CHINESE ZODIAC ANIMAL

The Chinese Zodiac is ancient, but it is just as meaningful today! Look up the year you were born — which animal are you?

RAT

2008, 1996, 1984, 1972

Your intelligence makes you a great speaker, and you have a very busy social life.

OX

2009, 1997, 1985, 1973

You are strong, steady, and reliable. But most importantly, you have a lot of patience.

TIGER

2010, 1998, 1986, 1974

Ambition and confidence make you a great leader. You are also brave and generous!

RABBIT

2011, 1999, 1987, 1975

You are strong-willed, elegant and kind — and you hate disagreements!

DRAGON

2012, 2000, 1988, 1976

You have an A+ imagination and like to meet all of your goals.

SNAKE

2013, 2001, 1989, 1977

You are a super organized communicator who likes to think serious thoughts.

HORSE

2014, 1990, 1978, 1966

You work very hard, but are always up for a wild, warm-hearted adventure.

RAM

2015, 2003, 1991, 1979

You stay calm — even in a crisis. You are always generous, too!

MONKEY

2016, 2004, 1992, 1980

You have a bright wit and know how to turn on the charm. You're always on the go!

ROOSTER

2017, 2005, 1993, 1981

You are very dignified, and usually love to be the focus of attention! You are also generous and well-meaning.

DOG

2018, 2006, 1994, 1982

You seem to have a lot of luck! You're also honest and wise beyond your years.

PIG

2019, 2007, 1995, 1983

Your determination and spirit helps others. You always know how to stay positive.

 DONE!

213 TEST YOUR PIZZA BRAIN

How good is your memory? Two players can take the tricky pizza test!

Pizza (left)

flour

salt

yeast

olive oil

garlic

cheese

tomato

oregano

salami

pineapple

pepper   egg

Pizza (right)

tomato

cheese

basil

flour

salt

spinach

prawns

anchovy   yeast

olive oil

chilli

celery

1 The first player should look at the ingredients on the pizza above for one minute. Then they must write down all the pizza ingredients they can remember.

2 When the second player takes their turn, they should look at the pizza on the right.

3 Play the game again, this time swapping pizzas.

Why Not?

Make up your own crazy recipes to remember. Each one should have 12 ingredients to remember.

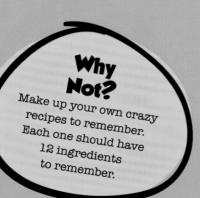

DONE!

Try this 10-question quiz on transportation if you on the road or on the couch! The questions are tricky, so you might need to make a guess if you don't know, and everyone has a chance of being lucky! The answers are upside-down at the bottom of the page.

1. Who invented the first wheel?
a) The Ancient Romans
b) The Ancient Greeks
c) Nobody knows

2. What was the name of the vehicle driven on the moon by the US Apollo missions?
a) Lunar Rover
b) Lunar Tracker
c) Lunar EVA

3. What is a coracle?
a) A type of bicycle
b) A type of airplane
c) A type of boat

4. What is an airship?
a) A yacht with electronic sails
b) A plane that can land on a lake
c) A giant balloon with a pilot cockpit

5. When was the first airplane flight?
a) 1603
b) 1903
c) 2003

6. What is a tram?
a) An electric carriage running on rails and cables
b) An electric train running on magnets
c) An electric car running on rails

7. What is an F16?
a) A type of car
b) A type of plane
c) The name of a famous road

8. Which of these can be used to make car fuel?
a) Recycled water
b) Vegetable oil
c) Sand

9. Who was Henry Ford?
a) A famous racing car driver
b) A famous pilot
c) A famous car maker

10. What is a trimaran?
a) A type of motorbike
b) A type of car
c) A type of yacht

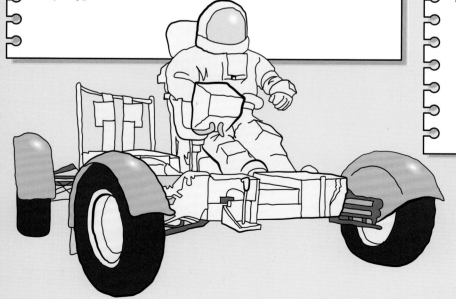

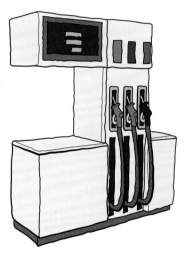

• 1.c, 2.a, 3.c, 4.c, 5.b •
• 6.a, 7.b, 8.b, 9.c, 10.c

DONE!

215 MAKE A TANGRAM

A tangram is a pattern picture made of seven pieces. Making different tangrams is a good travel game to play on a flat surface. Here's how to make the pieces for your next trip.

1 Copy or trace the lines shown on the square above. Use a ruler to make sure that the lines are straight.

2 Shade each section in a bright color. You will find it easier to make patterns if you color each one differently.

3 Cut out the shapes. Keep them safe in an envelope. Now you're ready to make some tangrams.

Ideas pictured include a dog, cat, or rabbit.

you will need
- Square of card 6 x 6 inches (15x15cm)
- Pen
- Ruler
- 7 colored felt-tips or crayons
- Scissors
- Envelope to keep pieces safe

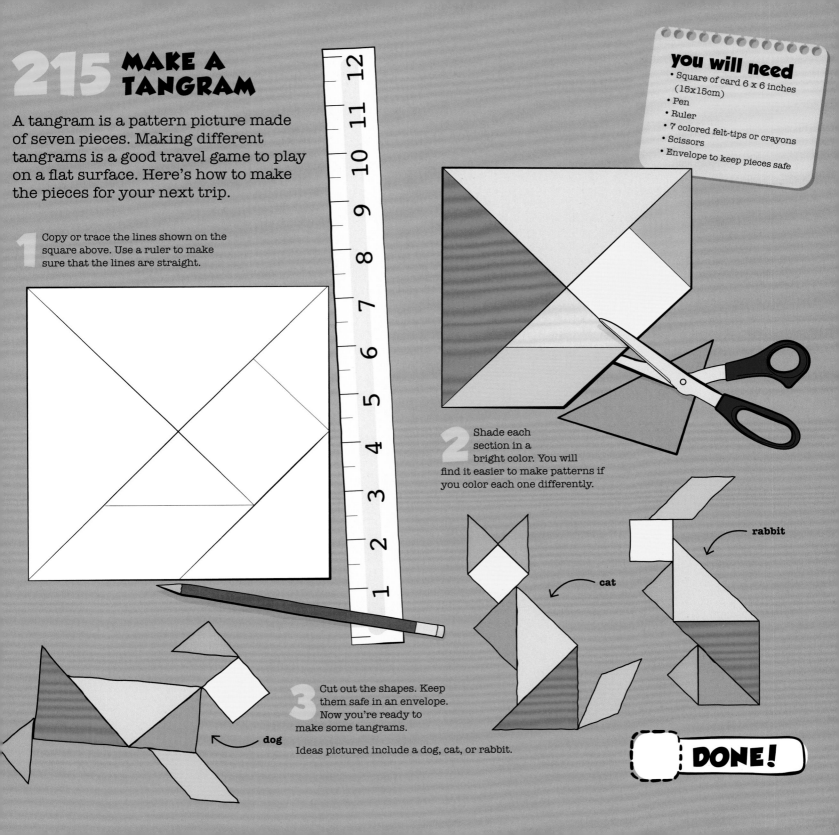

dog

cat

rabbit

DONE!

216 HAVE A SPELLING BEE

Have your own spelling bee, using words from a magazine or even this book.

1 When it's your turn, choose a word. Ask everyone else to write it down. Then read out the correct spelling to see if anybody got it right.

2 Any player who doesn't get it right loses a point (everybody starts the game with five points).

Why Not?
If there are people of different ages playing, ask an adult to choose a word for each player. They can choose one that is right for the age of each player.

3 Each player takes turns to choose a word to test everyone or, if you prefer, ask an adult who isn't playing to do this.

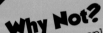

DONE!

217 BE A HUMAN LIE DETECTOR

Follow these top tips to uncover un-truths!

BODY LANGUAGE CHECKLIST

Read their body language! Check out these classic liar's tell-all traits.

✓ **Touching the face**
✓ **Rubbing the back of neck**
✓ **Playing with hair**
✓ **Blinking more than usual**
✓ **Wringing their hands**
✓ **Not looking directly at you**

Other signs to look out for

Note their tone of voice. Do they look happy when they're talking about something sad? Are they nodding but saying no?

Are they too still? If a liar is smart, they might try and stay still to avoid looking shifty. If you notice they aren't moving, or that they're talking in one tone of voice, then they could be up to no good!

DONE!

218 CREATE A SPY CODE

To bust your boredom on a rainy day or on a journey, create your own secret message code and pass messages to your fellow spies.

1 Write out the alphabet twice on a piece of paper.

2 Draw a symbol or write a different letter underneath each alphabet letter.

3 Do this twice, with the same symbols and letters under both alphabets. This is your code.

4 Now fold the paper in half and gently tear it into two between the alphabets. You can now have one secret code copy each. Keep it safe!

5 Write a message in your symbol code. Replace the letters of an ordinary message with the symbols and letters of your code.

6 Your friend must decode the message by matching the symbols and letters of the code to the alphabet they have.

Ideas for your code
Here are some symbols you could use to make your code.

^	•	Ω
@	|	≈
#	¢	≤
*	∞	≥
<	Ø	«
>	∏	»
+	∂	≠
/	◊	—
‡	Δ	%

DONE!

219 BE A KNOW-IT-ALL

Impress your friends with your amazing knowledge. Here are some too-cool facts to share!

Like fingerprints, everyone's **tongue** print is different.

Only 20% of the earth's deserts are covered in sand, while others are covered in **snow**.

Your **arm span** is the same length as your **height**. True story!

Frogs never close their eyes, even when they **sleep**.

It would take 1.2 million mosquitoes, all of them biting at once, to **completely drain** a human body of all its **blood**.

Most of the dust in your house is actually **dead skin cells**.

Cats sleep about **16 to 18 hours** each day.

Why Not?
Write down any new facts you find in your journal? Take a look at activity 60 to make your own!

DONE!

220 DREAM BIG

Scientists still don't fully understand why we dream, but the dreams that we do have, could have very specific meanings!

Being Chased
Someone is making you anxious.

Falling
You are feeling worried. Maybe it's about that big test coming up?

Invisibility
You need some love and attention.

Flying
You are happy and feel free. Life is good!

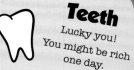

Teeth
Lucky you! You might be rich one day.

Monsters
Something is making you feel afraid.

Why Not?
Keep a dream diary next to your bed. Record the details of your dream to analyze in the morning.

DONE!

221 CREATE A SUPER PSEUDONYM

Sometimes, famous authors write under a different name, called a "pseudonym." Inventing a made-up name can be fun. Try it!

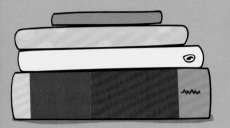

1 When selecting your pseudonym, you could mix and match some names from your favorite books or movies.

MIKE FOSTER
MKIEFSOTER
TOM FERSKIE

2 Or you could choose a name that's an anagram of your own. Like this!

3 Why not add a fancy title, like Sir or Queen? Theodor Seuss Geisel adopted a pseudonym to make his mother happy. She always hoped he'd be a doctor, so he called himself Dr. Seuss!

Why Not?
Make up different names when writing a scary book, a joke book or a dramatic book.

4 Try coming up with a pseudonym signature in a different style. Practice signing your new name with swirls and zigzags!

DONE!

222 BE A MYTH BUSTER

Put rumors to rest. Forget those superstitions. It's time to bust four popular myths!

Touch a toad and you'll get WARTS.

Give that toad a break. Just because its skin is covered in bumps doesn't mean you'll catch warts if you touch it. Actually, its bumps are for camouflage!

Lightning NEVER strikes twice.

Although it seems unlikely, lightning can strike in the same spot more than once. The Empire State Building in New York City has more than 100 lightning strikes every year!

If you swallow chewing gum, it takes SEVEN YEARS to digest.

Food we chew and swallow is broken down by enzymes in the digestive system. But here's the problem with gum: its basic ingredient is designed not to break down when chewed. If swallowed, it may take a little extra time to digest . . . but not seven years!

Bulls get mad when they see the color RED.

Bullfighters wave a small red cape to get a bull's attention. But believe it or not, it's not the color of the cape that matters to the bull. It's the movement of the fabric. In fact, bulls are color-blind, so don't see the color red the same way you or I would.

DONE!

6

MESSY

The projects in this chapter might be a little messy. Icky, sticky, but not too tricky! Whether you are melting some crayons or making a flower garden, you will turn something messy into something magnificent. Don't be afraid to get your hands a little dirty.

223 GROW PIZZA SAUCE

Okay, so you'll need to supply the pizza base and the cheese separately, but you can grow all of the ingredients for a truly delicious pizza sauce in just five to six weeks!

1 Put your container in a sunny spot and fill with compost, leaving 1 inch (3cm) free at the top. Make sure that your plants are well watered in the containers that they came in.

2 First, plant the tomato. Dig a hole in the center of the container that is slightly deeper than the tomato plant's pot. Plant the tomato carefully, pressing the soil down around its roots.

3 Divide the pot into six "slices" with your sticks or pebbles. Dig a hole for each plant in a different "slice." Unlike the tomato, the holes should be the same depth as their old pots.

4 If the plant has been in a small pot for a long time, the roots might be packed tightly together. You can carefully pull them apart with your fingertips. But be very gentle!

5 Plant the vegetables and herbs. Make sure that you press the soil down around the roots. The bottom of the stems should be at the same level as the top of the soil. Put labels next to each plant so that you remember which is which.

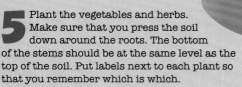

you will need
- Big container (ideally 1 foot [30cm] deep) with drainage holes
- Compost
- Plants: Tomato, onion, dwarf pepper, basil, chives, thyme, oregano
- Watering can
- Trowel
- Pebbles or sticks
- 3 stakes or bamboo canes
- Garden twine

6 Push the stakes into your container. Space them apart equally, near to the edge. Tie them together at the top like a teepee with garden twine. Take care not to disturb your plants. Carefully tie the tomato plant to the sticks, making sure not to tie them too tightly. You just want to tie them so that they can grow upwards and not fall over from the weight of the tomatoes.

7 Keep your pizza garden well watered, and watch it grow. Harvest your crop when it's ready to make an extremely delicious pizza sauce!

DONE!

224 BUILD A WILLOW TUNNEL

For a shady retreat, build a willow tunnel. Once you've got the hang of it, you could also try a dome. Or build a willow complex, joining domes and tunnels together!

Don't Forget
You need to make your tunnel when the willow rods are dormant — after leaf fall, and before leaf bud. After you've bought the willow stems, make a start as soon as you can.

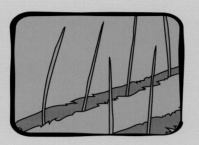
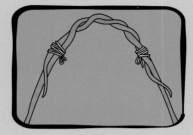
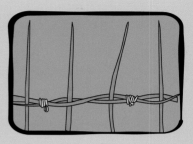

1 Decide where you will do this. Always make sure that you have permission to use the land. Now prepare the site. Use a spade to dig two trenches, 3 feet (1m) apart and 1 foot (30cm) wide and deep.

2 Plant the uprights. You will need 13 willow stems for each trench. Plant them about 1 foot (30cm) apart. Push each about 1 foot (30cm) into the ground. You might want an adult to help you to do this if the ground isn't very soft.

3 Bend each opposite pair of willow stems to form an arch. Twist them together. Fasten with string. You now have the main arch.

4 Now add the horizontals. Start at one end, about 2 inches (15cm) up, and carefully weave a single stem through the uprights. Use a "behind, in front, behind, in front" type pattern. Use the rest of your rods to weave horizontally on both sides of the tunnel, spacing them equally. Secure them all with twine.

you will need
For a 11-foot (3.5-m) tunnel
- 26 stems of heavy willow for the uprights, and another 12 for the horizontal walls (available from a garden center)
- Spade
- Tape measure
- Garden twine

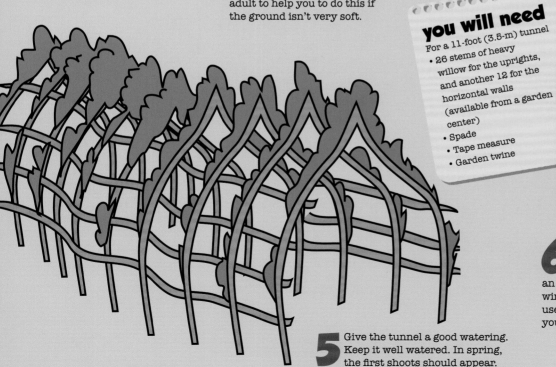

5 Give the tunnel a good watering. Keep it well watered. In spring, the first shoots should appear.

6 You can either let your tunnel grow shaggy and wild or ask an adult to help you to neaten it up with garden shears. You should ask an adult to help you cut it back each autumn or winter with garden shears in either case. Never use shears on your own.

DONE!

225 MELT YOUR CRAYONS

Melted crayon art is a great way to use up old crayons. It can get messy, so cover everything up. Working inside a box helps to keep things clean.

you will need

- Lots of newspaper and old clothes or an apron
- Tacky glue
- Blank canvas or thick white card stock
- Old crayons
- Large cardboard box (optional)
- Hair dryer
- Paints
- Paper flowers (optional)
- Piece of thin card stock (to make a flowerpot)

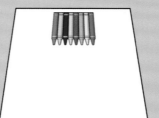

1 Lay newspapers down and put on your apron. Run a line of glue along the middle of the canvas (or card) at the top and arrange your crayons along it. Use greens and yellows for this flower picture.

2 Lean the canvas against the back of the box and heat the crayons with the hair dryer. Start with a low heat setting and turn it up if necessary.

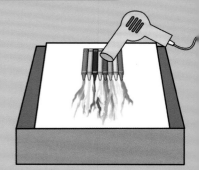

3 Work on one area at a time and concentrate the heat on the lower part of the crayons. Move the dryer around when they start to melt.

Top Tip
Peel the wrappers off the bottoms of the crayons so they melt faster.

4 When you're happy with the effect, lay your canvas flat to let the wax set. Don't touch it because it will still be hot.

5 Turn your picture the other way up and paint flowers or stick paper flowers on the tops of the stems.

6 Cut a piece of card into a flowerpot shape with tabs at either side. Paint it, then stick the tabs to your picture so it covers the ends of the crayons.

DONE!

226 ATTRACT BUTTERFLIES

Tempt butterflies into your garden or onto your balcony with a butterfly feeder. It's simple to make and works like a dream.

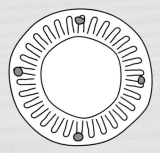

1 Make four holes around the rim of your paper plate. They should be equally spaced, just like the hour, half-past, quarter-past, and quarter-to positions on a clock face.

2 Cut four equal lengths of string and double knot the ends. Thread the string through the holes in your plate, making sure that the knots are underneath the plate. Tie the ends of the string together at the top.

Top Tip
Plant flowers to attract butterflies, too! Sunflowers are great because butterflies love them!

you will need
- Paper plate
- Scissors
- String
- Overripe (mushy) fruit

3 Chop some overripe fruit and put it onto the plate. Butterflies particularly like squishy banana! (If you put a banana in your refrigerator, it will go black and mushy more quickly.) Now hang up your feeder, and wait for some butterfly visitors!

DONE!

227 DIG A DINO PARK

Ferns have been around since the dinosaurs roamed the earth, so it makes sense to use them to make your very own Jurassic Park. Let your imagination and the dinosaurs roam . . .

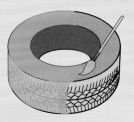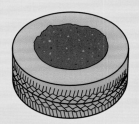

1 Wash the tire. Make sure it's dry before painting the outside. To get a good, strong color, you may need several coats. Let the paint dry between coats. Dry completely overnight.

2 Put the tire in a shady spot where the ferns will grow well. Line the tire with garbage bags, making a few drainage holes in the bottom. Fill with compost.

you will need
- Toy dinosaurs
- Old car tire (ask for an old one at an auto-repair shop)
- Outdoor paint
- Black garbage bags
- Bag of compost
- Prehistoric-looking plants, for example, ferns
- Moss or garden gravel
- Rocks and pebbles

3 Plant the ferns and water them. Add rocks and pebbles. You might want to pile up soil to make volcanoes, or add blue gravel as a lake. Cover the rest of the soil with moss or gravel.

4 Now all you need to do is add the dinosaurs!

DONE!

228 GROW POTATOES IN A BAG

Mashed potato, baked potato, chips? Yum! Get yourself some potatoes and get growing! If you can, you should "chit" your potatoes first — put them with the "eyes" facing upwards in an egg box for four to six weeks, and wait for them to sprout.

1 Take an old compost bag, and fill one-quarter of it with potting compost. Roll down the sides and carefully poke drainage holes into the bag with a knife. Keep the holes small so that you don't split the bag.

2 Put your potatoes on top with their "eyes" (the sprouted parts) up. Cover them with a little more compost, just to keep them in the dark. Water well and keep in a warm, sunny spot away from frost.

3 As green growth comes up, bury the foliage with more soil and roll a bit more of the bag up to accommodate. You'll need to do this every three to four weeks.

4 After 90 to 100 days, the potato plant will flower, and your crop will be ready to harvest. All you need to do now is tip the bag on its side (outside!) and shake out your potatoes.

Safety First!
Ask an adult to help you cut holes in the bag.

DONE!

229 MAKE A STICK FAMILY

When you're next in the park or the woods, try making your very own stick family. Add a few googly eyes and some other bits and pieces, and they'll really come to life.

1 Pick out your favorite sticks, and decide which to use for the bodies. Is there a cute little one for "baby"? Use thread or pipe cleaners to tie on smaller twigs for arms and legs.

you will need
- Sticks (found on the ground)
- Thread or pipe cleaners
- Googly eyes
- Glue
- Markers
- Bits of fabric
- Scissors

2 Stick on googly eyes. Knobbly bits might suggest open mouths or lips. You can also use the markers to draw on some facial features.

3 Wrap pieces of fabric around them for clothes. A ribbon tied under a "chin" makes for a good bow tie.

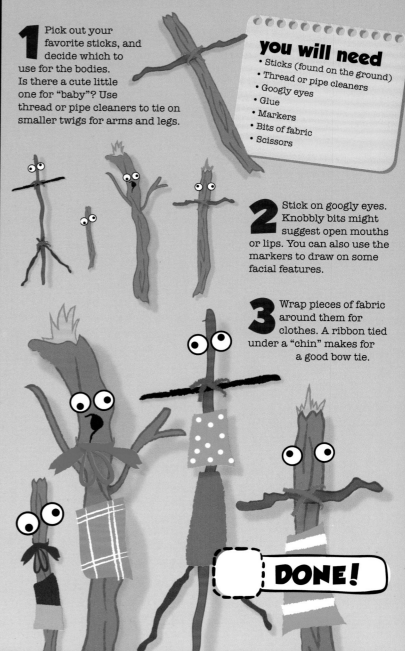

DONE!

THROW A SEEDBALL

"Throw it, grow it" is the seedballer's mantra. You can literally throw a garden into a place that needs a little bit of life and color!

Important!

Make sure that you don't throw seedballs onto other people's property if you don't have their permission first. But if you think your neighbor, school, or local business has a patch of ground that could do with livening up, find out who's in charge and see if they'll play ball — "seedball", that is . . .

1 Select seeds that are easy-to-grow without too much water or pampering. If you're mixing, choose plants that will look good together when they flower. Soak the seeds overnight and drain away the water in the morning.

2 It's best to mix your ingredients outdoors, as it can be quite messy. You need 5 cups of clay, 1 cup of compost, and 1 cup of seeds. Your cups can be as big or small as you like as long as you stick to these ratios — 5:1:1. Put the seeds and compost into your bowl and mix with the spoon.

3 Mix in the clay. Add water very slowly, drip by drip, and stir until you've bound everything together. The mixture should be moist, not dripping wet.

4 Knead the mixture with your hands. Take a handful of the mixture, and shape it into a ball — around the size of a golf ball. Use the rest of the mixture to make more balls.

you will need

- Seeds (easy-to-grow or native varieties)
- Clay (available from craft stores)
- Compost or potting soil
- Mixing bowl or bucket
- Spoon
- Water

5 Leave your seedballs to dry for a day or two. Then go to your chosen location, and . . . THROW! If they land on concrete or rock, don't worry — the seeds have everything they need to grow in the ball. Don't worry about watering either — nature will take care of that.

6 Return in a few weeks to check on your instant garden. Keep visiting to see it in full bloom.

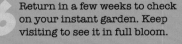

DONE!

231 BUILD A BUCKET POND

You don't need a big space for a simple outdoor pond. You don't even need to dig a hole! Try this simple project, and wait for the wildlife to visit.

You will need
- Watertight container, for example, an old bucket or baby bath
- Washed sand
- Washed pebbles
- Terracotta flowerpots
- Washed larger rocks and stones
- Water plants (available from garden centers — ask advice on the best ones to buy to oxygenate your pond)
- Rainwater

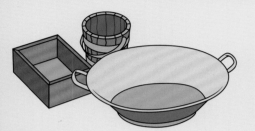
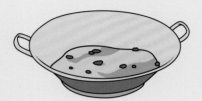

1 Find a container. You can use anything — from an old bucket or old-fashioned bathtub to an old baby bath or storage box — as long as it is watertight. It shouldn't be too deep so that creatures can get up to it easily. Wash it out thoroughly.

2 Pour washed sand into the bottom of your container until you've covered the base. Scatter pebbles over the sand. This will give the insects somewhere to bury and hide.

3 Put your flowerpots in upside down, then add the bigger rocks and stones. These will provide shelter for the wildlife.

4 Add some water plants. Check with the garden center when you buy them that you're including good oxygenators.

5 Put in a shady spot so it doesn't overheat in the sun. Pile stones around the edge to help frogs and other creatures climb up. Place other plants nearby.

6 Fill up with rainwater. Don't use tap water — it has chemicals in it that might harm your pond life. Then just wait for your visitors!

DONE!

232 FEED THE BIRDS

When food is hard to find in the winter, a peanut butter feeder will help to feed the local birds. If possible, hang it within view of your bedroom window.

1 Cut a length of string and tie it securely to the top of the pine cone.

2 Put the birdseed and any extras, such as sunflower seeds, corn, or nuts, into a bowl. Spread peanut butter all over the cone with a knife or spoon.

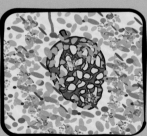

3 Dip the sticky cone into your bowl of seed. Roll it around until the peanut butter is completely covered with seed.

4 Ask an adult to help you to hang it from a tree branch or up high. Make sure that animals that like to eat birds can't reach it. Try to identify your visitors by looking them up in a birdwatching guide or on the Internet.

you will need
- String
- Pine cone
- Birdseed
- Peanut butter
- Scissors
- Butter knife
- Thread or pipe cleaners

233 MAKE DRIP CASTLES

You don't have to go to the beach to build these wild, magical towers — a sandbox will work just great!

1 Prepare a solid base. If you're on the beach, pile up wet sand and flatten it. If you're at home, you could just work on a patio or stepping stone.

2 Half-fill your bucket with sand. Then fill to the top with water. Stir with your hand to get a gooey mix.

you will need
- Sandy beach or a tray of sand in your outdoor space
- Bucket

3 Collect a handful of your gooey sand mixture. Point your sand-filled hand thumb down. Then let some of the goo drip through your fingers. As the sand drips, it will build up into a stalagmite structure.

4 Keep dripping, moving your hand up and away from the tower as it gets taller. Group lots together, or build towers on top of towers to create one big one. Arrange in a circle for a ring of mountain peaks, or make a castle!

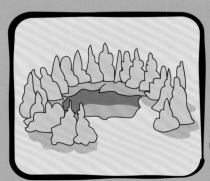

234 LAY A STICK TRAIL

Are you a good trailblazer? Head for the local woodland or park and lay a trail for your friends to follow and find you. If there's a big group of you, split into Trailblazers and Trackers. The Trailblazers set the trail for the Trackers.

you will need
- Sticks, stones, and other natural objects (found on the ground)
- Bucket
- A few friends

1 Gather together sticks, stones, pine cones, feathers, leaves, and any other natural objects you can find, and put them in your bucket. Don't pick anything from the trees — there will be plenty on the ground.

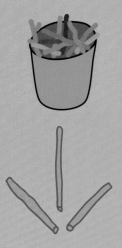

2 Decide on where your track will start and finish, and lay trails along the route. You can make up your own symbols, or use some of the examples on the right.

3 Now it's time for your friends to track you down. Use a few sticks to show them what to look out for and what your symbols mean. Ask them to count to 100 while you race to the end of your trail and hide. Can they follow your trail to find you?

Turn Right

Go Straight Ahead

3 Steps to the Right

Wrong Way

Go Over an Obstacle

Turn Left

Follow the Stream

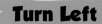
DONE!

235 CARVE A PUMPKIN

It's traditional to have a jack-o'-lantern on your porch for Halloween. How scary can you make yours?

1 Ask an adult to cut off the crown (top) of the pumpkin with a sharp, serrated knife. Put the top to one side.

2 Scoop out the pumpkin flesh, pulp, and seeds with a spoon. (If you wash and dry the seeds, you can use them later to make art or jewelery.)

3 Use your marker pen to draw a spooky face. Make it as simple as possible. Ask an adult to use a small, serrated knife to cut out the eyes, nose, and mouth.

4 Put a tea light in the bottom of your pumpkin to light after dark. Pop on the lid, place on your doorstep, and ward away all evil!

DONE!

236 MAKE MUD FACES

After a rain shower, there's plenty of mud around. It's the perfect time to create a mud face. Will it be a beast or a beauty? A friend or a foe?

1 Dig up some mud and put it in a bucket. The stickier the mud is, the better. Add water to make it stickier if you need to.

2 Make a mud ball in your hands, and squash it onto the tree trunk, shaping it into a face.

3 Use natural materials to add features like eyes, teeth, a mouth, a nose, hair, and horns. Moss and fern leaves are perfect for shaggy hair, and pine cones are great for noses, horns, fangs, and eyes.

4 Name your beast, sprite, monster, or goddess, and leave it for someone else to find. When you go back, maybe another face will have appeared!

DONE!

237 BUILD A BOTTLE TOWER GARDEN

You don't need a big garden to grow vegetables and flowers. In fact, all you need to make this garden is a trellised wall or fence and lots of large plastic bottles!

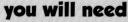

you will need
- Large plastic bottles with screw tops (2-litre soda bottles are perfect)
- Scissors
- An adult with a drill and a sharp knife
- Compost
- Handful of clean sand
- Seeds, seedlings, or small plants
- A trellised wall, fence, or freestanding trellis
- Garden twine
- Watering can

1 Clean the bottles and remove any labels. Ask an adult to help you to cut off the bottoms with a pair of sharp scissors.

2 Keep the lid on your first bottle. Ask an adult to help you make a small drainage hole at the top, at the bottle neck. Make another hole on the opposite side.

3 Fill the bottle with potting compost, leaving 0.9 inch (2.5cm) at the top of the tower. Stand the bottle on the ground, lid down, next to the fence or wall to make the bottom of the tower.

4 Take the lid off your second bottle and fill it with compost. Place it on top of the first bottle. Use garden twine to secure the bottles to your fence or trellis.

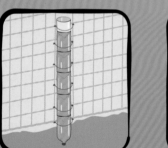
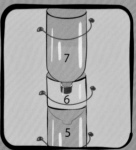

5 Add a third, fourth, and even fifth bottle to your tower in the same way. The sixth bottle will be the funnel. It should have no soil and no lid. Cut it down a little more than the others and put it into the top bottle.

6 Bottle number 7 needs its lid. Ask an adult to drill a very small hole into the lid. Add a handful of sand to the bottle to filter the water. This is your filling-up bottle, which drops water through all of the other bottles.

7 Ask an adult to make windows in each bottle by cutting three lines into the plastic with a sharp knife. Pull down a rectangle of plastic. Push a hole into the compost and plant a seed, seedling, or small plant inside.

8 Keep your filling-up bottle well watered, and watch your garden grow!

DONE!

238 GROW A BAG OF STRAWBERRIES

Instead of taking your shopping bag to the grocery store to buy strawberries, fill it with compost and grow them instead! They're delicious with whipped cream when they're ripe.

you will need
- A sturdy reusable shopping bag
- Scissors
- 1 bag of potting compost
- 8 strawberry plants
- Broken eggshells
- Petroleum jelly

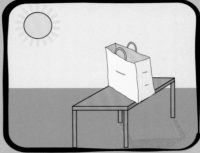

1 Ask an adult to help you cut drainage holes in the bottom of your shopping bag with the scissors. It's easiest to snip a hole, and then cut a cross shape.

2 Cut a horizontal slit about 2 inches (5cm) across in the middle of the bag's front and back. Then cut two slits in the middle of each side of the bag.

3 Put your bag in a sunny, sheltered spot. It needs to be at least 1 foot (30 cm) above the ground, so you might want to rest it on a crate or small table. This will allow the plants to hang down without touching the ground.

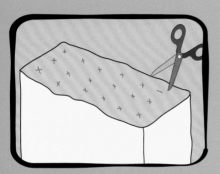

4 Fill your bag with potting compost up to the level of the slits. Put six strawberry plants inside. Working from the inside, poke the leaves and crown (the part where the stems of the leaves meet in the middle) of each plant carefully through each slit. Spread the roots out in the bag.

5 Fill the bag almost to the top with the potting compost, and plant your remaining two plants at the top. Make sure that their roots are completely covered. Sprinkle broken eggshells onto the soil at the top (eggshells add calcium to your fertilizer) and smear petroleum jelly onto the sides of the bag to keep snails and slugs away.

6 Water until the compost is evenly moist. Keep well watered. Every few days, rotate your bag so that all the plants get the same amount of sunshine. Then just wait for your strawberries to appear! After flowering, you should get ripe berries in just a couple of weeks. Don't be impatient — wait until they're red all over before picking the fruit.

DONE!

239 CREATE A SAND PALACE

Build a showstopping sandcastle fit for a king or queen.
You'll need lots of wet sand and a bucketful of imagination!

you will need
- Sandy beach
- Long shovel
- Dustbin with no bottom (an adult will need to cut off the bottom)
- A bucket or container with no bottom (an adult will need to cut off the bottom)
- Funnel
- Sculpting tools, whatever you can find at home; cake decorating tools, spatulas, make-up brushes, and craft sticks are all great
- Spray bottle

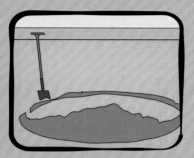

1 Find a good spot on the beach just above the tide line (where the dark sand becomes lighter). Use a long shovel to dig a circle in the sand, piling the sand up into the middle to make a hill. Don't forget to bend your knees!

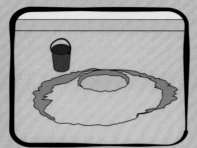

2 Stamp the top of your hill into a volcano crater shape. Pour water into your crater. Use your feet to push down the sand. This will be the foundation for your sand palace.

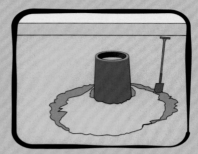

3 Now put your dustbin on top. Fill it three-quarters full with sand. Pour in a few buckets of water, and press down the sand with your hands or a bucket. Add more sand and water. Keep going until it is full.

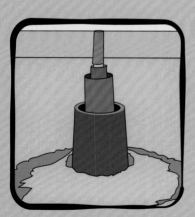

4 Add a slightly smaller bottomless container on top. Add sand until it's three-quarters full. Add water and push down, as in step 3. Continue to add and fill the smaller containers on top of one another.

5 Carefully pat the sides of the top container, and pull it off the top tower very slowly. Release all your containers from the top down.

6 Add a turret. Fill the funnel with very wet sand, and put it on your top tower. Smooth the sand down. A make-up brush or spatula is good for this. You can add wet sand to finish off edges, too.

7 And now for the detail. Always start carving from the top down so that the sand falls away from your finished areas. Keep the sand wet with your spray bottle. Join towers with spiralling ramps, using craft sticks to make steps. Cut archways, doorways, and windows . . . and don't forget to put flags on the top!

DONE!

240 THREAD A FLOWER GARLAND

In Hawaii, a flower garland is called a lei and is used to welcome visitors. Why not make your own to greet your friends?

you will need
- Fresh flowers (with big receptacles — the thicker green part at the top of the stem)
- Scissors
- Strong thread
- Thick darning needle

1 Pick or buy the flowers that you'd like to use. If you're picking, check with the person who planted them first! You'll need about 40 flower heads for a full garland.

2 Cut the flower buds from the stem by snipping them at the bottom of the receptacle. Set the flowers aside, making sure that you don't crush the petals.

3 Measure a double length of thread around your neck to decide on the length of the garland. Add about 10 inches (25cm) for tying off. Thread the needle and knot the ends.

4 Divide your flowers into two equal piles. For the first half, insert the needle through the flower from head to stem.

5 For the second half, insert the needle the other way around — from the stem through to the flower.

Top Tip
Alternate the type and color of flowers in the garland for a burst of color.

6 Push the flowers together on the thread. Then tie the garland into a circle by knotting the ends. Now greet your friends with a lei!

DONE!

241 TAKE LAVENDER CUTTINGS

Lavender smells lovely in your garden or on a windowsill. If you have a plant already, take cuttings in the summer, and you'll have more plants in the spring.

1 Choose a plant that is nice and healthy, with no pests or diseases. Look for a straight, healthy stem without any flower buds. Make sure that the stem is hard, not soft, and carefully cut it off with scissors. Remove the lower leaves so that the cutting has a bare stem.

2 Fill your pot with potting compost (first, mix it with grit if you have some). Push your cuttings into the side of the pot between the pot and the compost.

3 Water well and cover the pot with a plastic bag to keep it humid. Put it in a warm, shady place. Once the rooting has started, remove the plastic bag. When your cuttings are well rooted, move them into their own pots.

DONE!

242 USE NATURAL DYES

Try out nature's very own dyes. Experiment with different leaves, berries, and vegetables to see which colors you can make and which work best.

1 Pick the vegetables or berries that you want to use. Ask an adult to help you chop them up. Put them in an old saucepan, and then half-fill it with water. Ask an adult to bring it to a boil, simmer for about an hour, and strain.

2 Adding salt and cold water will help the dye stay on the fabric. Add half a cup of salt to every 8 cups (1.8L) of water. Soak your T-shirt in the fixative (the salt and water) for about an hour. Rinse your T-shirt in cool water until it runs clear.

you will need
- Plants, fruits, or vegetables (like blueberries, carrots, and beetroot)
- Old saucepan
- Salt
- Sieve
- Rubber gloves
- Light-colored old T-shirt or scarf

3 Wearing gloves, put your T-shirt into the dye. Press it down until it's completely covered. Leave overnight. Wearing gloves, remove it from the pan, wring it out, and hang it up to dry.

DONE!

243 BUILD A WOODLAND DEN

If you go down to the woods today . . . why not build yourself a den? You don't need to take anything with you — all the materials will be in the woodland itself. A couple of friends would be a great help, though!

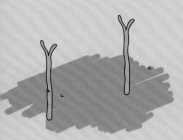  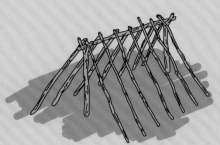 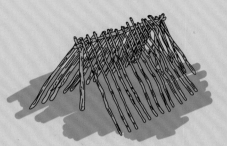

1 Find some open woodland to build your den. Look for a place with flat ground. Find two strong branches with forked ends for uprights. Drive them into the ground, 6.5 feet (2m) apart, making sure they're at the same height.

2 Now you need to find a strong branch to sit across the forked uprights. This will be your ridge pole. Make sure that your structure is sturdy. If not, drive your uprights into the ground a little more.

3 Gather up lots of strong, long sticks from the woodland floor. Only use dead wood — don't break any branches from the trees. Lean the sticks up against your ridge pole. Place them evenly on both sides. It's best to put a few on one side, then a few on the other, and so on, so that one side doesn't get too heavy and fall down.

4 Continue to add sticks and branches until you have made a tent-shaped structure. Use as many sticks as possible to fill in the gaps. You can either close off one end in the same way, or leave both ends open.

5 Now you're going to thatch. Collect leaves from the forest floor, and pile them up against your structure. Start from the bottom, and work your way up. You can also use moss, pine needles, or bracken — anything you can find that is dead. Don't pull branches or leaves from the trees.

6 When you've finished thatching, go inside! It should be snug and warm in your woodland den — a perfect place to while away the hours with good friends.

DONE!

244 MAKE SLIME

Start with a basic slime to get a feel for the process and an understanding of how the different ingredients work to create your goo. This recipe uses three simple ingredients from home.

Top Tip

Many slime recipes don't have perfect measurements. Add small amounts of ingredients at a time to find what works for you.

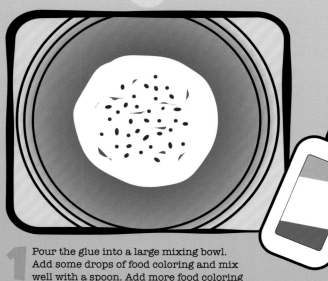

1 Pour the glue into a large mixing bowl. Add some drops of food coloring and mix well with a spoon. Add more food coloring if needed to get the color desired.

2 Add a small dash of laundry detergent and mix well. Continue mixing in small amounts of laundry detergent until the mixture starts to come off the sides of the bowl.

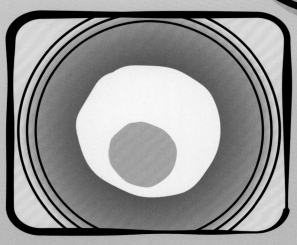

3 Use your hands to knead the mixture for at least five minutes, until it turns into a slime consistency (solid, stretchy, and not sticking to your fingers).

you will need
- 2 cups (500ml) white or clear glue
- Liquid laundry detergent
- Food coloring

DONE!

245 MAKE RANGOLI PATTERNS

Swirling bright colors in intricate patterns are laid on doorsteps and courtyards in India during the festival of lights — Diwali. They are called rangoli, and they welcome guests into people's homes.

you will need
- Table salt (the more you have, the bigger your design)
- Runny paints (craft/poster/tempura paint) in 3 different colors (you can use whatever 3 colors you like)
- Doorstep, paved area, patio, or driveway outside your home
- Bowl
- Spoon

1 Pour one-third of your table salt into a bowl. Add a spoonful of one of your runny paints and stir until it has mixed into the salt evenly. Add more paint if you want a stronger color. Make the other two colors with the rest of the salt, then leave to dry out overnight.

2 Find a place to display your rangoli. It is traditional to put it near the entrance to your home, so maybe on your driveway, pavement, patio, or courtyard. Make sure that it won't get in anyone's way. Sweep the area first so you have a clean surface.

3 Take a handful of the first colored salt, and place it in the center of your chosen space. Shape it into a circle.

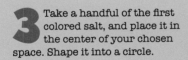

4 Take a little of the next colored salt in the palm of your hand. Use your thumb and forefinger to sprinkle it neatly around the edge of your circle. Neaten it with the tips of your fingers.

5 Take a handful of the last colored salt, and place it above the circle. Add another six handfuls, and round them off to become petals.

6 Use the rest of your first colored salt to create a frame around the petals.

7 Add handfuls of salt to the dips in the flower's frame, and shape to finish off. You can add night lights around your rangoli pattern to make it especially welcoming. When you want to make a different design, simply sweep the salt away and start all over again!

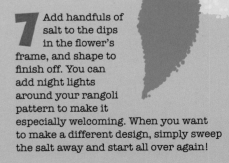

DONE!

246 CREATE A WALK OF FAME

Since the 1920s, famous movie stars have left their handprints in paving stones on Hollywood Boulevard. It's part of the Walk of Fame. Why not re-create it in your own backyard, but this time, you and your family are the stars?

1 Put on your gloves, and then mix the powdered cement and water in the bucket according to the instructions on the packet. It should become a thick paste.

2 Brush a little bit of vegetable oil into the base of your container. Pour in the cement and smooth the top with the trowel. Let it sit for about an hour.

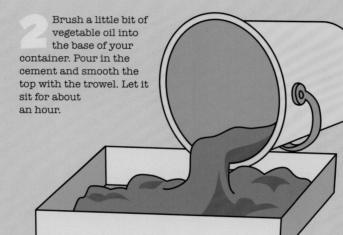

3 Leaving a space that will be large enough for your handprints, decorate the rest with your trinkets and pebbles. Try to use objects that say something about you. For example, an old but special toy car, or something that is your favorite color.

4 Use the stick to write your name or initials. You could also add the date. Remove your gloves, spread out your fingers, and press firmly to make a print in the cement. Wash your hands thoroughly immediately after.

5 Let the stone sit for a few days before getting it out of its container.

6 When you've made a stone with each member of the family, lay them out on your lawn or backyard, and celebrate with an opening ceremony!

you will need
- Disposable plastic gloves
- Powdered cement mix
- Disposable container (for example, plastic plant dish, or even a sturdy cardboard box will do)
- Bucket
- Vegetable oil and brush
- Trowel or putty knife
- Small toys, trinkets, or glass pebbles
- Stick or pencil

DONE!

247 MAKE A PAPIER-MÂCHÉ BOWL

Follow these simple steps to transform old newspapers into these colorful bowls. Why not make one as a gift for a friend?

1 Cover the outside of a bowl with cling film. The cling film will stop the papier-mâché sticking to the bowl once it's dried.

2 Start by brushing the newspaper strips with the watered down PVA glue and overlapping them on the outside of the bowl.

3 Once you've covered the bowl in newspaper, leave it to dry for a couple of hours before adding another layer. Make sure they aren't too wet or they won't dry flat.

4 After you've built up a few layers of paper, allow them to dry out completely before removing the papier-mâché from the mold. Trim the edges with scissors.

Why Not? Try making a matching set of bowls in different sizes.

5 Now it's time to decorate your creation! You can use paint, glitter, or even add on a few more layers of colored paper for a cool collage effect.

6 Finish your bowls with a coat of clear varnish. If you don't have varnish, then a coat of normal PVA glue will also give a shiny finish.

DONE!

248 GROW MINT TEA

Mint tea is refreshing, delicious, and good for you! A pot of freshly grown mint makes your house or garden smell wonderful, too.

1 If you can, plant your mint in spring, or in the fall if you're in a climate that is free of frost. Plant your mint 2 inches (5cm) deep in a 1-foot (30-cm) pot.

4 For your mint tea, pinch a stem or two of mint from your plant, and rinse under cold water. Crush the leaves a bit as you put them into the bottom of your mug to help bring out the minty taste and smell.

2 Put your pot in a sunny position. Ideally, it will receive morning sunlight and have some shade in the afternoon. Keep it well watered so that the soil is always damp.

5 Ask an adult to boil a kettle and pour the boiling water over your leaves. Leave it to cool down a little before you try it!

3 Keep the top of your plant well trimmed to stop it from growing too tall. This will encourage growth at the sides.

Why Not?

Add to new potatoes or carrots? Mint can be used for all sorts of cooking. You can add it to cold drinks such as lemonade, too.

6 Add sugar or honey to taste. You can even add a squeeze of citrus (lemon or lime) if you want to add a tasty zing!

DONE!

249 GO POND DIPPING

Discover a hidden world in a pond. You'll need a net, a shallow tray, a magnifying glass, rubber boots, and a pond field guide.

1 First, fill your tray with pond water. Then gently sweep your net around the pond through the vegetation. Creatures live on the top, the middle, and the bottom of the pond, so make sure you sweep in all areas. You want to disturb some of the sediment at the bottom.

2 Turn your net inside out over your tray so that any creatures and plants fall out. What can you see? Don't forget to look under and on the vegetation. Creatures will hide in your tray just as they do in the pond. Can you identify any of them in your field guide?

Safety First!

Always go pond dipping with an adult. Stand at the edge of the pond rather than wading in, and don't lean over too far. Always put the creatures back where you found them when you're done.

add air holes

3 For a closer look, scoop up a creature and some water into a smaller pot with a lid—be sure to put holes in the lid! Use your magnifying glass and check your field guide to see what you've found!

DONE!

250 CREATE A BOOT GARDEN

Don't get rid of your old rubber boots — use them to create an awesome garden! If you want to get really carried away, find more boots and shoes in your local charity shop.

1 Find some old rubber boots. If there aren't holes in them already, ask an adult to make some holes in the bottom to allow for drainage (using a hand drill and large drill bit).

2 Pour sand or grit into the bottom of each foot to add weight and stop them from falling over. It will also help with drainage. Fill them to the top with potting soil or compost.

Why Not?

Would you like some mystery flora? When you next get home from a muddy walk, scrape the mud off the bottom of your boots and plant that. You'll be amazed at what might pop up!

3 Plant them with seeds, bulbs, or potting plants, and arrange them artistically in your garden. Don't forget to water them if it doesn't rain!

DONE!

251 MAKE BOUNCING SLIME

Make your very own bouncing ball out of a very basic slime recipe. Keep the recipe simple so the slime comes out thick and more solid than usual.

you will need
- ½ cup (120ml) clear glue
- Contact solution
- Glitter

1 Pour the glue into a large mixing bowl.

2 Add the contact solution one squirt at a time, mixing it in as you go. Use a spoon until it starts sticking together. Then knead with your hands.

Extra Stuff

How many times will your slime ball bounce?

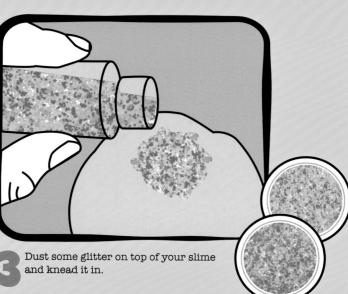

3 Dust some glitter on top of your slime and knead it in.

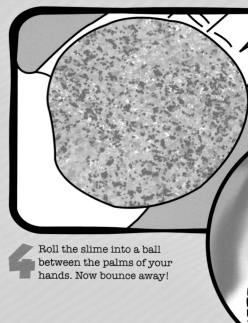

4 Roll the slime into a ball between the palms of your hands. Now bounce away!

DONE!

252 MAKE SPOOKY BLACK FLOWERS

These flowers will look awesome displayed at Halloween, and they're super-simple to make.

1 Take your flowers and carefully snip off the end of the stems.

2 Fill a vase around one third full of tap water, then add four to five drops of food coloring. You can use any color, but black is perfect for Halloween!

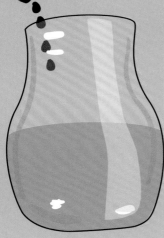

3 Place your flowers into the vase and leave them for a few hours, or overnight if you can. The flowers will soak up the black water and dye the petals black. Spooky!

you will need
- White flowers (carnations or roses work well)
- Scissors
- Vase
- Black food coloring

Why Not?
Forgot flowers for Mother's Day? Use this technique to dye celery sticks. Try pink food coloring instead of black!

MULTI-COLORED FLOWERS

Once you've mastered this technique, try making two-colored flowers. Cut the stem into two halves with your scissors and place each half in a different colored water and food coloring mixture. The petals will soak up both colors separately!

DONE!

253 GROW A WORM FARM

Make your own worm farm and watch these squirmy creatures dig, eat and make their way down into a new home!

1 Ask an adult to help you cut off the top of the bottle and tape the rim so there are no sharp edges. Also, poke a couple of small holes in the bottom for drainage. (Keep the cut-off top — you will tape it back on top of the worm farm when you're done!)

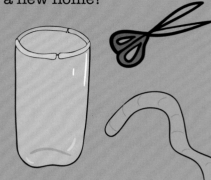

2 Layer your materials. Put the pebbles at the bottom, then sand, soil, more sand and even more soil until you get to the top. You can use soil from your garden or a nearby park. Find worms in your garden or buy compost worms at a garden center. Once the worm farm is ready, add the worms.

3 Wrap the black paper around the bottle to help re-create the worms' natural habitat, and glue the top back on with sticky tape. After a day, check to see how far your worms have tunnelled into their new home.

you will need
- Empty, 2-litre plastic bottle
- Scissors
- Sticky tape
- Small pebbles
- Sand
- Soil
- Worms
- Black craft paper

DONE!

254 MAKE A DAISY CHAIN

Flower power! Garlands, crowns, necklaces, bracelets, rings . . . you can make them all with these cute little flowers.

1 Find a daisy patch. Pick a few flowers with really long stems.

2 Use your thumbnail to carve a small slit into one daisy stem. (It's best to do this at the thickest part of the stem.)

3 Thread another daisy through the slit. Then make a slit in the stem of that daisy. Thread a daisy through that, and so on. Keep on going until your chain is the right length for your daisy jewellery.

4 To finish off, just make a slit in the last stem and thread the first daisy back through it. Wear your daisies with pride!

DONE!

255 MAKE A RECYCLED BIRDHOUSE

Looking for birds in your backyard? Encourage winged visitors to stop by for a rest or a snack!

you will need
- Empty, clean cardboard juice carton
- Paint and paintbrush
- Scissors
- Glue
- Hole punch
- Popsicle stick
- Bird seed
- Strong string

Why Not?
Keep a diary of all the different types of birds that visit your garden!

1 Paint and decorate the outside of the carton and let it dry.

2 Carefully, cut a rectangle in the bottom of the carton for your birds to go in and out of!

3 Take your popsicle stick, and glue it to the bottom of your carton. This will make a perch for your birds to land on!

4 Punch a hole in the top of your carton, and feed some strong string through the hole.

5 Fill the bottom of the carton with bird seed and hang it from the branch of a tree. Watch as the hungry birds come to visit!

DONE!

256 SPIN A PICTURE

Watch out for flying paint! You should wear old clothes that you don't mind getting dirty for this project. If you don't know Damien Hirst's spin paintings, look them up on the Internet, and see if yours match up.

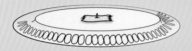

1 Stick some tape onto the back of the plate, in the middle. Push the thumbtack through the center of the other side of the plate, through the tape.

2 Put the modeling clay into the middle of the bottom of the box. Push the plate onto the clay blob with the drawing pin. Try spinning the plate. Adjust it up or down to spin as smoothly as possible.

3 Take some paint onto your brush and drip it onto the plate, spinning the plate at the same time. Add as many colors as you like, but keep spinning! When you have a spin picture that you like, let it dry. Then make enough to make a spin picture gallery.

Top Tip
If you have a salad spinner, you could use that! Just put your plate inside, drip on the paint, and spin!

DONE!

---

257 BUILD A BUG HOTEL

Bugs are great for the garden, and they're fascinating, too. Make a "hotel" for them to shelter in during the cold winter months, and see who checks in. But be patient! It might take several months before your visitors decide to stay.

1 Get some large, plastic soda bottles and remove any labels. Ask an adult to help you to cut off the bottoms with a pair of sharp scissors. Keep the lids screwed on.

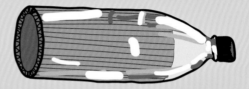

2 Line each bottle with corrugated card stock. This will make it dark inside the bottle.

3 Fill each bottle with nesting materials like straw, dry leaves, small twigs, moss, and bark. Pack them in as tightly as possible so they don't fall out.

4 Stack the bottles into a pyramid shape, and cover them with felting or plastic. Weigh the "roof" down with logs or tent pegs so that it doesn't blow away. Check your hotel regularly to make sure that it's intact, as well as to spot the visitors!

DONE!

258 MAKE A BIRDBATH

Birds might fly several miles to find clean drinking water. Why not tempt them into your garden or onto your balcony with a birdbath?

Why Not?
Set up a wildlife camera to record your visitors? You can note which birds come to visit during different times of the year!

1 Find an old plant pot or bucket. Turn it upside down and paint it. Be imaginative with colors, patterns, and pictures.

2 Now paint the saucer. Ideally use one with a rough surface for the birds' feet to grip without slipping. Terracotta plant saucers are perfect. Leave the pot and saucer to dry overnight.

3 Glue around the top of the upturned pot. Place the saucer on top, making sure that it is positioned in the middle. Press firmly, and allow the glue to set.

you will need
- Plant pot or bucket
- Saucer (ideally with a rough surface)
- Garden paint
- Waterproof glue or tile adhesive
- Pebbles
- Water

4 Find a safe place to put your birdbath. Nearby branches are useful for birds to hop to safety from a swooping bird of prey or a hungry cat!

5 Pile up some pebbles on one side of the saucer. The birds can perch on these. They will also provide a spot for insects to lie in the sun.

6 Fill the saucer with water, making sure that the pebbles are slightly above the waterline to make a perch. Perfect! The birds now have a spot to drink.

DONE!

7

SPORTY

Forget screen time. How about scream time? Cheer your friends and high-five as you score that goal or win the championship race. It's time to get up, get moving, and make some noise. The tricks, stunts, and games in this chapter are great ways to get out there and get on the go.

259 DO PERFECT PUSH-UPS AND SIT-UPS

By doing these two simple exercises a few times each day, you give your body the tools it needs to stay strong.

PUSH-UP

1 Get into the plank position. This means just what it sounds like: you need to let your torso become as stiff as a board. Put your hands under your shoulders, with your torso and legs extended straight back. Be sure your back is straight.

2 Bend your arms to lower your body. Don't stick your bottom into the air or arch your back. You need to keep the strong plank position as you lower your body. Then push yourself back up again.

Why Not? You can kneel with your feet off the floor to make it easier.

SIT-UP

1 Lie on the floor with your back straight and your arms crossed over your chest. Bend your knees up, keeping your feet flat on the floor.

2 Slowly use your stomach muscles to raise your back off the floor into a sitting position. Then use your tummy muscles to guide you back to your first position again. Repeat!

Keep your feet on the floor!

DONE!

260 BUNNYHOP ON A BMX

Impress your friends by mastering this awesome trick! Remember to always wear a helmet, in case you fall off.

Safety First!
Be sure to wear a helmet!

Why Not?
Get a friend to film your new BMX skills. Try making a short film!

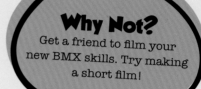

1 Start by pushing forward slowly. Get ready to pull the front of the bike up.

2 Pull the front wheel up. As it starts to fall back toward the ground, use your legs to kick the back of the bike up.

3 With both of the wheels off the ground, you can hop over your obstacle!

4 For a smooth landing, bend your arms and knees as you land back on the ground. You should always try to land on the back wheel, or both wheels.

DONE!

261 RELAX WITH YOGA

Find a quiet spot in a garden, in the park, or at the beach, and try some of these basic yoga moves. Repeat them as many times as you feel comfortable.

1 Sit cross-legged. Raise one hand into a fist. Breathe in while counting to five and uncurling your fingers. Breathe out to the count of five while slowly curling your fingers back into your fist. Repeat on the other side.

2 Stand straight with your legs spread out and your arms at your sides. Breathe out and bring your right arm over your head while the left arm slides down your left leg. Repeat on the other side.

3 Stand straight with your hands together above your head. Breathe in deeply. Stare ahead. Breathe out, bending one leg slightly as the other comes up to rest the foot just below the knee of the standing leg. Hold as long as possible. Bring the bent leg down. Rest. Repeat.

4 Lie flat on the floor with your arms and legs stretched out. Breathe out and lift your arms and legs a couple of inches off the ground. Stay as long as you feel comfortable, then rest and try again.

 **DONE!**

262 MASTER A RIBBON MAZE

Pretend you're a secret agent trying to find your way through a maze of laser beams as you wriggle and climb through this web of ribbons.

1 Find a room that's not too wide with safe places to tie your ribbon. A hallway is good because there are usually lots of door handles.

you will need
- Ribbon (or yarn or elastic)
- A room with plenty of anchor points

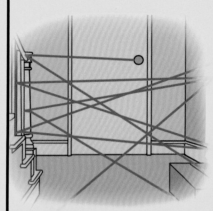

2 Zigzag the ribbon across the room, choosing high and low anchor points. You can loop it around doorknobs, boxes, chair legs, the bottom of a bannister, etc. Avoid heavy furniture that might topple over, or the top of a staircase, where you could trip.

Why Not? Attach bells to the ribbons so the slightest touch will sound an alarm.

3 Ask an adult to check that it is safe before you start to play. (Adults are useful for tying the ribbon to high anchor points, too.) Now navigate your way through the maze without touching the ribbon.

 **DONE!**

263 TRY CHINESE JUMP ROPE

For this ancient Chinese game, you'll need skipping elastic and two friends. Stay focused and you might complete all three levels!

1 Decide which two of you are the "enders." If you're the ender, then stand with the elastic around your ankles and feet shoulder-width apart. Be far enough away from each other for the elastic to be pulled tight above the ground.

2 The third person is the jumper. Start with your feet inside the rope, in the middle of the enders.

3 Jump with both feet out. Then jump with both feet back in.

4 Jump so the right foot lands on the rope, and the left foot lands outside it. Do this again, but the other way around with the left foot on the rope, and the right foot outside it.

5 Jump so that both feet land on the rope. If you've completed this without missing a step or standing on the elastic when you shouldn't have, you've completed level 1!

Why Not?
When you've played levels 1–3, you can try levels 4 and 5, where the rope is at calf height and knee height. Can you jump that high?

6 For level 2, the enders lift the elastic to calf height, and the jumper tries to complete the sequence again. If at any point the jumper misses a step or stands on the elastic, it's someone else's turn, and the jumper and ender swap places.

7 Don't worry if you have to swap — it'll be your turn again soon, and you can start from where you left off. See if you can get to level 3, which is knee height. The winner is the first to complete all levels.

DONE!

264 PLAY GLOW-IN-THE-DARK RING TOSS

Have you ever played glow-in-the-dark ring toss? All you need are a few empty drink bottles, a bunch of glow sticks, 12 inches (30cm) and 6 inches (15 cm) long, and a couple of friends. How good is your aim?

1 Wait until dark. Fill each bottle three-quarters full with water. Bend and shake six 6-inch (15-cm) glow sticks to activate them. Drop one into each bottle. Screw on the bottle tops.

2 Each player should now take five to ten 12-inch (30cm) glow sticks and their connectors and make them into rings. Bend and shake them to activate the glow.

3 Set the bottles about 12 inches (30cm) apart, in a triangular shape. Decide on your throwing line and all stand behind it.

4 Now play! Take it in turns using all your rings to get as many points as possible. You get 3 points for each ring that lands over a bottle, and 1 point for a ring that touches a bottle. Remember to keep behind the throwing line!

DONE!

265 GET THE GOAL

Ever dreamed of scoring goals like Cristiano Ronaldo? It'll take a bit of practice! Get your soccer career going in your garden or local park.

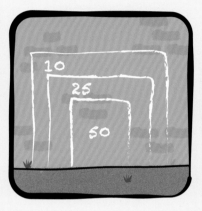

1 Chalk goalposts onto a wall at different heights and widths. Mark the scores onto the wall — write 10 points for the easiest, 50 points for the hardest, and so on.

2 Mark a kick line for you to place the ball. Aim at the goalposts to win the points. Chalk your points on the pavement.

Remember
Don't forget to wash off the chalk marks afterward — especially if you are using a public space.

3 After 10 kicks, add up your scores. How did you do? Take another 10 kicks, and see if you can beat your original score.

DONE!

266 SHOOT A BOW AND ARROW

Make mini bows and arrows, and perfect your aim. It'll take practice, but don't give up — even Katniss Everdeen had to start somewhere!

you will need
- Craft sticks
- Nail scissors
- Dental floss
- Cotton swab

Safety First!
Never aim your arrow at people or animals.

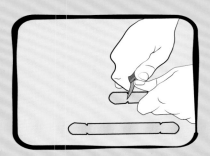

1 Ask an adult to carve notches into your craft sticks with the scissors. Working about 0.375 inch (1cm) from the ends, you need a notch on each side, on both ends. You should have four notches on each stick.

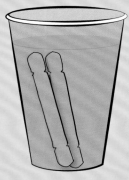

2 Put your sticks into a cup of warm water. Leave for at least an hour. This will soften the wood, allowing it to bend.

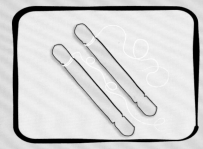

3 Remove the sticks from the water and dry them off. Wrap dental floss around one end of each stick about four times. Knot in place, leaving the rest of the floss to wrap around the other end of the stick.

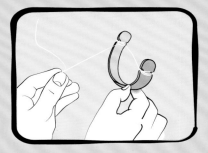

4 Holding the stick in one hand, stretch the dental floss to the notch on the other end. Make sure that you keep the floss on the same side. Carefully bend the stick as you stretch the floss tightly across it.

5 Wrap the floss around the notch at the other end of the stick about four times, and knot it in place. Your bow is ready!

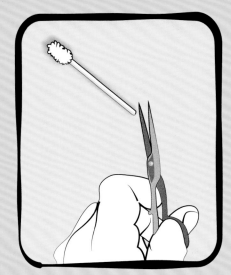

6 To make the arrows, simply snip one end off your cotton swab with nail scissors. Ask an adult to help you to do this.

7 Aim and FIRE! Line up rows of targets to practice on. They'll need to be small and light, such as toy figurines or pine cones. As you get better at hitting your targets, position them farther and farther away.

DONE!

267 HAVE A WATER CUP RACE

If you don't feel like getting soaked through with yet another water fight, use your water pistols for a cup race instead. All you need are plastic cups and string. Load . . . aim . . . go!

1 Ask an adult to help you make holes in the bottom of some plastic cups.

2 Set up a string line for each player by tying one end of each string to a post or a tree. Thread a cup onto the string before tying the other end. Make sure that each player's string is the same length — no cheating!

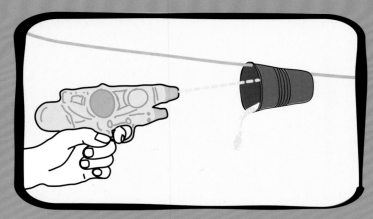

3 Pull the cups to equal starting positions. Place the bucket of water between each starting string line. Load your guns, and race your way to the finishing line!

Why Not?
Practice on your own using a stopwatch. What's your best time?

DONE!

268 THROW PAPER-PLATE FRISBEES

If you don't own a Frisbee, don't worry — it's very easy to make one with a couple of paper plates. So, how far can you throw it?

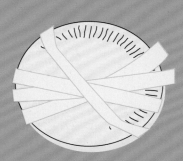

1 Cover one side of each plate with adhesive tape. Place the plates right side up, as if you're going to put food on them. Cover them with strips of tape, letting them overlap the edges.

2 Trim around the outer edge of each plate to remove the extra tape. Make a hole in the center of one of the plates. Use a protractor or draw around a lid or a saucer to get a perfect circle. Ask an adult to pierce the center of the circle with scissors to cut it out and cut a hole in the other plate in the same way.

3 Turn the plates over and decorate with markers. Now cover the decorated sides of your plates with tape. Let the tape hang over the sides, and trim it on one plate as before. Leave the overhanging tape on the other plate and use it to join the two plates together. Now you're ready to play!

you will need
• 2 paper plates
• Tape
• Scissors
• Markers

DONE!

269 PLAY BEANBAG LADDER TOSS

Are you better at throwing overarm or underarm? Can you throw blind? Practice your aim using just a step ladder, sheets of paper, colored markers, and beanbags.

1 Write the scores onto different sheets of paper with colored markers. You will need to write the scores: 10, 20, 30 (×2), 40, and 50. Make sure you draw the numbers big and bold so that you can see them easily.

2 Ask an adult to put up a step ladder in a large space outside. Tape the score papers onto the steps, with one of the 30 points sheets hanging from the bottom step, and then in ascending order (10, 20, 30, 40, 50) as you travel up the steps. Ask an adult to hold the ladder for you, and to help you to tape the scores onto the higher steps.

3 Now it's time to play! Either take turns with friends or play solo, trying to beat your best score each time. Your aim is to throw the beanbags between the steps of the ladder and win the number of points hanging above that hole. If your beanbag lands on a step, you lose 5 points.

DONE!

270 SAIL A LEAF BOAT

If you happen to be near a pond, stream, or lake, you can launch your leaf boat there. An upturned garbage can lid or wheelbarrow full of water will do just as well!

1 Collect your materials. You will need a "seaworthy" piece of bark, flat and broad enough to form the hull (the base) of your boat. If there's no bark on the ground, you could peel it away from a fallen, rotting tree trunk.

2 The bark may already have a hole in it, made by insect larvae. If not, make a small hole with a twig. (It helps if the bark is wet and softened.) Make the hole as central as possible, and push a twig into it, making sure it fits snugly. This will be your mast.

3 Thread a big leaf or series of leaves onto the stick for a sail. Find some water and launch your boat!

Why Not?
Add a passenger! Find a small pebble or flower head. Place it on the hull or on top of the mast, as if in a crow's nest. Will it stay aboard?

DONE!

271 TRANSFER A SPINNER FROM FINGER TO THUMB

Perform a finger pad or fingertip balance with a literal twist. Thumbs up!

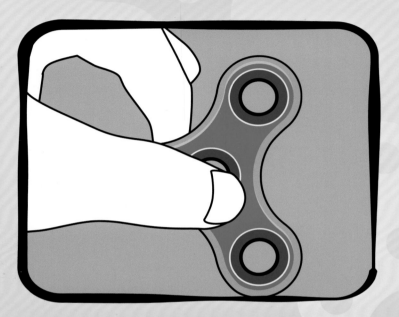

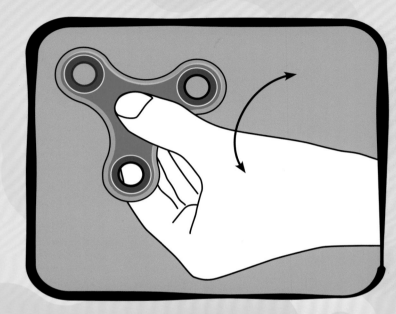

BASIC SKILLS

1 Hold the spinner in its center, with your thumb on the top and your index finger on the bottom. Then place your middle finger of the same hand between the spinner's spokes. Move your middle finger toward you very slightly and then flick it in the opposite way. This should set your spinner spinning. Slowly lift your thumb off the spinner. The spinner should be spinning and balancing on your fingertip only.

2 Place your thumb back on the spinning spinner while flipping your hand so that your thumb is now on the bottom of the spinner.

3 Remove your finger and let the spinner spin on your thumb.

4 Repeat, flipping back and forth from finger to thumb, with the spinner spinning the whole time.

DONE!

272 PLAY SAND DARTS

Are you a devil on the dartboard? Try this version the next time you're on the beach. Try to beat your best score!

 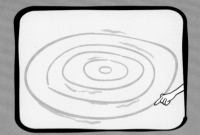

1 Collect a pile of small pebbles and shells. These will be your "darts." (Avoid large and heavy pebbles or rocks that could hurt someone by mistake.)

2 Use your finger or one of the pebbles to draw a circle in the sand, about the width of your foot. Draw 4 bigger circles around that circle.

3 Mark the circles with the points you can earn for each ring: 10, 20, 30, 40, and 50 (for the "bull's-eye" in the center). Draw a line in the sand to stand behind for each throw.

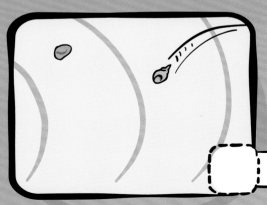

4 Take turns throwing your sand darts into the ring. Always throw underarm. Keep scores in the sand, and play to win!

DONE!

273 GO ROCK POOLING

Rock pools are great little open-air aquariums. When you're at the seaside, pick up a bucket and take a look!

1 Before you set out, get a bucket and a net, and make sure that you've checked the tide times carefully. Stay away from any cliffs. Put a little seawater into your bucket, and start hunting!

2 Think like a marine creature — they like shady, protected spots, so look under rocks, among seaweed, and between cracks in the rocks. Carefully dig with your fingers to see what you can find.

Safety First!

Check the tides on the Internet or at your local tourist office before you go. The best time to go is during the very low tides. Head out an hour or two before low tide to give yourself plenty of time to get back safely. Be careful of the slippery rocks near the shore.

3 Pick up creatures carefully and put them in your bucket or container for a closer look. Some may be very small or camouflaged against the sand or weeds. Always put creatures back where you found them, and make sure that you return them the right way up.

DONE!

274 PLAY HOPSCOTCH

It's thought this game began in ancient Roman times. Soldiers ran courses over 100 feet (30.4m) long in full armor to improve their footwork. Don't worry — yours can be much shorter, and you can wear anything you like!

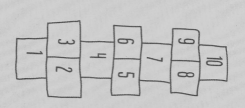

1 Draw a hopscotch course on the ground. Make sure the squares are big enough to fit one hopping foot!

2 Throw a stone to land on square 1. It can't bounce out or touch the border! If you don't get within the lines, you lose your turn and pass the stone to the next player.

3 If your stone lands in the first square, you can start your hopscotch. Hop over the first square, planting both feet on squares 2 and 3. Then hopscotch your way to number 10, hopping in single squares with one foot, and planting both feet on the side-by-side squares.

4 When you reach number 10, turn around on one foot and go back again. Don't forget to hop over square 1! If at any point you step on a line or lose balance, it's the next person's turn.

Don't Forget
to wash away your course at the end of the game.

5 Now its time to throw your stone into square number 2. This time, you'll need to hop into squares 1, 3, and 4 before you plant both feet onto 5 and 6. Keep throwing your stone into the squares in order, and hopscotch your way through the course. You can just count up to 10, or do the countdown (from 9 to 1), too. Always hop over the squares with stones!

Why Not?
Change the shape of the hopscotch course! You could try a spiral shape, or even try separating the boxes and jumping between them!

6 If you're really good, you'll finish the course before the next person even has a chance to take a turn, and you WIN! But it's more likely that you'll take turns until one person has finished.

you will need
• Chalk (or a stone that leaves marks on a pavement)
• Small stone
• Pavement or area you can chalk on
• Any number of players — you can do this solo, too

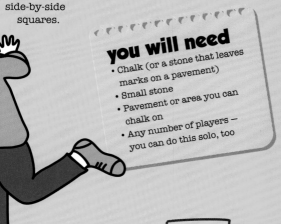

DONE!

275 BUILD A SNOW PENGUIN

I bet you've built a snowman, but how about a snow penguin? It can look very cute in all that amazing snowfall and is actually based on the traditional snowman shape.

1 Wrap up warm, and don't forget your gloves! (In fact, take a spare pair or two for when they get wet.) First, make the base. Roll a large ball of snow, just as you would for building a snowman. Leave it where you want your penguin, with the flattest side up.

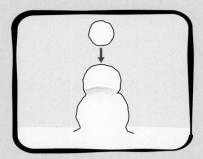

2 Roll another ball of snow that is about two-thirds the size of the first ball. Put it on top of your base. Now make one more ball of snow that is about half the size of the second one. It should be as round as possible. Put it on top.

3 Fill the gaps between the snowballs with more snow. Smooth and pat the snow down. Keep adding more snow and smoothing it down until you have a pear-shaped "body."

4 Gather snow around the base, and shape it into two feet. Use your fingers or a stick to make gaps between the "claws" so the feet look webbed.

5 Now add the penguin's wings. Draw a wing shape on each side with your finger. Carve out the shape so the groove is clear, and then add snow. Pat and shape the snow to fill out the wings.

6 The beak is the most delicate bit, so don't worry if it takes a few tries. It's easiest to have a stick support to build around. Find a stick that's a little longer than the length you'd like for your beak, and stick it into your penguin's head. Pack snow around the beak and shape it into a beak shape as you go.

7 And lastly, the tail! Gather up snow to form a tail shape directly from the penguin's base on the snow. Now the body is finished! If you spray your penguin lightly with water from a spray bottle or hose, it will freeze solid and last longer.

8 Now add eyes with small stones and maybe a hat and a scarf for fun! Don't forget to take a photo!

DONE!

276 DO THE PINCH-GRIP TOSS

Pinch me! There are so many ways you can take advantage of the simple pinch grip and up your spinning game. This one is just a hint to your fans of what you're capable of . . .

INTERMEDIATE SKILLS

1 Hold the spinner in your left hand, with your thumb on top and index finger on the bottom of the center piece.

2 Use the index finger of your right hand to set the spinner spinning.

3 Give the spinner a little toss, letting go of it with your thumb and index finger at the same time.

4 Quickly catch it with the same hand, using a pinch grip with your middle finger on the bottom and thumb on the top of the center piece.

5 Keep tossing and catching, using steps 3 and 4, using a different finger to catch the spinning spinner each time. Try to toss from index to middle to ring to little finger — and back again!

Top Tip
Always pinch the center piece only when you catch, to avoid stopping the spin.

DONE!

277 TRY STONE SKIPPING

When you visit the seaside, a lake, or a river, try to beat the stone-skipping record of 51 bounces. It takes practice, but if at first you don't succeed, try, try again!

1 Find a flat stretch of water with a good supply of rocks. Look for skinny, flat, oval rocks about the size of your palm.

Safety First!
Watch out for people around you.

2 Hold a stone between your thumb and forefinger in your strongest hand. Imagine the rock's path, choosing a spot ahead of you where you want the first bounce to be. Angle your hand so the front of the stone is pointing slightly upwards.

Top Tip
The smoother and flatter the stone, the better it will skip across the surface of the water without breaking the surface tension.

3 Keep your elbow close to your body and swing out from your hip. Swing your arm in an arc. As your arm reaches the bottom of the arc, straighten it and flick your wrist to release the stone.

DONE!

278 WIN AN EGG AND SPOON RACE

Have you ever been in an egg and spoon race? Gather a few friends to race against, or compete against the clock to become an egg-spert!

you will need
- Enough eggs for each of your competitors
- Spoons to balance the eggs on
- Sticks and/or ropes

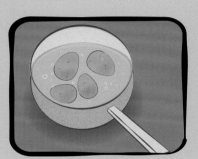

1 Cook the eggs in boiling water for about 8 minutes so that they're hard. Let them cool down before you use them. It's best to have an adult around for this step!

2 Decide on your racecourse, and mark the start and finish lines with ropes or sticks. Pick out a spoon that's big enough to fit your egg on it but not so big that the egg rolls around.

3 Hold one arm out in front of you with the egg and spoon almost at eye height. Keep your head and arm as still as you possibly can while running as smoothly as you can. Avoid any sudden movements! Keep your eye on the finish line, and try not to drop your egg. If you drop your egg, you must go back to the beginning!

DONE!

279 BUILD A SPUDZOOKA

Air pressure can be extremely powerful. It's even been used to launch satellites into space! This potato cannon (or spudzooka) uses the power of pressure to send potato pieces a long way!

you will need
- A length of copper piping, 12-24 inches (30-60cm)
- Dowel or garden stake
- Large raw potato
- Metal nail file

Safety First!
Never fire your spudzooka at people or animals. Do this with an adult. You must always be in a large outdoor space.

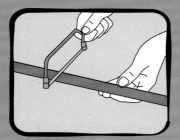

1 Find a length of copper piping. If you don't have any, ask for an offcut at your local hardware store. They may cut it to size for you, too. Otherwise, ask an adult to cut it to between 12-24 inches (30-60cm) long.

2 Make sure that the pipe is straight and that the ends are smooth. If there are any rough edges, ask an adult to file them down for you. Do not touch the ends before they are filed down, as they may cut you.

3 Time to "load" your spudzooka. Put the potato onto a table (make sure you protect the table first) and hold it with one hand. With the other hand, push one end of the pipe all the way through the potato.

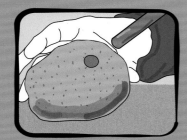

4 Push the other end of the pipe through the potato in the same way as before. Take the pipe out. Now you should have potato in both ends of the piping.

5 Line the pipe up and aim at a target. Poke one end of your spudzooka with the dowel and keep poking until it "fires."

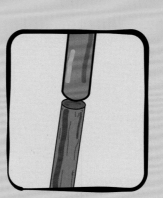

6 To use your spudzooka again, push out the potato that's still there with your dowel, and reload, as in steps 3 and 4.

Why Not?
Make a target for your spudzooka. Dip the end of the potato in paint so you can see where it hits. Bull's-eye!

DONE!

280 WALK YOUR CAMERA

When you walk to school or go shopping, do you really notice everything that's around you? If you take your camera for a walk, you might just start to see everything in a brand-new light.

1 Decide on a walk. It might be a routine journey to school or the walk to a friend's house. It could be somewhere new, for example, when you're on holiday. Always let an adult know where you're going.

2 As you walk, keep your eyes peeled for great photo opportunities. What catches your eye? Is there something you always look out for? Do you meet the neighborhood cat? Is there anything funny?

3 It's always exciting to look at the pictures you've taken. You could print them out, order, and write on them, or make a slide show on your computer. Share them with your friends and family, and ask them to guess where the photos were taken.

DONE!

281 RACE MINI JUNK RAFTS

Get creative with recycled trash, and build the ultimate mini raft. Get your friends to make one too, and race them in the park on a breezy day.

you will need
- Recycled and found bits and pieces — plastic trays and bottles, straws, corks, bamboo, craft sticks, bottle tops, twigs, pine cones, feathers, etc.
- String or rubber bands
- Inventive and competitive friends!

1 Gather lots of useful stuff. Think about whether they will float. Cardboard will soak and sink, but an old flat cheese grater might stay above the water if fixed to a couple of plastic bottles. Combine man-made and natural materials. Be inventive, and think outside the box!

2 Decide on your raft's shape. It doesn't have to be square. Lay the materials out and arrange them. Fix the pieces together with string or rubber bands, or both.

3 Name your raft and challenge your friends to a race. A breezy day on a shallow pond in the local park is perfect. But make sure that it is safe to wade in afterwards to retrieve your inventions!

DONE!

282 CATCH THE DRAGON TAIL

This is a traditional Chinese game inspired by the legendary Chinese dragon of ancient mythology. It's best played in a large group — perfect for a party! You need at least 10 people, but the more the merrier!

1 Choose a referee. Everyone else should make at least three teams. If possible, each team should have the same number of members. Line up the teams to face each other.

2 Tie or loop a scarf to the back of the last person in the line of each team. These are the dragons' tails. The people at the front of the lines are the dragons' heads. Everyone should hold onto the waist or shoulders of the person in front of them.

3 When the referee shouts "Catch the dragon tail!" the game begins. The dragon heads need to get the scarves, or tails, from the other teams. The team lines must not break, and no one but the dragon heads are allowed to catch the tails.

4 When a tail is caught, the head shouts "Caught!" and the referee awards the team a point. If a line is broken or anyone but the heads catches the tail, the team loses a point. The referee needs to write down the scores.

5 The scarf is given back to the "tail," and the game continues. You can either play for a set amount of time or until one team has reached 5 points. The team with the most points is the winner!

DONE!

283 LEARN TO JUGGLE

Juggling is the perfect skill for showing off. With just a little focus, practice, and rhythm, you can be the life of any party!

1 Grab a small ball or beanbag. Throw it from hand to hand in an arc. Toss it so that it's level with your eyes.

2 Throw the ball from one hand to the other without reaching out to grab the ball. Practice until you've got a good rhythm.

3 Now try tossing two balls at once. As the first ball is coming down, throw the second ball and catch both.

Why Not?
Substitute one of the balls for an apple. During the juggle, try to take a bite from the apple!

4 Now add a third ball, so you are holding three balls in total. Your dominant hand should be holding two.

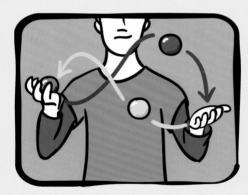

5 Throw the first two balls just as before, holding the third ball in your dominant hand.

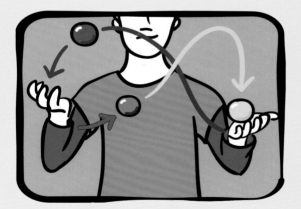

6 Add a third throw just when the second ball is at its peak and keep throwing the balls in a continuous loop.

Safety First!
First things first: the primary rule of juggling is safety. So don't even THINK about juggling flaming torches or knives! Learn to juggle with small beanbags or balls. With the right objects, and the right technique, you'll be ready to toss and twirl in no time at all — and look mighty cool doing it!

DONE!

284 PLAY RED LIGHT, GREEN LIGHT

Can you react quickly and stay as still as a statue? Grab some friends, find a big playing area, and give it a try!

1 Decide who is going to be the "traffic light." He or she stands at one end of the playing field. All of the other players stand behind a line at the other end of the playing field facing the "light."

2 The "light" turns away from the other players. When he or she shouts "Green light!" the players run toward the "light." When the "light" shouts "Red light!" he or she turns around and the players must freeze.

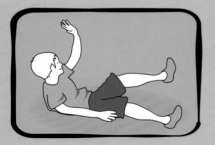

3 If players wobble or fall, they are sent back to the starting line.

4 The goal is to tag the "light" on the shoulder and become the "light" yourself. The "light" needs to try to trick the other players into wobbling or falling by turning around suddenly and quickly.

DONE!

285 SPOT FIVE ANIMAL FOOTPRINTS

Locating and identifying animal tracks is so exciting. You just need to know what to look for — and where to look.

1 Look for prints on soft ground. This could be mud, sand or snow in the winter!

2 Tracks will be different depending on what the animal was doing. You can see whether it was walking or running, heavy or light, or even if it slipped!

3 Check out this chart to discover a few prints you may find in the wild, or even in your own backyard.

ANIMAL	TYPE OF PRINT
Cat	🐾
Dog	🐾
Rabbit	
Seagull	
Squirrel	

DONE!

286 GET TIED UP IN KNOTS

Here's the thing about knots: they are NOT uncommon. We use knots for tons of things in our daily lives, so learning how to tie one is very important. Here are three useful and easy knots for you to try.

SQUARE KNOT

The square knot is used to tie two ropes together.

1 Lay the left hand end of one rope over the right hand end of the other. Pass the left hand end under the other rope and pull it to the top.

2 Point the ends inward. Pass the right hand one over the left, then take it down behind it and up to the front through the loop which has now been formed.

3 Pull the knot tight. To remember this knot say: "left over right and right over left."

BOWLINE (pronounced "bo-lin")

The bowline is used to form a nonslip loop in the end of a rope. It was traditionally a waist knot used by climbers before harnesses were used.

1 Form a loop in the rope by passing the working (bottom) part of your rope up over the standing part (the attached part).

2 Pass the working end back up through the loop from behind and then around the back of the standing part.

3 Pass the working end back down the loop and pull tight.

CLOVE HITCH

Use this to tie a rope to a rail.

  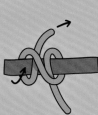 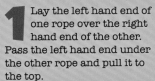 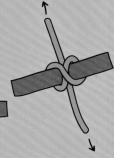

1 Pass the working end over and under a rail or post. Run it across the standing part.

2 Go round the rail again, bringing the working end back. Tuck it under the cross.

3 Pull tight. The two ends of the rope should lay next to each other under the cross, in opposite directions.

DONE!

287 TOSS HAND-TO-HAND

Let's get vertical... Switch it up with another kind of hand-to-hand toss.

INTERMEDIATE SKILLS

1 Hold the spinner vertically in your left hand, using a pinch grip with your thumb on the front and index finger on the back of the center piece.

2 Use the index finger of your right hand to set the spinner spinning.

3 Lower your hand for momentum, then toss the spinner up and over toward your right hand.

4 Toss the spinner back and forwards between your hands, keeping it vertical and spinning the whole time.

5 Catch the spinner with a pinch grip, with your right thumb on the front and index finger on the back of the center piece of the spinner. Avoid touching the outer section of the spinner so that you don't stop its spin.

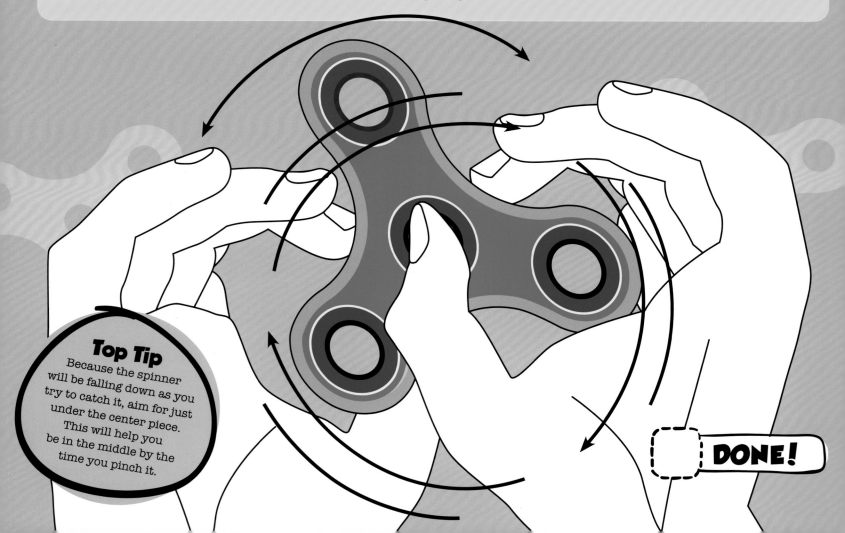

Top Tip
Because the spinner will be falling down as you try to catch it, aim for just under the center piece. This will help you be in the middle by the time you pinch it.

DONE!

288 PLAY ELBOW TAG

You've probably played tag, but have you played this version? It's quite a challenge and best with a big group of friends in a large space.

you will need
- A group of friends (at least 8, but the more the better!)
- Large area to run around in

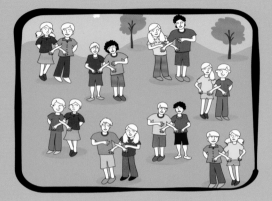

1 Split into pairs. If there's anyone left over, have one group of three. Stand in your pairs with your elbows linked. Spread out in the play area.

2 Choose one pair to unlink elbows and become "It" and the Runner. Whoever is "It" chases the Runner. If the Runner is caught, he or she is tagged and will become "It." In turn, "It" will become the Runner.

3 To escape "It," the Runner can link elbows with one of the pairs to make a threesome. He or she is now safe. But the person at the other end of the threesome is now the Runner.

4 "It" must chase the new Runner. The new Runner can link onto a pair to pass on the role, but it must be a different pair from the one they were in before.

Why Not?
Change the rules a little. You could speed-walk or hop instead of run.

5 At any point, if "It" tags the Runner, the roles reverse. Play until you're all so exhausted that you fall down in a big heap!

DONE!

289 WALK THROUGH PAPER

Amaze your friends by walking through a single sheet of paper!

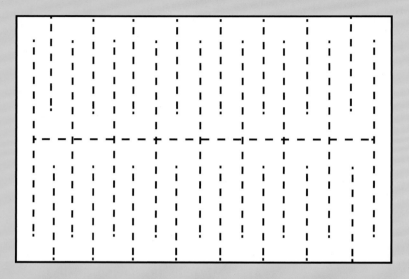

THE PERFORMANCE

1 Ask the audience if they think you can cut a hole in a letter-size piece of paper large enough to walk through.

2 Cut along the lines carefully in front of the audience. Tell some jokes to keep them entertained!

3 Stretch the paper apart carefully and walk through it. Ta-da!

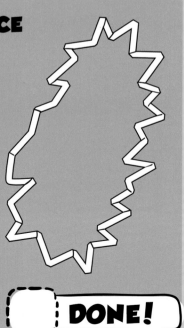

DONE!

290 GET WET IN A WATER RELAY

This is a fun game to play with a couple of friends on a hot day. You'll need a plastic drinking cup and a bucket each, as well as a giant bucket of water. And yes — the water is supposed to drip down your nose!

1 Ask an adult to poke six holes into the sides of each cup using a thick sewing needle. Make sure there are the same number of holes in each player's cup!

2 Choose a grassy area with a lot of space. Put the empty buckets in a line on the ground a little apart from one another. Put the giant bucket full of water at the other end of that area.

3 Players start at the big bucket of water. When someone shouts "Go!" they fill their cups with water at the same time. The players hold their cups above their heads and run to their empty buckets.

4 As the players reach their buckets, they should tip any water left in their cup into it and race back to the other end. The first to fill his or her bucket right up to the top wins! On your marks, get set . . . GO!

DONE!

291 GO ON A GHOST HUNT

Want a scary adventure? Grab some friends and search for ghosts! Here's how to track down spirits lurking in your neighborhood . . .

GET READY

Once you are in the room or space that you're ghost-hunting in, be as calm and peaceful as possible. Turn out the lights, or dim them if you're feeling a bit wobbly! Take notes of everything you see, hear, and feel.

SERIOUS SPOOKS!

Edinburgh, Scotland
The famous Edinburgh playhouse has a friendly ghost called Albert who wears a gray coat. He's believed to be an old stagehand who can't resist helping out now and then!

Banghar Fort, India
People say a wizard put a curse on this Indian village, and soon after that, the place was invaded. To this day, people there think that the ghosts keep nosy visitors away.

The Charles Bridge, Prague
In the Middle Ages, ten lords were beheaded on the bridge. Their ghosts still linger on there, singing in the night to scare off anyone who dares to cross the bridge.

ASK QUESTIONS

Once the room or space is as quiet as possible, ask the ghosts questions, such as "Is anyone there?" or "Can you give us a sign?" See what happens after you've asked your question.

is anybody there?

Why Not?
Bring along a camera, and see if you can capture any spooky things on film!

UH-OH!

Once you've heard, felt, or spotted a ghost, ask around to see if anyone else has had the same experience. If you start getting too spooked just say "Spirit, I release you!" and turn on the lights. Compare notes with your friends to see if you have experienced a collective spook!

DONE!

292 SPIN A BASKETBALL

Practice makes perfect with this tricky skill, but soon you'll impress everyone with your spinning style!

1 Holding the basketball in one hand, take the opposite hand and spin the ball, fast. Use any of the fingers on that hand to hold up the ball as it spins, but your index finger might be the easiest.

2 Gently pat the ball on the side as you spin it on the pad of your index finger. Wait for one second, and then spin again.

Top Tip
Deflate the ball slightly before you begin. This will create a larger surface area when you touch the ball, and will help you to control it better!

3 Keep your elbows bent and tuck your chin under so you remain steady. Try to lengthen the spin each time!

DONE!

293 DO TRANSFER TRICKS

Try this cool trick to see how the energy from one falling ball can be transferred into another.

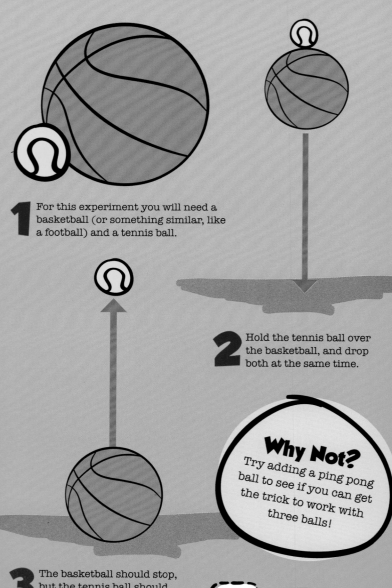

1 For this experiment you will need a basketball (or something similar, like a football) and a tennis ball.

2 Hold the tennis ball over the basketball, and drop both at the same time.

Why Not?
Try adding a ping pong ball to see if you can get the trick to work with three balls!

3 The basketball should stop, but the tennis ball should launch itself upward as the energy from the basketball transfers in to it.

DONE!

294 PLAY WATER BALLOON VOLLEY

This is the perfect game to play on a hot day at the beach, in the park, or even in your backyard. But watch out — you're going to get wet!

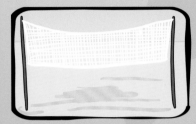

1 Set up your net, and gather together your players. You'll need at least four people to play this game.

2 Get a pile of water balloons ready.

3 Each team grabs a beach towel or blanket, and uses it to launch a balloon over the net for the other team, who have to try and catch it in their towel. The winning team is the one that bursts the fewest balloons (and stays the driest!).

Why Not? Double the fun, and try playing with two water balloons at the same time!

DONE!

295 MAKE YOUR OWN BOOMERANG

Boomerangs are throwing sticks traditionally used by Australian Aboriginals. Try making this cool three winged version from a simple sheet of card stock.

1 Take a sheet of thin card stock and copy the basic shape below onto it.

2 Cut out the shape and fold down each of the three edges along the dotted line.

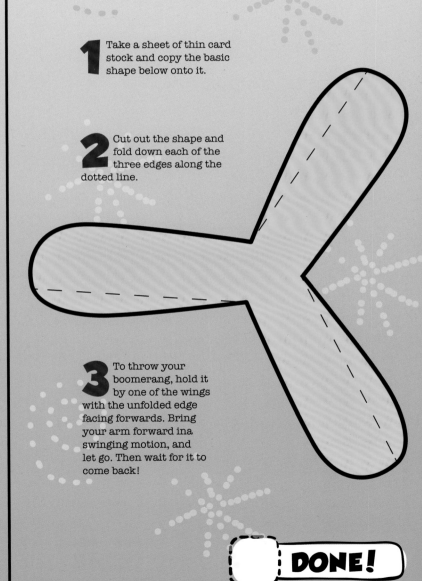

3 To throw your boomerang, hold it by one of the wings with the unfolded edge facing forwards. Bring your arm forward in a swinging motion, and let go. Then wait for it to come back!

DONE!

296 PLAY UP-DUCK!

This game will keep you on your toes! Play it while you are on a road trip — drivers don't play, for obvious reasons.

1 Every player has five lives. If you go over a bridge, you must lift your feet up. Anyone who doesn't lift up their feet loses a life.

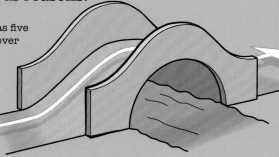

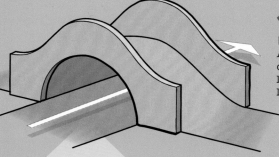

2 If you go under a bridge, you must duck. Anyone who doesn't duck loses a life. The last person with a life left wins.

DIFFERENT UP-DUCKS

If your trip doesn't have bridges you could try these variations, or make up your own up-ducks.

- Feet up every time you hear the word "traffic" on the radio.

- Duck when you hear the word "weather" on the radio.

- Feet up whenever you pass a gas station.

- Duck whenever you pass a broken-down vehicle.

- Feet up whenever you see a fuel truck.

- Duck whenever you see an airplane.

DONE!

297 THUMB WRESTLE

Here's a fun game to try for two players who have roughly equal-sized hands.

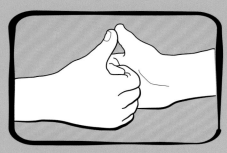

1 Place your thumbs in midair, facing each other. Lock your fingertips together.

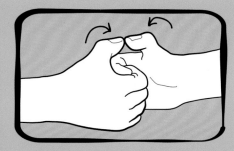

2 Bow your thumbs, to respect your opponent. Then let the game begin!

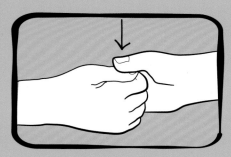

3 You must try to push your opponent's thumb down and hold it there for a count of five.

4 The winner could say "One, two, three, four. I win the thumb war!"

DONE!

298 PLAY PENCIL SPIN

For this stunt, you'll need a pencil, mechanical pencil, or pen with a flat bottom. You'll also need a spinner with removable center caps.

SPINNING WITH PROPS

1 Pull the center caps off both sides of your fidget spinner.

2 Push a pencil or pen through the center hole, starting at the pointy end, as far as it will go.

3 Hold the pencil or pen by the barrel above the spinner and set the spinner spinning with your other hand.

4 Put the pen or pencil flat end down on a flat surface. Watch it spin!

5 Try flicking the top of the pencil or pen as it spins. If it's got enough momentum, it should stand itself up straight again!

DONE!

299 DO A SKATEBOARD TRICK

One of the key tricks in skateboarding is a jump called the Ollie. Remember to always wear a helmet when using your skateboard!

1 Bend your knees. As you roll (slowly!), slam your right foot down as hard as you can on the kicktail and then jump into the air (above skateboard) with both feet.

2 As you go up into the air, drag your left foot up the deck. It will take time and practice to get the feel for this, so keep trying.

3 Bend your knees as you come down to soften the impact. Soon you will be doing an Ollie everywhere you skate!

Skateboard Parts

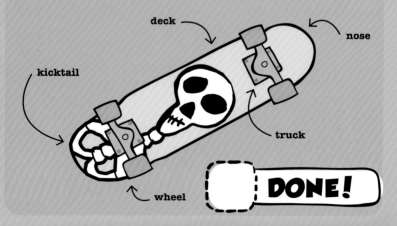

deck

nose

kicktail

truck

wheel

DONE!

300 READY YOUR CAMPING GEAR

Going camping needs lots of planning and organization — get clued up by reading below!

Safety First!
Make sure that you tell someone where you are at all times, and never camp alone!

tent

camping chair

map of the area

flashlight

ground mat

first-aid kit

food

Be Prepared
Pack essential items you need for a good night's sleep in the wild, such as a tent, a sleeping bag, and a ground mat. Think about where you are planning to camp and what the weather is like, and take the right clothing to keep you warm. Also, remember a first-aid kit, food, a flashlight, and a map for the ultimate (and safe) outdoor experience!

DONE!

301 PLAY ROCK, PAPER, SCISSORS

Remind yourself how to play the well-known "rock, paper, scissors" game, and then try some secret winning tips! You need two players.

ROCK

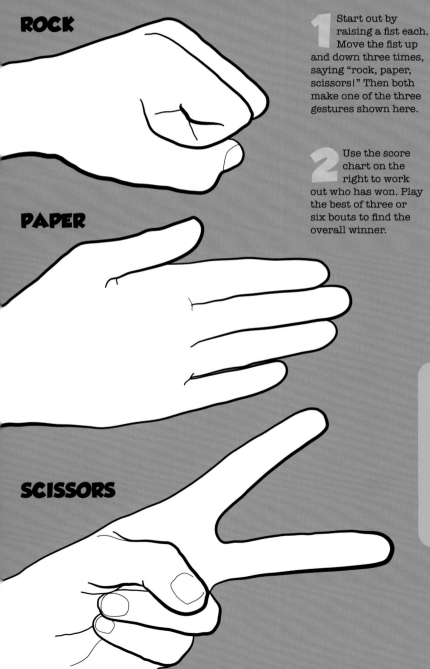

1 Start out by raising a fist each. Move the fist up and down three times, saying "rock, paper, scissors!" Then both make one of the three gestures shown here.

2 Use the score chart on the right to work out who has won. Play the best of three or six bouts to find the overall winner.

PAPER

SCISSORS

Here's How to Score

Rock wins — **Rock Smashes Scissors**

Scissors win — **Scissors Cut Paper**

Paper wins — **Paper Covers Rock**

If both players make the same gesture, it is a draw and you play again.

Winning Tips

(Keep these hidden from your opponents!)

- Most people tend to start a game with scissors.

- If someone says the same thing twice, they are unlikely to say it again. Their next choice might well be the gesture that will beat their previous double choice.

- Watch your opponent. Do they have a favorite choice they use a lot? Remember for the next time you challenge them.

DONE!

302 PLAY BOTTLE SPIN

Spin on a bottle to add more tricks to your repertoire. Just place a plastic bottle on the table, and raise the spinner to new heights!

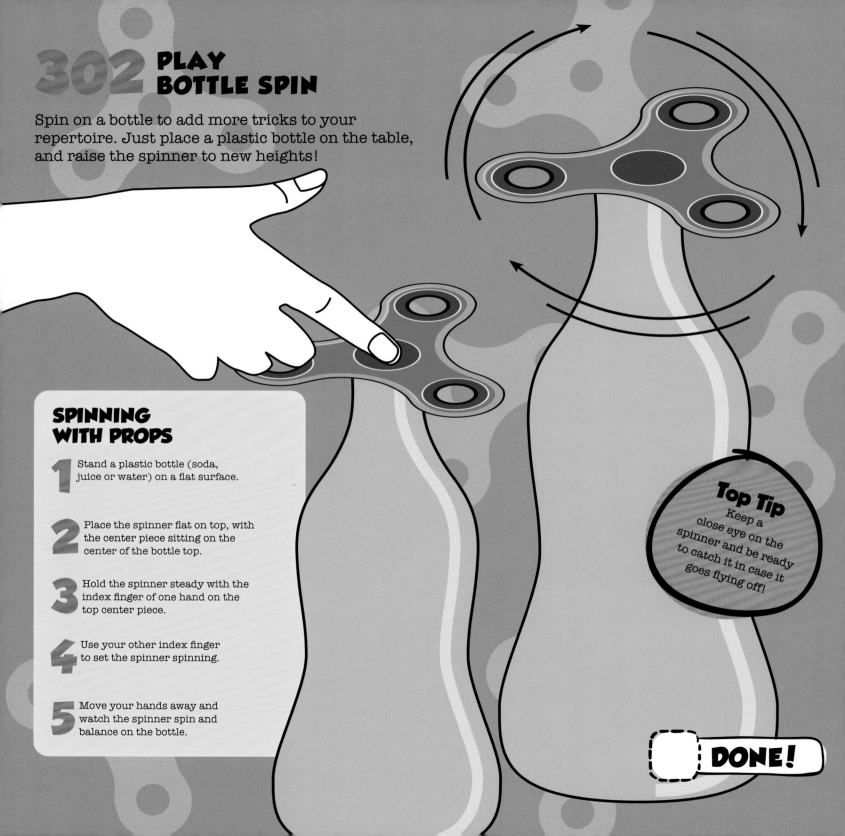

SPINNING WITH PROPS

1 Stand a plastic bottle (soda, juice or water) on a flat surface.

2 Place the spinner flat on top, with the center piece sitting on the center of the bottle top.

3 Hold the spinner steady with the index finger of one hand on the top center piece.

4 Use your other index finger to set the spinner spinning.

5 Move your hands away and watch the spinner spin and balance on the bottle.

Top Tip
Keep a close eye on the spinner and be ready to catch it in case it goes flying off!

DONE!

303 MAKE SNOW ANGELS

Here's how to make perfect angels in the snow. If you go out right after a snowfall, you'll have a blank canvas to work on.

1 Find a patch of snow that's at least as tall as your body and as wide as your outstretched arms. Fresh powdery snow is best, so if possible, do this immediately after snowfall. Carefully fall back onto the snow with your arms outstretched.

2 Move your arms and legs back and forth, keeping them straight as if you're doing a jumping jack. Press your head back hard enough to make sure that you're leaving a good imprint.

3 Get up carefully so you don't spoil your masterpiece. If a friend is with you, ask him or her to help you up. Stand back and admire your snow angel. Take a photo!

DONE!

304 PLAY H-O-R-S-E

You just need a basketball, a basketball hoop, and a group of friends to play this game. Who will spell H-O-R-S-E first?

1 Stand in a line — this will be the order for you to take your turn. The first player takes a shot at the basketball hoop. If he or she makes the shot, then the second player has to make the same type of shot, from the same place as the first player.

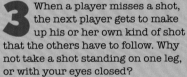

2 If player 2 makes the shot, then the third player has to make the same shot, and so on. If player 2 misses, then he or she gets a letter — first H, then an O, and so on, until it spells HORSE. If players spell out the whole word, then they are out of the game.

3 When a player misses a shot, the next player gets to make up his or her own kind of shot that the others have to follow. Why not take a shot standing on one leg, or with your eyes closed?

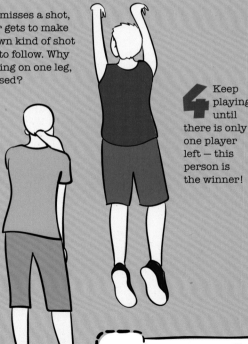

4 Keep playing until there is only one player left — this person is the winner!

DONE!

305 PLAY DROP CATCH

How good are you with a ball? Can you catch one on two knees, with one hand on the floor and both eyes closed?

1 Stand in a circle with some friends and space yourselves out equally. The farther apart you are, the more challenging the game will be. Decide who is going to start, and give that person the ball.

2 The first person should throw the ball to another player in the circle. If that player catches it, he or she then throws it to another player, and so on.

3 The ball is thrown back and forth in the circle until someone drops it. The "dropper" has to pay a penalty and continue to play on one knee. Any other "droppers" pay the same penalty.

4 If players on one knee catch their next ball, they can stand back up again. But if they drop that one too, they pay another penalty and go down on two knees.

On a third drop, the player on two knees should also put one hand to the ground; on a fourth drop, close one eye; and on a fifth drop, close both eyes! If players with penalties catch the ball again, they can remove one penalty — for example, if they're on two knees, one knee can come up again. The last player still in the game wins!

DONE!

306 PLAY CUP CATCH

This game is strictly hands-free. Anyone caught touching the ball must pay the price.

1 Roll the foil up to make a small ball and put it into one of the cups.

2 Players stand in a circle and use their cups to throw and catch the ball — no one is allowed to touch it with their hands.

you will need
• Aluminum foil
• Plastic cup for each player

3 Make players do forfeits, such as five star jumps, if they touch or drop the ball.

DONE!

307 SKIP YOURSELF FIT

Skipping is a great workout. It's lots of fun, too! If you haven't done it for a while, build up slowly.

1 Warm up gently with a slow Double Hop. This is when you skip with your feet together, turning the rope slowly. Jump twice between each rope turn. Try 10 of these.

2 Next, do the Shuffle. This is when you put one foot in front of the other and switch feet as you skip. Jump twice between each rope swing. If you feel ready, try to speed it up with just one jump between each rope swing. Do 10 of these.

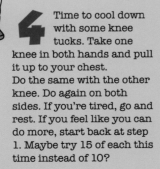

3 Now for the High Knee. Pick up one knee at a time while you skip. Again, start off by jumping twice between each rope swing. When you're ready, jump just once, as if you're running with your knees up high. Do 10 of these.

4 Time to cool down with some knee tucks. Take one knee in both hands and pull it up to your chest. Do the same with the other knee. Do again on both sides. If you're tired, go and rest. If you feel like you can do more, start back at step 1. Maybe try 15 of each this time instead of 10?

DONE!

308 GO SLEDDING

There's nothing like zooming down the slopes on a sled, but make sure you do it safely. Wheee!

1 Wrap up warm, with a waterproof coat, trousers, gloves, hat, and boots. Wear lots of layers underneath to keep toasty and dry, but don't wear a scarf. Wear lip balm, and put some in your pocket to reapply. Put on your helmet.

2 Choose a good sledding hill: one that is not too steep with a long flat area at the bottom, away from any roads and ponds, is perfect. It should be snowy rather than icy and free of obstacles such as rocks or trees.

Safety First!
Always take an adult with you. Make sure that your sled can brake and steer. Practice braking before taking your sled on a hill, and only sled in the daytime.

3 Put your sled on the top of the hill. Sit on it facing forward, with your arms and legs inside the sled, not dangling over the sides. Push off with your hands, and hold on tightly to the sides. If you fall off, move out of the way of your sled and any other sledders. If you can't stop, roll off the sled and get out of the way.

GERONIMO! Time to go again? Walk back up the side of the hill, leaving the middle open for other sledders.

DONE!

309 PLAY WATER-BALLOON DODGE

Cool off on a hot day, and invite your friends to a friendly water-balloon fight. But be prepared to get wet — VERY wet!

1 Get your ammunition ready. Before filling up each balloon with water, blow it up and stretch it a little. This should stop it from popping. Stretch the neck of the balloon over the end of a tap or hose. Turn on a medium stream of water so that it doesn't shoot off! Turn the water off before the balloon is filled to the top.

2 Tie the balloons tightly, about 1 inch (3cm) from the top. Put them in buckets. This can take a while, so ask your friends to help!

3 Select a referee and scorekeeper, and divide the rest of your friends into two teams. Agree on the rules before you start. When someone is hit, the other team scores a point. Will the teams take turns, or is it a free-for-all? Will you play until all the balloons are gone, until everyone has been hit, or when one team has reached a certain number of points?

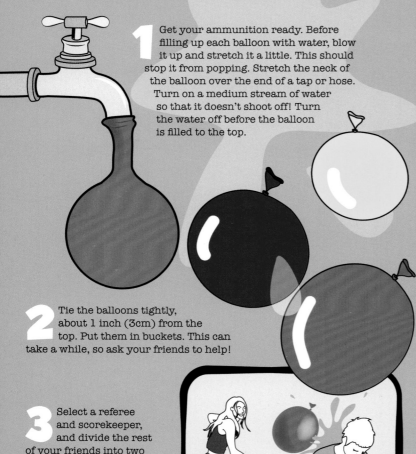

DONE!

310 GO HILL ROLLING

Want an exciting activity that is faster and more fun than walking? Try Mother Nature's very own roller coaster — go hill rolling!

1 Find a grassy hill. It needs to have a good slope, but make sure that it's not too steep. Make sure there are no rocks, litter, or animal droppings!

2 Empty your pockets and hand everything over to a friend. (It's pretty uncomfortable rolling over and over your things, plus you might lose something!)

3 Lay down on the ground at the top of the hill. Either cross your arms in front of you or put your arms above you.

4 And . . . roll! If there are other rollers, shout out "Wheeee!" so they know you're coming. Did you have fun? Okay, so walk to the other side of the hill, get up to the top, and roll again and again!

Safety First!
To be super-safe, wear a helmet and knee pads.

DONE!

311 DO THE TABLE SPIN

Gather a bunch of fidget spinners to create a tower of spinning awesomeness. How high can you go?

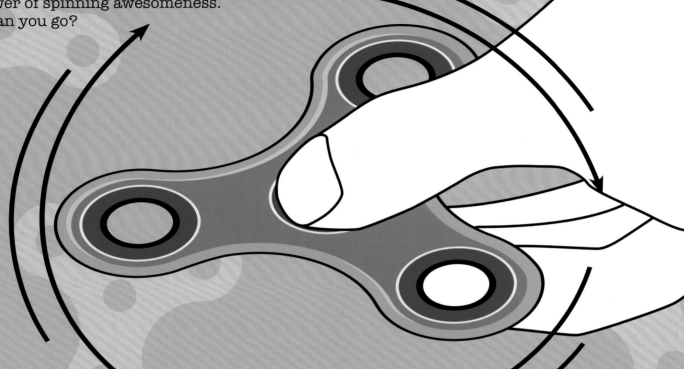

BASIC SKILLS

1 Start with one spinner flat on the table. Place the index finger of one hand on the center piece of the spinner and use the other hand to set it spinning. Remove your index finger.

2 Carefully place another spinner on top of the spinning first one.

3 Place your index finger on the top spinner's center piece and use your other index finger to start it spinning too. Remove your fingers.

4 Repeat with as many spinners as you can, adding one at a time.

Top Tip
This is a great one to do with friends — you'll have more spinners!

312 STICK THE SPIDER'S WEB

Set up your sticky web in a narrow space, such as a doorway.

1 Stick masking tape across the doorway to form a web, with the sticky side facing you.

2 The balls of newspaper are your flies. Try to throw them through the gaps in the web without them getting caught. If most of your flies make it through to the other side, try adding more tape to make some of the gaps smaller.

you will need
• Masking tape
• Balls of crumpled newspaper

Top Tip
When you're setting up the web and making the newspaper balls, check that they will fit through the gaps.

DONE!

313 GO ON A NATURE HUNT

Get together with a couple of friends and challenge them to a nature hunt. Decide as a group what to look for and what to do with your treasures at the end.

Ideas List
Things that are:
Round, fuzzy, green, hard, soft, beautiful, red, orange, light, heavy

Something you can: Fly, spin, twirl, make a noise with

Make something from:
A pine cone, 3 different leaves, 5 seeds, a flower, a berry, a feather

1 Make sure that each hunter has a grocery bag, a pen, and some paper. Sit and agree on a list of things to look for. As you agree on an item to hunt, write it down. You'll each need a copy of the list.

2 Agree on where you'll go — perhaps in your back yard or in the park. Make sure that an adult always knows where you are.

3 Find every item on the list and put it in your bag. Do not pick flowers or leaves — try to find them on the ground.

4 When you've finished, make sure that everyone else has, too. Take your stuff home to compare — you can make a little exhibition with the best finds.

DONE!

314 RIDE THE WAVES

If you've never been surfing, why not start with a boogie (or body) board? Just lie on top of the board and ride a wave to the beach. Surf's up!

1 Watch someone else boogie board first to get the idea. Then practice on the beach, using your feet and arms to paddle. This will give you a nice warm up, too.

2 Now it's time to get into the water! Make sure you're wearing your leash. Lie flat on your belly holding the side of the board with your hands. Keep your shoulders parallel to your hands, with your elbows bent, resting close to the outer edge of the board. Kick your feet, keeping them underwater.

Top Tip

Make sure that you have the right size board. They range from 3–4 feet (90–120cm) long. Stand the board upright. It should come up to your belly button, or about 1 inch (3cm) on either side of it. E.g., if you're 4 feet (120cm) tall, then your body board would be 3 feet (90cm) long.

you will need
- Waves
- Sunblock
- Body board
- Leash
- Wetsuit (it needs to fit snugly but still allow movement)
- Booties
- Fins
  (A wetsuit, booties, and fins can all be rented with a body board)

Safety First!

The beach can be very dangerous if you're not careful. Always take an adult with you, and do not try to boogie board unless you are a good swimmer. Always make sure that you don't go too far out so that you don't get caught in a strong ocean current.

5 If you've caught the wave, it'll take you all the way to the beach. Was that fun? Time to go back in!

3 Kick and paddle to where the waves are breaking. Choose the wave you want to ride, starting with a small one. A few seconds before the wave starts to break, point the nose of your board toward the beach.

4 Just as the wave reaches you, push off toward the shore. Let the board take your weight and lean up on your elbows with your head up and your back arched.

Don't Panic!

If you fall off your board, don't worry — pull on your leash until you get hold of it again. Your board will keep you afloat.

DONE!

8
BUSY

There's no reason for you to plug-in if you're stuck on a plane, train, or automobile. Hit the road with these challenges, quizzes, and games, and the miles will pass by in no time. You don't even have to take your seatbelt off to enjoy a rip-roaring fun ride.

315 MAKE A CHECKLIST

Plan for fun while you are on the go! Here are some things to take with you.

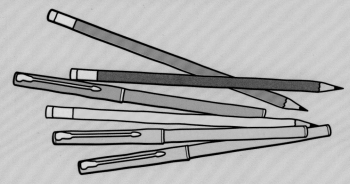

1 Take pens and a small pack of colored pencils. Make sure the pen tops are on securely. There's nothing worse than a leaky pen making a mess on bags and clothes!

2 Take plenty of paper for playing games. You can buy blank sketchbooks in different sizes.

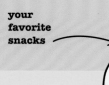

your favorite snacks →

CHECKLIST

- Pens and pencils
- Plenty of blank paper
- This book!
- Your favorite snacks
- Drink
- MP3 player or tablet and headphones for listening to music or watching movies (don't forget to pack a charger for phones and tablets, too)
- Small pack of hand wipes (great for cleaning sticky fingers)

Top Tip
If you're going on an airplane, there will be special rules for the things you can take on board. Check before you go.

3 Here is a checklist of things (above) to take, to help you as you pack.

DONE!

316 SET SOME GOALS

When you need to plan a vacation, you can ramp up the excitement by setting some goals.

I WANT TO:

Speak a new language

Send a postcard

Go on a hike

Try riding a bodyboard in the sea

Build a sandcastle

Collect some beautiful pebbles and shells

Try a new flavor of ice cream

Take a selfie by a famous building

Take a picture of an animal I've never seen before

1 Make a list of all the things you want to do when you get to the end of your journey. There might be some sights you want to see, or activities you'd like to try. This list outlines some goals you could aim for.

2 You don't need to complete all your goals, but the list will help you come up with ideas for enjoying your trip.

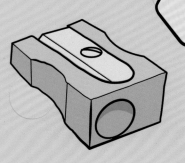

3 When you get home, take a look through your list and check off any you achieved. Any that are left over can wait until your next adventure!

DONE!

317 MAP IT

All the best explorers spend time studying their destination. Before you set off on your vacation, check out where you're going on a map.

1 Type your destination into Google Earth online, and see if you can get a street view. If so, you can do a little bit of on-the-ground exploring before you go.

2 Work out your route. You could ask your driver which way you are going or look online to see if you can find details of your train, boat, or plane route.

3 Are there any interesting features on your route? There might be mountains, lakes, rivers, and bridges, for example. Note them and then get ready to spot them if you can. You could check them off as you see them.

Top Tip
Don't go on the Internet without asking for your parents' help. They'll make sure you stay safe, and they'll probably enjoy researching your journey too.

4 Do you know how to read a map? Here are some tips to help you:

• Look on a map to see if the compass points are marked. Then you will be able to tell north, south, east, and west.

• Your map may have contour lines. They show hills. The closer together the lines, the steeper the ground.

• Your map may have a key, showing symbols such as rivers and roads. The key will help you understand the pictures on the map.

• Your map may be marked with a scale, which explains the distances shown. Here's an example:

0.5 inches (1.3cm) of the map = 1 miles (1.6km) in real life

DONE!

318 PLAY EYE SPY

This classic travel game is perfect for players of different ages! There are also some variations you can try to make the it harder.

2 Say the classic line: "I spy with my little eye something beginning with . . ." (then say the first letter of the word).

1 Choose an object that you know every player can see for the whole of the game. It could be inside or outside.

Why Not?
Spy colors as well as letters — "I spy something red." Spy shapes as well as letters — "I spy something round." Describe objects you spy — "I spy something shiny and see-through."

3 The other players must guess your choice. You could give them a time limit of two minutes, if you like.

DONE!

319 TRY TRAVELSPEAK

Make up a silly language to speak while you travel. Here are some ideas.

1 Verbs are "doing" words. Spend a few minutes replacing every verb you say with the word "banana."

Shall we banana at the next turn?

I'm going to banana as soon as we arrive.

2 For ten minutes put the word "frogface" at the end of every sentence. If you forget, it means you are a frogface!

plogalog

3 Make up a completely new word to use instead of one you all know. For example, "car" could be "plogalog." Use the new word throughout your whole trip.

DONE!

320 FILL YOUR FARM

If you're driving through the countryside, create your own farm by spotting animals. Draw them on your farm when you see them. Photos of animals on billboards and trucks count!

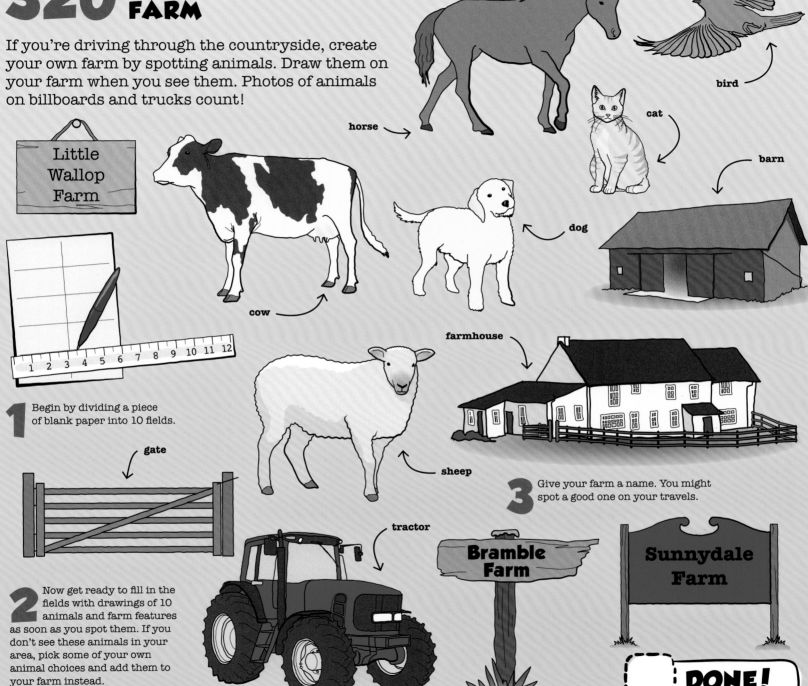

bird

horse

cat

barn

Little Wallop Farm

cow

dog

farmhouse

1 Begin by dividing a piece of blank paper into 10 fields.

gate

sheep

3 Give your farm a name. You might spot a good one on your travels.

tractor

2 Now get ready to fill in the fields with drawings of 10 animals and farm features as soon as you spot them. If you don't see these animals in your area, pick some of your own animal choices and add them to your farm instead.

Bramble Farm

Sunnydale Farm

DONE!

321 PLAY TRAVEL BINGO

Here's a quick-fire spotting game for two or more people on the go. You need to make a bingo grid for each player. Make a few grids before you leave on your trip.

3 One person acts as the bingo caller, looking around to spot things from the grid. As they call things out, cross them off your grid.

4 The winner is the first person to get a horizontal or vertical line of crosses. They should shout out "Bingo!" You could then continue to see who comes in second.

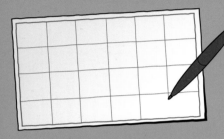

you will need
• Pad of scrap paper
• Pens or pencils for everyone
• Two or more players and a caller

1 For each bingo grid, you need to roughly draw a rectangle and then divide it into squares as shown. Six squares across and four squares down is a good size. Make a grid for each player.

2 Write a word in each square — an object to spot on your trip. Each grid should have the same words, but put in different squares.

BINGO LISTS
Here are some different travel bingo subjects to try.

• Objects that you are likely to spot on a trip

• People you are likely to spot, such as a person wearing a hat, walking a dog, someone wearing red, etc.

• Different colored cars and trucks

• Different colors on any object

• Different numbers

• Road signs

• Words used in songs or chatting on the radio

motor-home	fuel pump	store	bridge	coach	stop light
speed sign	mileage sign	fir tree	farm	billboard	open-backed truck
restaurant	motorbike	red car	yellow car	white car	black car
blue car	fuel tanker	food truck	white van	bumper sticker	roof rack

DONE!

322 PLAY ALIEN, ALIEN, ROCK STAR

Spot people in cars alongside you while you are on a road trip. Don't point at them but, between you, decide who they are and what they're called.

WHO TO FIND

A billionaire — What's their name and how did they become a billionaire?

An alien in disguise — What's their name and what is their home planet like?

A rock star — What's their name and the name of their band?

A time traveler — What's their name and which time in history did they come from?

A famous artist — What's their name and their most famous painting?

A supermodel in disguise — What's their name and what disguise are they wearing?

A top inventor — What's their name and what have they invented?

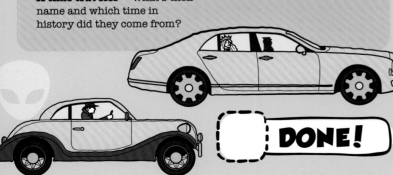

DONE!

323 PLAY WHY? BECAUSE!

It's a silly, silly world! Make it even sillier with this laugh-out-loud game.

1 Write down six sentences each, without showing anyone. The sentences should start with: "Why did the ..." Number them 1 to 6. Here's an example:

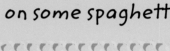

Why did the bear jump up?

2 Now write down six sentences that start with: "Because..." You can write anything you like. Number them 1 to 6. Here's an example:

Because she sat on some spaghetti.

you will need
• Paper
• Pens or pencils
• Two players and some silliness

3 Now it's time to interview each other. Ask the other player your "why" questions. They should reply with their "because" answers, matching numbers. Then get the other player to read out their "why" questions and reply with your "because" answers.

DONE!

324 PLAY WHO AM I?

This is a game to play if you're facing each other, perhaps on a train or at a rest stop.

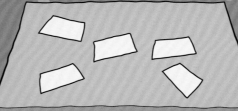

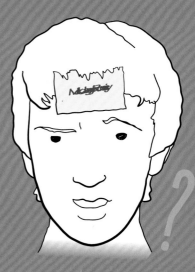

1 Each player must take a piece of paper. Without anyone else seeing, write down the name of a person that everybody is likely to have heard of. It could be a famous real-life person or a fictional character, but it's best to agree on a category of person before you start. Look at the category board to the right for some ideas.

2 Place the papers face down on a table. Each player should choose one but not look at the name written on it.

3 Stick the paper to your forehead (lick the back of the paper if it isn't already sticky). This way, everyone can see your name and you can see theirs.

you will need
- Blank paper, cut into small squares, or a mini pad of sticky papers
- Pen or pencil
- Two or more players

Am I a boy or a girl?

Am I a real person or a made-up person?

4 The first player must then ask 20 questions that can be answered with either a "yes" or a "no" to find out who they are supposed to be.

5 When the first player has guessed correctly, move on to the next player. When everyone has guessed their names, you can start again!

CATEGORY IDEAS
Here are some ideas for name categories:
- Sports stars
- Characters in kids' movies
- Famous children's book characters
- TV stars
- Music stars

DONE!

325 NAME THAT PLACE

Here are some activities using place names that you can play while traveling. If you have GPS navigation or a roadmap, look for place names or take them off road signs you see along the way.

Why Not? Make time limits longer or shorter if you want. The limits in this book are only suggestions.

Come to LOVELYTOWN

now
tool
won
vote
not
tone

Welcome to Spotterville

1 Pick a place name and see who can make the most words from the letters. You could have a time limit for the challenge of, say, five minutes.

3 Pick a place name and tell a friend. They must shut their eyes and say the place name backwards. If they get it wrong, they could have a forfeit. In a big group, they could be "out" of the game.

THIS WAY TO PLEASANT HEATH

VISIT SUNNYPLACE

2 You could score the words you make, if you like.

0 points for a two-letter word (try harder!)

1 point for a three-letter word

2 points for a four-letter word

3 points for a five-letter word

4 points for any longer words

NICEVILLE 5 KM

4 Can you think of place names that have shorter words hidden in them? For instance, a town called Sunnytown would have "sun," "sunny," "town," and "own" in it. Who can think of the name with the most hidden words?

DONE!

326 GUESS THE WEATHER IN SKYWAY

It may be sunny every day where you are, or perhaps it's chilly and icy, but it doesn't have to stop you playing a travel weather game. Here's how.

SKYWAY STUFF

If you like the game but you've played the weather version, here are some variations to try. Play the game the same way, making lists and reading them out.

• Imagine seven different buildings being built in Skyway.

• Imagine seven places for children to visit in Skyway (such as a cinema, park, swimming pool, etc).

1 Get every player to imagine seven days of weather in the imaginary land of Skyway. They should write down the weather for each day. The weather can be anything you want. It changes all the time in Skyway!

2 You could have a tornado one day and a sunny day the next, then a hurricane, a rainstorm, a snowstorm, fog, and finally a rainbow! It might be frosty, foggy, cloudy — or anything unusual you can think of.

3 Read out your week of weather. If someone else has chosen the same weather anywhere in their week, cross it off. The winner is the player with the least number of crosses.

DONE!

327 FIND THE FOOD COUNTER

This game is good for a journey through a small town.

1 Split into two teams. One team takes the left-hand side of the road. The other team takes the right-hand side of the road.

2 Start counting up the restaurants you see. The first team to get to 10 wins (you can make this less or more if you want).

3 You could play another version of the game by spotting different types of restaurants. Who will spot the most burger restaurants, Italian restaurants, or coffee shops, for example?

DONE!

328 SPOT THE CRAZY HOUSE

Do a bit of house-spotting and then try designing some crazy homes yourself.

1 Look at the list below of things to spot on houses. As you see them, check them off.

- Red door
- Blue door
- Black door
- Yellow door
- Green door
- Satellite dish
- Numbers 1 to 10 on the front door

2 Now turn architect and design a house for one of these owners. Label your ideas for their crazy home!

- A werewolf
- A vampire
- A fairy
- A wizard
- An alien

3 Think up a house name for each of the characters in the list.

DONE!

329 PLAN A PLANET

Imagine you are visiting a faraway planet. What will it be like?

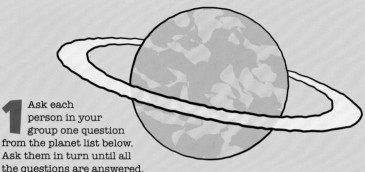

1 Ask each person in your group one question from the planet list below. Ask them in turn until all the questions are answered. Write the answers down.

2 Read out all the answers. Between you, you will come up with a crazy new world!

Why Not?
Feel free to add more questions of your own!

PLANET LIST

1. What is the planet called?

2. How long would it take to get there from Earth?

3. What is the weather like there?

4. What does the planet surface look like?

5. What are the aliens who live on the planet called?

6. What do they look like?

7. What do they eat?

8. What superpower do they have?

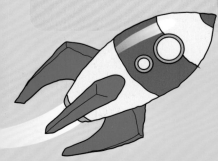

DONE!

330 MAKE UP A FAST STORY

Create a lightning-fast story plot. The faster you do it, the sillier it is likely to be!

1 Write down the numbers 1 to 12. Quickly write the name of a story character by the number 1. Here's an example:

2 Now write one short line of the story by each number. You can write anything. Just do it quickly! You could give yourself a time limit of 60 seconds.

3 Read out your silly story. You could do a drawing of it, too.

Here's an example, done quickly.

1. a blue cat

2. ate a lemon

3. it turned into a yellow dog

4. it ate a banana

5. it turned into a red monkey

6. hey, stop eating my picnic! said a wizard

7. the red monkey was very unhappy

8. he wanted to be a cat again

9. the wizard felt sorry for him

10. he gave the red monkey a magic apple

11. the red monkey turned back into a blue cat

12. he only ate fish after that

Top Tip
Try to give your story an ending on number 12. The ending may well become clear to you as you work through the numbers.

DONE!

331 KNOW YOUR TRUCKS

There are so many great trucks around. Here are some truck-spotting challenges to try if you're on a busy road journey, with plenty of trucks to choose from.

1 What is the most number of wheels you see on a truck? Work together as a team to spot the highest number you can.

2 What will be the best- decorated truck you see on your trip? Decide between you and award a "great truck" award to the best ones.

draw your design here →

3 What is the most unusual cargo you see written on the side of a truck? Make a list of the contenders you spot.

4 Come up with an imaginary trucking company that you run. What will you be selling? Design the side of your trucks.

5 Who will be the next player to spot a red truck?

6 Truckers like to stop every now and again for a meal. Create a list of ingredients for an imaginary trucker burger to serve in your imaginary trucker's restaurant. You have to have 6 ingredients plus a burger and bun.

DONE!

332 BE A WORLD TRAVELER

Test your knowledge of the world by playing these geography games together as a group. (The answers to questions 3, 4, 5, and 6 are at the bottom of the page.)

3 Can you name the world's seven continents? Point out each one on the map above.

4 Is Antarctica in the far north or the far south of the world?

5 Can you name the world's five oceans? Point out each one on the map to the left.

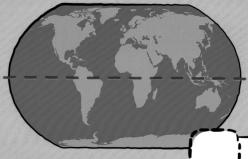

6 What is the name of the imaginary line around the middle of the Earth?

1 Think of a country or a city around the world beginning with every letter of the alphabet.

2 In your own country, see if you can think of a location beginning with every letter of the alphabet.

Answers:

Seven continents: Africa, Antarctica, Asia, Europe, Oceania, North America, South America

Five oceans: Arctic, Atlantic, India, Pacific, Southern

Antarctica is in the far south.

The Equator is the imaginary line around the earth.

 DONE!

333 CREATE NAPKIN ORIGAMI

If you stop at a restaurant while you travel, you might be offered square paper napkins. Save one to make an impressive origami lily!

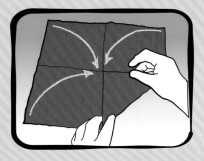

1 Open out the napkin flat. Begin by folding all four corners into the center.

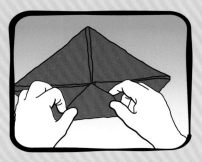

2 Press down on the edges and then fold all four corners into the center again.

3 Press down again and then fold all four corners into the center a third time.

4 Turn the napkin over and press down with your hand. Then fold all four corners into the center.

5 Fold over the tip of one corner, as shown below.

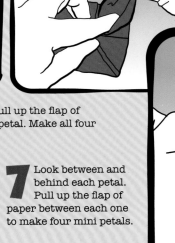

6 Reach behind the corner and pull up the flap of napkin lying behind to make a petal. Make all four petals in this way.

7 Look between and behind each petal. Pull up the flap of paper between each one to make four mini petals.

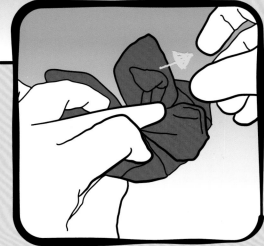

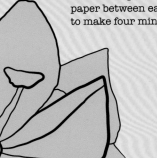

DONE!

334 ASSIGN A LETTER

Your brain will amaze you in this game! By the time you've played it a few times, you'll realize you know more words than you imagined.

1 Begin by choosing a letter from the alphabet.

2 Now, in 60 seconds, write as many four-word sentences as you can beginning with that letter. If you chose B, for example, you might begin like this:

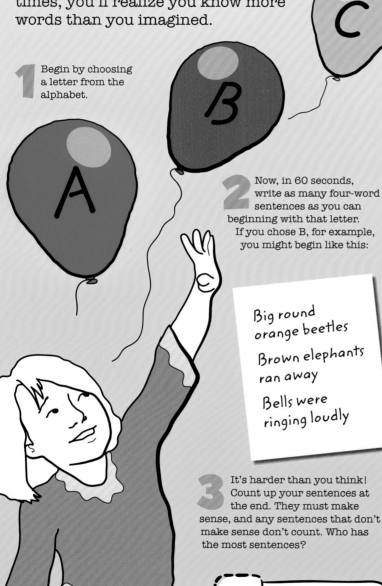

Big round orange beetles

Brown elephants ran away

Bells were ringing loudly

3 It's harder than you think! Count up your sentences at the end. They must make sense, and any sentences that don't make sense don't count. Who has the most sentences?

DONE!

335 PLAY DESCRIBOTRON

Describing things can be lots of fun! Here's how to make it into a game to play with your traveling companions.

1 Quickly choose a noun — a name word. It could be something you can see. Here's an example:

Door

2 Now spend a minute writing words that describe that noun. Here are some examples for "door." (You can't use colors. That would be too easy!)

Open
Old
Wooden
Metal
Broken
Locked
Big
Tiny

Door

3 Now read out your words. If anyone else has the same word, cross it off. Who has the most left in their list?

DONE!

336 TAKE A TRAVEL QUIZ

How brainy are your traveling companions? Here's a quiz to test them. One person can be the quiz master, reading out the questions and then the answers. Players should keep their own scores. The answers are at the bottom of the page.

3. History

a) Where did the Ming emperors once rule?
b) What do you call someone who digs up historical remains?
c) In what country would you find the remains of the Roman city of Pompeii?
d) Where did the Vikings come from? Was it Scandinavia or Africa?

4. Nature

a) What is a chameleon? Is it a lizard or an insect?
b) What is the biggest land animal in the world?
c) How many legs does a bee have?
d) In which continent would you find a sloth living in the wild?

1. Space

a) How many moons does the earth have?
b) What is the closest star to the earth?
c) What is the name given to a large lump of rock hurtling through space?
d) What would you look through to see space more closely?

2. Geography

a) What is a glacier made of?
b) Is the center of the earth hollow or solid?
c) Which is the world's largest country in size (area)?
d) Which is the tallest mountain on Earth?

5. Food

a) What is baklava? Is it a type of fruit pie or a pastry?
b) What is a korma? Is it a type of curry or a type of bread roll?
c) What is borsch? Is it a type of meat stew or a type of soup?
d) What is feta? Is it a yoghurt drink or a type of cheese?

6. Dinosaurs

a) Which was bigger, a T. rex or a brachiosaurus?
b) Did dinosaurs ever eat people?
c) Which of these two prehistoric creatures could swim — a pterosaur or an ichthyosaur?
d) Which of these two dinosaurs ate plants — an allosaurus or a triceratops?

Answers

1 Space a) One b) The sun c) An asteroid d) A telescope
2 Geography a) Ice b) Solid c) Russia d) Mount Everest
3 History a) China b) An archaeologist c) Italy d) Scandinavia
4 Nature a) A lizard b) An elephant c) Six d) South America
5 Food a) A type of cake — made from pastry, honey and nuts b) A type of curry — creamy and spicy c) A type of soup — made from beetroot
6 Dinosaurs a) A brachiosaurus b) No — not in real life, anyway! Humans and dinosaurs never lived at the same time c) ichthyosaur d) triceratops

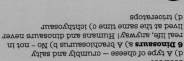
DONE!

337 BE A DESIGN GENIUS

Get creative and start designing the travel machines of the future. Use paper and pens to begin inventing!

1 Design a car of the future and label its interesting features. Here are some ideas to get you started.

Cars of the future may be driverless – steered by computers not people. Will yours be computerized?

Cars of the future may be surprising new shapes to help them go faster, use less fuel, or carry more people and luggage. Give your car a futuristic shape.

3 Design a spaceship to get astronauts to Mars. Then design a space home for them to live in once they arrive.

2 Design a train of the future. It could be super-fast, or perhaps even hover above the rails. Put your name on the side.

Cars can be powered by unusual fuels such as solar power, vegetable oil, or even fuel made from algae. What will power your car?

4 Perhaps we will one day travel around in an entirely new vehicle – a rocket-powered pod or a solar chair, for instance! Can you think of a crazy idea for a completely new type of vehicle?

DONE!

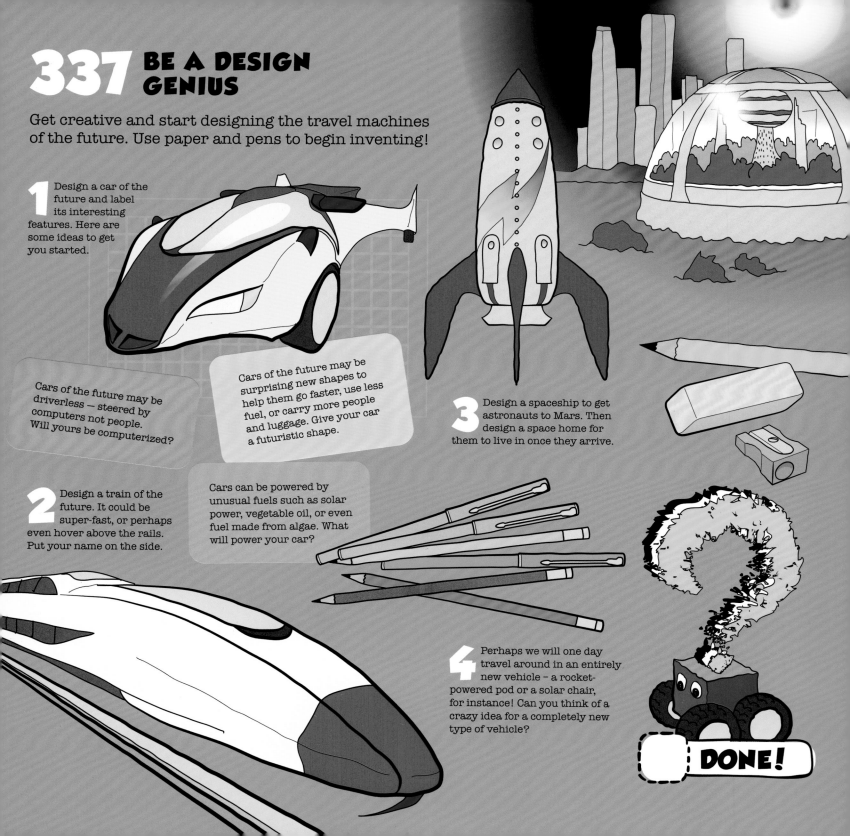

338 LIST IT

Work out some lists of your favorite and not-so-favorite things. Thinking about them and making decisions can take a surprisingly long time, and quite a few journey miles.

1 Write a list of your all-time top three, then a list of your all-time bottom three:
• Movies
• Books
• TV shows
• Popstars

2 Write a celebrity list and imagine giving your own awards:
• Best sportsman
• Best sportswoman
• Funniest person on TV
• Coolest movie star
• Coolest rock star
• Best website
• Best superhero

3 Write a list of your best and worst-rated stuff in daily life:
• Piece of clothing
• Color
• Time of day
• Teacher
• Toy
• Computer game
• Food

DONE!

339 COLLECT TICKETS

A great way to remember your trip is to collect any paper items you are given and stick them in a scrapbook when you get home. So whatever you do, don't throw those tickets and receipts away!

1 You will get receipts for food and objects you buy, and ticket stubs for places you visit.

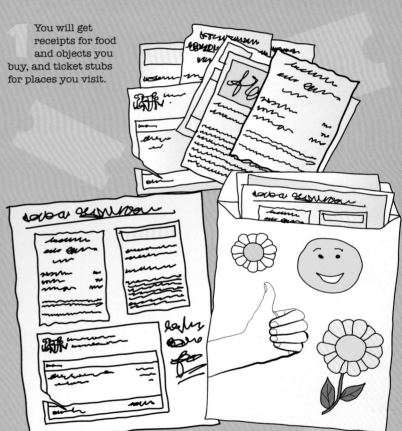

2 At the end of each day, collect up the paper trail pieces you have and stick them on a piece of paper. Write the date on the top, and label any ticket stubs.

3 Keep your paper trail pages in an envelope (you could decorate it). If you don't have an envelope, slip the pages inside a book or magazine (don't forget to take it home!).

DONE!

340 LOOK FOR SYMBOLS AND FLAGS

Countries and regions of the world have their own flags and symbols. Find out more while you are on your trip.

1 Countries have their own flags, and regions often have them, too. Keep an eye out for flags that you see often as you explore your vacation location. You could ask a local person to explain what they represent if you are not sure.

2 Countries and regions often have their own official animals and flowers. See if you can find out what they are in the location you are visiting.

3 Design your own flag for the place you are visiting, and also for your own home. Flags often have patterns on them, such as stripes. They sometimes have symbols, too.

DONE!

341 CREATE A MEMORY CORNER

While you're away, collect some small 3-D objects that you could display in a "memory corner" of your room on your return.

1 Bring back items that mean something to you and that will help you to remember your trip. They could be anything you like, from a bottle top to a candy box.

2 Look out for pretty pebbles and shells on a beach. Gently wash them in warm soapy water to get them ready for display.

3 Flowers can be pressed between two paper towels and put between the pages of a book to dry out.

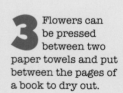

Why Not?
When you get home, remove the lid from a shoe box, then cut the side off to make a stage set for your memory corner. Glue photos from your trip inside.

DONE!

342 MAKE TRAVEL ART

You might like to try drawing a picture on your trip. But how can you make it look more 3-D? Here are some art tips to try.

1 Draw a horizontal line near the top of your picture. That will be your horizon line, far away in the distance.

2 Objects down near the bottom of the page should be bigger than objects farther up toward the horizon line. They will appear closer, in the foreground.

Overlapping objects in your picture will help to give a 3-D effect. You could draw one bush in front of another, for instance.

4 In the foreground, draw things with sharp and distinct edges. Make outlines softer if things are further away, up near the horizon line.

5 If you color in your picture, make colors stronger in the foreground and paler in the background.

6 Try drawing a view through a window. The window will make a good frame in the foreground, and the rest of the picture will look farther away.

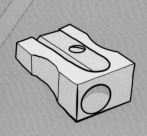

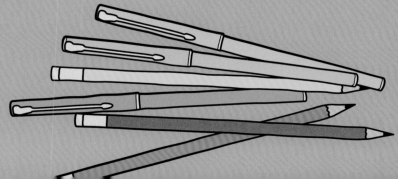

DONE!

343 FRAME HOLIDAY PHOTOS

If you have a favorite vacation photo, spend time making a collage frame to display it.

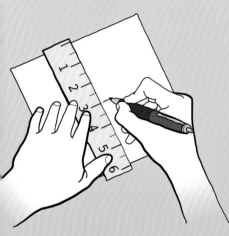

1 Using a ruler to help you, mark the centers of the two card stock sheets to help you position your photo.

2 Lay your photo on one of the card stock sheets, in the middle, and draw around it. Do the same on the second sheet.

3 Glue your photo onto one of the card stock sheets. Cut a photo hole out of the second sheet, which will be the front of your frame.

you will need
- Ruler
- Pencil
- 2 sheets of card stock that are longer and wider than your photo
- Your photo printed out on thick glossy photo paper
- Magazines, leaflets, or photo printouts to cut or tear up for the collage
- Glue stick
- Piece of recycled thick cardboard (corrugated cardboard is good for this piece)
- Scissors

4 Tear up collage pieces and glue them to the front of the frame to make an interesting effect.

5 Glue the front of the frame on top of the back.

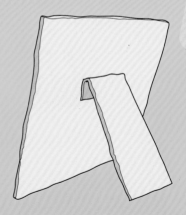

6 Cut a piece of the thick cardboard to make a stand at the back of the frame. Bend over one edge and glue it to the frame. When dry, it should stand up.

Why Not?
Decorate your frame with 3-D objects such as shells, beads, sequins, or buttons, glued onto your collage background.

DONE!

344 PLAY QUICK-FIRE CARS

Here are some quick-fire games to play in a car.

1 Take turns to guess the color of the next car to come the other way.

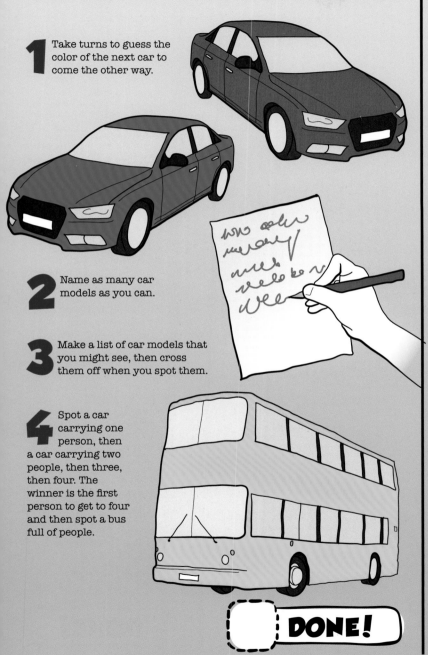

2 Name as many car models as you can.

3 Make a list of car models that you might see, then cross them off when you spot them.

4 Spot a car carrying one person, then a car carrying two people, then three, then four. The winner is the first person to get to four and then spot a bus full of people.

 **DONE!**

345 TRY 60-SECOND SPEAK

You don't need paper for this wordy list game — just a watch with a way of timing one minute.

1 Get ready to time a player. Just before they start, give them one of the categories listed on this page (or one that you think of yourselves).

2 The player must name as many things in the category as they can in 60 seconds. One of the other players will need to count up the score as they speak.

CATEGORY IDEAS

1. Things that are a specific color, such as red or blue, etc.

2. Things beginning with a letter of the alphabet — such as animals, food, or place names in your country

3. Countries around the world

4. Things to wear

5. Girls' or boys' names

 **DONE!**

346 PLAN A MOVIE

Use some time on your trip to plan a blockbuster movie that you might make in the future.

1 Start by thinking about what type of movie your masterpiece will be. It could be sci-fi, a jungle adventure, or a school story, for instance.

2 Make a list of characters and the famous stars you would choose to perform the big parts.

3 Storyboard an important scene. That means drawing the action that goes on in one scene. Draw it like a cartoon comic. You could write some script for that scene, too.

4 Now you know your movie a bit better, decide on a title. Choose something that people will like the sound of and want to see.

5 Design and color a movie poster advertising your blockbuster.

6 If you have access to a video camera on a smartphone or tablet, you could film a scene with some help from your friends when you get home.

DONE!

347 GET MAP SMART

Learn how to read three different types of map — without the need for GPS!

TYPES OF MAP

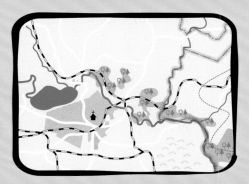

Regional

Regional maps are the most common maps we use. They show us where places are and how to get from one place to another. You will find country borders, roads, and railways, as well as parks, lakes, and rivers.

LEGEND
★ Capital city

Canada
Ottawa ★

Washington D.C ★

United states of America

Nassau ★

Mexico

Havana ★

Political

Political maps are color-coded to show different information such as population, languages, or countries. There is a key to the map, called a legend, to explain what's being shown.

Physical

Physical maps show the way the land is shaped. Ragged, bumpy areas show where the land is mountainous or hilly. Green areas show where there are densely packed forests or jungles.

MAKE YOUR OWN MAP

Draw a map of your surrounding area using some pens, paper, and a few cool symbols! Include important things that can help you find your way, such as buildings, roads, bus stops, and green areas. Once you've finished coloring in your map, you can add paths you use often, such as your way to school, a friend's house, or to your local park.

MAP SYMBOLS

Here are some important symbols you'll find in many regional or city maps. Can you add some to your map?

Train

Airport

Hospital/ First-Aid

Forest or Woodland

Church

Camping Ground

Café

Mountain Peak

DONE!

348 BUST YOUR BOREDOM

If you need to pass the time, delight your friends and family with these boredom-busters. They will keep everyone entertained!

Eat the alphabet

Come up with funny things to eat for each letter of the alphabet. Announce, "I'm so hungry, I could eat an alligator." The next player continues with a B word. They might say, "I'm so hungry, I could eat an alligator and a beach ball!" Keep it going until everyone in the car is eating zippers!

The place name game

The first person thinks of the name of a place (town, city, or country anywhere in the world), for example, "London." Then, the next person has to try and think of a place name beginning with the last letter of that place name, for example "Nepal." See how long you can keep it going!

Guess the theme tune

Each player takes turns to hum (no singing the words!) a TV theme song. The first person to guess the song gets to go next.

DONE!

349 SPOT THE SOUVENIR

Look out for funny souvenirs sold in your location. The weirder, the better!

1 Have a fun competition between you to spot the craziest souvenir on the trip.

2 Look out for dolls in local costumes, and then try to draw the costume yourself. When you get home you could print out a photo of your head, cut it out, and glue it to the top of your drawing.

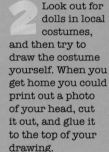

With love from home

3 If you were selling a souvenir of the place where you live, what would it be? Design something you think visitors would like to buy.

DONE!

350 GO ON A SCAVENGER HUNT

Go searching for items and collect everything on your list before your friends do!

WHERE TO PLAY

Your backyard or a local park would be perfect places to hold a scavenger hunt, but they work indoors, too. Once you've chosen a place to play, make sure all of your players know where they should be looking, and not to go outside that area. Always make sure that an adult knows where you are if your hunt is outside of your home.

MAKE A LIST

Start by coming up with a list of things for your player to find. Here are some suggestions:

On an outdoor hunt

- Pine cone
- Flower
- Leaf larger than your hand
- Leaf smaller than your palm
- Something that smells nice
- Something round
- Feather
- Piece of bark
- Twig shaped like a "Y"

On an indoor hunt

- Toothbrush
- Book
- DVD
- Cushion
- Pillow
- Spoon
- Odd sock
- Rubber duck
- A clothespin

SECRET ITEMS!

Hide some funny items (like an egg cup or a rubber duck) around the search area. Tell your players that whoever finds these bonus items gets a special prize! If you want to join in the hunt, ask an adult to do this for you.

THE WINNER IS...

The first person to collect all the items on his or her list is the winner! When everyone comes back, take a good look at your collection.

Why Not?

Give extra prizes for the biggest leaf, the most unusual item, and the nicest flower.

DONE!

351 WORD CHAINS

Word games are a perfect way to pass the time on a trip. How quickly can you make a chain of word connections? If you hesitate, you're out!

1 The first player says a word. The second player must quickly say another word that is connected in some way through its meaning. There is an example below of how a game might start.

2 The next player must quickly say another connected word in the chain. Keep going, thinking of words quickly to keep the connection chain going. Here's how a chain might start developing and changing:

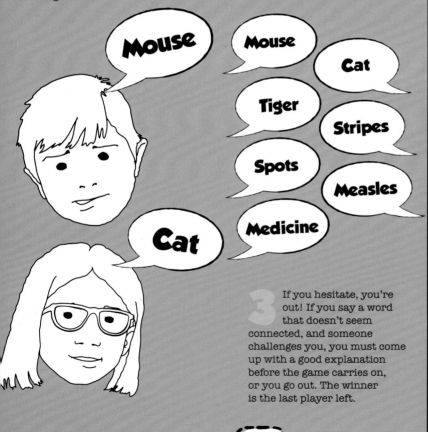

3 If you hesitate, you're out! If you say a word that doesn't seem connected, and someone challenges you, you must come up with a good explanation before the game carries on, or you go out. The winner is the last player left.

DONE!

352 DESIGN YOUR OWN STICKER

Design your own bumper sticker that is unique to you or your family. There are some sticker ideas below to inspire you.

STICKER INSPIRATION

- A symbol of the place where you live
- The name of your family
- Your name, decorated in some way
- A bumper sticker based on your favorite hobby

1 Draw a circle, an oval, square, or rectangle on a piece of sticker paper or poster board.

2 Write in the words or letters you want. You can choose whatever you like.

3 Decorate around the letters with colored pens to make your design stand out.

Why Not? Take a look at some stickers on other people's cars, to get inspiration.

DONE!

353 DRAW A SELF-PORTRAIT

A self-portrait is when an artist paints himself or herself. They can be done anywhere. Look at yourself in a mirror, grab a pen and paper, and start your own!

1 To start your portrait, map out your features. Your hand is about as large as your face, so put your hand on the page.

2 Mark the top finger with a dot and then the heel of your palm with another dot. Connect them with an oval shape.

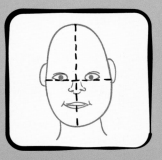

3 Draw a dotted cross inside the oval. Eyes sit on top of the horizontal line, the nose is in the center, and your mouth is below that.

4 Add more details, such as eyebrows, ears, and hair. Then, erase the dotted cross and... voilà! You have a portrait!

DONE!

354 PLAY A TRICK ON YOURSELF

Can you trick your own body? Why not test yourself on a boring journey with these amazing tricks.

Apples and Oranges

Take an apple and an orange, and while taking a bite of the apple, hold the orange under your nose. Does the apple taste different? Your sense of smell and taste are very closely linked, so you might find that the apple starts to taste like an orange!

The Tap Test

Place your hand palm down on a flat surface, like a table top. Without moving your other fingers, try tapping your ring finger. Easy, right? Now tuck your middle finger under your palm and try again. You should find it impossible to move! This is because your middle and ring fingers share a tendon.

Why Not?
Put on a magic show for your family and friends.

DONE!

355 ONE DAY I'LL...!

It's time to start planning a dream trip of the future!

1 Before you start, there's something that's really important to do. You need to thank the people who organized your last trip because they showed you a great time. You might even like to give them a little thank you card with a vacation photo on it. It will mean a lot to them to know you enjoyed it.

Thank you!

I'd love to go surfing again.

I'd rather not go camel riding again.

2 Make a list of the best things about your last trip. What would you like to do again? Are there one or two things you'd rather avoid in the future?

3 Make a list of the top five types of vacation you'd love to go on. Just have fun and daydream!

4 Make a list of the top five places in the world you'd like to see. One day you may make your dream come true.

5 Now draw a picture of your ideal vacation. Label it, date it, and put it up on your wall when you get home. You'll get there one day.

LET'S GO!

DONE!

356 DOODLE DUDES

Here's some quick doodling and cartoon fun for two players. The idea is to create some crazy people who say funny things.

1 Doodle a line or random shape.

2 Hand it over to the other player. It's their task to turn it into a person or an animal.

3 When the second player has completed their masterpiece they should add a speech bubble and hand it back to you to add some words.

Boo!

DONE!

357 I SAW ELEPHANTS

All you need for this game are three or more players, and your imagination to create a silly story.

I...

1 The first player says one word to begin a story. For instance, they might say "I".

saw...

2 Players then take it in turns to say one word each, to carry on the story. In our example the next player might say "saw" and the next one "elephants". The story goes on from there.

elephants...

3 If you hesitate or say something that doesn't make sense, you're out. The winner is the last player left telling the story.

DONE!

358 FOLD AND FLY A PERFECT PAPER PLANE

Ready for take-off? While waiting for a flight, why not grab a piece of paper and construct your own awesome aircraft to send soaring into the sky.

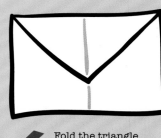

Why Not?
Decorate your airplane with a unique design.

1 Fold the paper in half lengthways and open it up again.

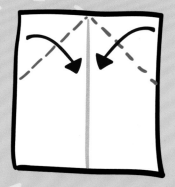

2 Take the top right corner and fold it so it meets the center crease. Do the same with the top left corner.

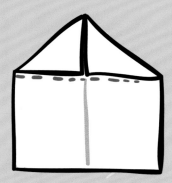

3 You should now have a triangle at the top of the paper.

4 Fold the triangle down toward the center of the paper.

5 Take the right corner and fold it in toward the center. Do the same with the left corner. Make sure the two corner points touch.

6 Fold the paper in half along the crease you made in step 1.

7 To make the wings, fold the corners down toward the bottom of the airplane.

8 Grip the plane on the bottom and launch it. Now watch it fly!

DONE!

359 LEARN A NEW LANGUAGE

Learn these useful phrases and show off your new language skills. Letters often sound different in other languages, so the words in brackets show how they are pronounced.

SAY HELLO

This is one of the most important things to learn, because if you go abroad you'll use it all the time.

French: Bonjour (bonjoor)

German: Guten tag (gooten tahg)

Italian: Buongiorno (bonjiorno)

Spanish: Hola (ola)

Hola !

YES/NO

These are two essential words.

French: oui/non (wee/non)

German: ja/nein (yah/nine)

Italian: si/no (see/noh)

Spanish: sí/no (see/noh)

Ja !

PLEASE/ THANK YOU

You'll need to know these if you want to be polite.

French: s'il vous plaît/merci (seel voo play/mair-see)

German: bitte/danke (bitter/danker)

Italian: per favore/grazie (per favor-ay/ graht-see-eh)

Spanish: por favor/gracias (poor favor/grah-seeahs)

Grazie

SORRY !

This is a very useful word if you step on someone's toe.

French: Pardon! (par-dohn)

German: Entschuldigung! (ent-shul-di-gung)

Italian: Scusi! (skoosi)

Spanish: Perdón! (pehr-dohn)

Pardon !

TEST YOURSELF

How would you say?

Yes please in German

No thank you in French

Hello in Spanish

Sorry in Italian

Now tell someone you are sorry in French!

Top Tip

If you've enjoyed mastering these phrases there's no need to stop here. There are lots of books and websites to help you learn more.

DONE !

360 NEW NAMES

Have some fun with your names, and turn yourselves into new people for the duration of your journey.

Claire...
erialc

Pete...
etep

Kath...
htak

Cameron...
noremac

1 Spell everyone's name backward. Read out the new names.

2 Now call each other by your backward name for the rest of the day.

3 Think of some friends and family you all know. Spell their names backward and read them out. Who will be the first to guess who they are?

DONE!

361 TODAY I AM...

Vacation is the perfect time to get prepared in case you're ever asked to be a movie or TV star. Here's an acting game to play for five minutes.

Today I am a spy!

Today I am a vampire!

1 Everyone in your group should choose a character from the list below.

2 Everybody should play their character for five minutes.

?

TODAY I AM...

- 100 years old
- 1 year old
- A vampire
- A fairy godmother
- A person who is scared of everything
- A spy
- A superhero
- A movie star
- President of the world
- A zombie

3 To vary the game, you could keep your choice a secret, and other players must guess who you are from the list.

DONE!

362 MASTER THE ART OF ORIGAMI

Origami is the ancient Japanese art of paper folding. You'll be amazed at what you can make from just a simple square of paper. Why not start by making this cute rabbit?

Why Not?
Try using different colored paper and draw some details on your new creation!

1 Take a square of paper and fold it in half, diagonally.

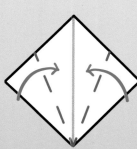

2 Open the paper up, then fold the corners inward toward the center fold.

3 Fold down the top corner to make a triangle.

4 Fold the tip of the top flap back to make the tail.

5 Fold in half along the center fold.

6 Your paper should now look like this.

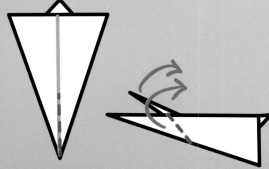

7 Use scissors to make a small cut a third of the way along the center fold. This will make the rabbit's ears.

8 Next, bend back each of the ears.

9 Fold the bottom corners under. This will make your rabbit sit up.

10 Fold the ears down. You now have your very own origami rabbit!

DONE!

363 EYE IN THE SKY

This is a good activity to play on a long trip! See how many of these sky sights you can spot and tick them off as you go.

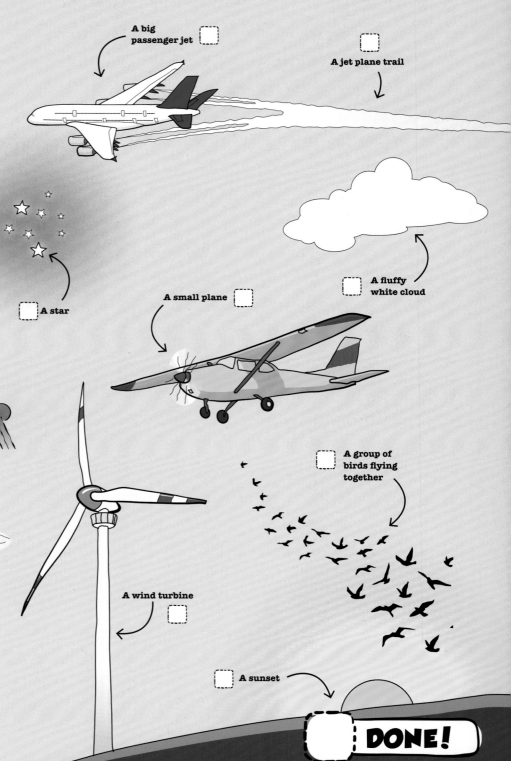

A big passenger jet ☐

A jet plane trail ☐

The moon ☐

A star ☐

A small plane ☐

A fluffy white cloud ☐

A grey raincloud ☐

A group of birds flying together ☐

A wind turbine ☐

A helicopter ☐

A sunset ☐

DONE!

364 RETRO POST

Before electronic communication, sending a postcard from a vacation spot was the traditional way to say "hello" to your friends and family back home. Go retro and surprise someone by sending something old-style!

1 Choose a fun postcard. Then write a message, buy a stamp, stick it in the top right corner, and post it to a friend. If you're traveling abroad, the stamp will look very different from the ones you've seen back home.

2 Design some ideas for postcards yourself. They could show a place or person representing your trip.

3 Design some ideas for new stamps. Draw a square or rectangle, and add a price in one corner. Then add a picture. It could show you and your family, your holiday location, or maybe your home.

DONE!

365 LANGUAGE LAB

If you travel to different parts of the world, you'll find people speaking different languages and using different accents. Try thinking up your own language to use among yourselves.

1 What will your language be called? It could be your name plus "ian", for example. What will your accent be? Practice a new one.

2 Think up a few phrases and write them down. Here are three common ones:

> Hello. My name is ......
>
> I live in ......
>
> I am on vacation.

Hi. I speak Sophian.

I speak Mikeian.

3 If you do go to a place where the language is different, see if you can learn some basic words before you finish your trip. "Please", "Thank you", and "Hello" are useful phrases to know.

DONE!

STAYING SAFE: DO'S AND DON'TS

 DO: Have an adult help in the kitchen

DO: Stay hygienic and wash your hands thoroughly and regularly.

DO: Take care while using scissors and other sharp objects.

DO: Wear a helmet while riding a sled, bike, or skateboard.

DO: Always wear old clothes or an apron when doing art projects.

DO: Carefully follow the instructions and pay attention to any safety warnings.

DO: Pay attention to local guidelines on social distancing.

 DON'T: Start a messy project without asking an adult.

DON'T: Go anywhere without telling an adult first!

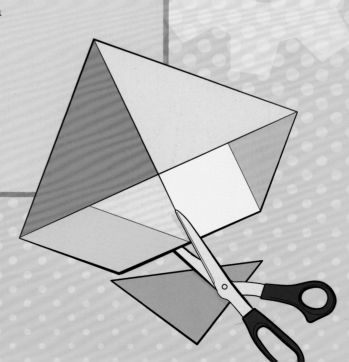

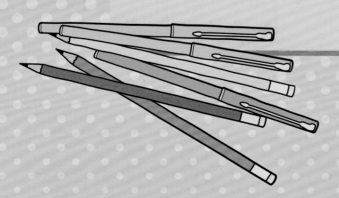

CREDITS

Written by Pat Jacobs; illustrated by Dynamo Limited: 1, 2, 3, 4, 5, 6, 7, 8, 9, 10, 11, 12, 13, 14, 15, 19, 20, 26, 47, 48, 49, 50, 51, 52, 53, 54, 55, 56, 57, 58, 59, 60, 61, 62, 63, 89, 90, 96, 97, 98, 99, 100, 102, 104, 105, 116, 119, 120, 121, 122, 123, 124, 125, 126, 127, 128, 129, 130, 131, 132, 133, 134, 135, 136, 137, 138, 139, 140, 141, 142, 143, 145, 164, 165, 166, 167, 168, 169, 170, 171, 172, 173, 174, 175, 176, 177, 178, 225, 262, 306, 312, 359

Written by Susan Hayes; illustrated by Shahid Mahmood: 16, 17, 18, 43, 44, 45, 46, 64, 65, 66, 67, 68, 69, 70, 71, 72, 73, 93, 106, 117, 144, 146, 147, 148, 150, 151, 152, 153, 163, 179, 180, 181, 182, 183, 184, 185, 186, 223, 224, 226, 227, 228, 229, 230, 231, 232, 233, 234, 235, 236, 237, 238, 239, 240, 241, 242, 243, 245, 246, 248, 249, 250, 254, 256, 257, 258, 261, 263, 264, 265, 266, 267, 268, 269, 270, 272, 273, 274, 275, 277, 278, 279, 280, 281, 282, 284, 288, 290, 303, 304, 305, 307, 308, 309, 310, 313, 314

Written by Laura Dower, illustrated by Dan Bramall and Katie Knutton: 21, 22, 23, 24, 25, 27, 28, 29, 30, 31, 40, 41, 42, 74, 75, 76, 77, 78, 79, 80, 81, 82, 83, 84, 85, 86, 87, 88, 91, 92, 101, 107, 108, 109, 110, 111, 112, 113, 149, 154, 155, 156, 157, 158, 159, 187, 188, 189, 190, 191, 192, 193, 194, 195, 196, 197, 198, 199, 200, 201, 202, 203, 204, 205, 206, 207, 208, 209, 210, 211, 212, 217, 219, 220, 221, 222, 247, 252, 253, 255, 259, 260, 283, 285, 286, 289, 291, 292, 293, 294, 295, 299, 300, 347, 348, 350, 353, 354, 358, 362

Written by Moira Butterfield; illustrated by Dynamo Limited: 32, 33, 34, 35, 36, 37, 38, 39, 94, 95, 114, 118, 160, 161, 162, 213, 214, 215, 216, 218, 296, 297, 301, 315, 316, 317, 318, 319, 320, 321, 322, 323, 324, 325, 326, 327, 328, 329, 330, 331, 332, 333, 334, 335, 336, 337, 338, 339, 340, 341, 342, 343, 344, 345, 346, 349, 351, 352, 355, 356, 357, 360, 361, 363, 364, 365

Written and illustrated by Cloud King Creative:
103, 115, 244, 251, 271, 276, 287, 298, 302, 311

Published by Weldon Owen Children's Books
An imprint of Weldon Owen International, L.P.

A subsidiary of Insight International, L.P.
PO Box 3088
San Rafael, CA 94912

www.insighteditions.com

Weldon Owen Children's Books:
Publisher: Sue Grabham
Creative Director: Bryn Walls

Insight Editions:
Publisher: Raoul Goff
President: Kate Jerome

Produced in conjunction with:
CAMERON + COMPANY
Publisher Chris Gruener
Creative Director Iain Morris
Art Director Suzi Hutsell
Designer Emily Studer
Managing Editor Jan Hughes

ISBN: 978-1-68188-389-2

Manufactured in China

23 22 21 20 19 1 2 3 4 5